CONTEMPORARY DEBATES IN EDUCATION STUDIES

Contemporary Debates in Education Studies gives the reader a vital and nuanced understanding of the key debates surrounding the field of education today. Exploring important educational themes such as issues of sexuality, extremism and mental health through a variety of viewpoints, this wide-ranging book questions what the nature and purpose of education is, and how this can be understood in contemporary contexts.

From eradicating child poverty in schools, to considering how education should rise to the challenge of the digital world, the book covers an extensive range of topics designed to inspire discussion and debate. Examining a variety of perspectives, each chapter looks at these topics through key research, thinkers, theorists and policies, and, featuring discussion questions and case studies throughout, it forms a truly accessible and interactive guide to the issues that can not only help students access the debates, but also provide lecturers with questions to stimulate seminar discussions.

Challenging current thinking on a number of topics, this book's original and distinctive ideas consider how education should meet some of the trials and tribulations of the 21st century, and its wide-reaching and all-encompassing discussion will be essential reading for all students on undergraduate and postgraduate education studies courses.

Jennifer Marshall is Senior Lecturer in Education Studies and MA Education, University of Derby, UK.

CONTEMPORARY DEBATES IN EDUCATION STUDIES

Edited by Jennifer Marshall

Routledge
Taylor & Francis Group
LONDON AND NEW YORK

First published 2018
by Routledge
2 Park Square, Milton Park, Abingdon, Oxon OX14 4RN

and by Routledge
711 Third Avenue, New York, NY 10017

Routledge is an imprint of the Taylor & Francis Group, an informa business

© 2018 selection and editorial matter, Jennifer Marshall; individual chapters, the contributors

The right of the editor to be identified as the author of the editorial material, and of the authors for their individual chapters, has been asserted in accordance with sections 77 and 78 of the Copyright, Designs and Patents Act 1988.

All rights reserved. No part of this book may be reprinted or reproduced or utilised in any form or by any electronic, mechanical, or other means, now known or hereafter invented, including photocopying and recording, or in any information storage or retrieval system, without permission in writing from the publishers.

Trademark notice: Product or corporate names may be trademarks or registered trademarks, and are used only for identification and explanation without intent to infringe.

British Library Cataloguing in Publication Data
A catalogue record for this book is available from the British Library

Library of Congress Cataloging in Publication Data
A catalog record for this book has been requested

ISBN: 978-1-138-68023-4 (hbk)
ISBN: 978-1-138-68024-1 (pbk)
ISBN: 978-1-315-56371-8 (ebk)

Typeset in Interstate
by Wearset Ltd, Boldon, Tyne and Wear

Printed and bound in Great Britain by
TJ International Ltd, Padstow, Cornwall

This book is dedicated to all the students for whom the debates presented here are real. The challenges and concerns you face have not gone unnoticed. We have a long way to go, but know your voice is heard.

CONTENTS

List of figures ix
List of tables x
List of contributors xi
Preface xiii
Acknowledgements xiv

1 **Introduction: The nature and purpose of education in contemporary society** 1
   Jennifer Marshall

2 **Child poverty: Trends, causes and responses** 16
   Ihsan Caillau-Foster

3 **Terrorism, extremism and radicalisation** 32
   Ihsan Caillau-Foster

4 **The marketization of education** 52
   Trevor Cotterill

5 **Creativity in the classroom** 63
   Matt Edinger

6 **The NEET debate** 81
   Jade Murden

7 **Sexuality and education** 97
   Trevor Cotterill

8 **Special educational needs and disability: Categorisation and naming** 119
   Deborah Robinson

9   **Self-harm – dispelling the myths**   129
    Ang Davey and Anna Davey

10 **The mental health needs of refugee pupils**   141
    Shirley Hewitt

11 **The role of education in resilience**   156
    Andy Marshall

12 **Education and the digital revolution**   171
    Tom Staunton

13 **The future of education**   182
    Vanessa Cottle and Anne O'Grady

    Index   195

FIGURES

1.1	What is education?	2
2.1	Attainment at Key Stage 4 by FSM eligibility, percentage of pupils achieving each indicator, England, 2013/2014	23
5.1	Steps of creativity	64
9.1	Ball and chain by Sophie Harward	131
10.1	Predictors of mental health issues	142
10.2	Bronfenbrenner's (1994) ecological framework	143
10:3	Interventions which shape the microsystem	144
10.4	Factors faced during the migration process	146
10.5	Characteristics of prevalent mental health disorders	148
10.6	School and community responses	149
11.1	Resilient personality characteristics	157
11.2	The five main areas of resilience	164

TABLES

5.1	Definitions of creativity	65
5.2	Characteristics of creative children	65
5.3	What can teachers do to foster creativity?	67
5.4	Barriers to creativity	73
7.1	Strategies for disclosing sexual identity	112
12.1	Elements of digital literacy	172

CONTRIBUTORS

Ihsan Caillau-Foster, PhD, is Senior Lecturer in Education at the University of Derby and a researcher exploring social issues such as crime and crime reduction, schools facing challenging circumstances, home–school relations, children and citizenship, and communities and childhood. Her recent research investigated social development in childhood.

Trevor Cotterill has 40 years of experience working in education and his current teaching and research activities centre around the field of special education.

Vanessa Cottle is currently Programme Leader for the MA Education part-time programme at the University of Derby and coordinates the independent study. Her interests are eclectic having previously managed post-16 teacher education programmes and worked for a short while in prison education. Currently she is researching into the implications of the masterly journey for education students.

Ang Davey is an HE manager in Education, Childhood and SEND. Her research interest lies in how people can help themselves and others through understanding underlying causes of behaviour.

Anna Davey is Learner Voice Co-ordinator in an FE college with 16 years' experience working with post-14 learners. Her previous roles have included Safeguarding Officer where she developed an interest in self-harm.

Matt Edinger, PhD, has a background in Gifted and Talented education, and he has taught and studied the concept of creativity for many years. Most recently he has examined the effect that standardised testing within secondary education has on creativity in high school classrooms.

Shirley Hewitt is a qualified teacher who has taught in a range of educational settings over the last 25 years. She now works in teacher education and has a particular interest in inclusive provision for all learners.

Andy Marshall is a practitioner of contingency planning and disaster management with extensive experience of resilience planning in both the public and private sectors. He has written and presented widely on resilience and is a Member of the Editorial Advisory Panel of *Crisis Response Journal*.

Jennifer Marshall is a senior lecturer in the fields of Teaching English to Speakers of Other Languages (TESOL) and comparative and international education. Her recent research projects have centred on the internationalisation of higher education and subject-specific language acquisition.

Jade Murden is a senior lecturer at the University of Derby who has extensive experience of working with vulnerable young people who are excluded, or at risk of exclusion, from mainstream education.

Anne O'Grady is Principal Lecturer in Academic Studies in Education at Nottingham Trent University. She researches in the field of educational social justice within adult education and lifelong learning. She is particularly interested in the educational experiences of groups who might be considered on the margins of mainstream society, including prisoners, children in challenging circumstances and unemployed adults with low levels of literacy.

Deborah Robinson, EdD, is the Director of the Centre for Educational Research and Innovation at the Institute of Education at the University of Derby. She has a particular interest in teacher education for inclusive practice. Her most recent research focused on the inclusion of children and young people with learning disabilities in pleasurable reading and enjoyment of books.

Tom Staunton is a careers adviser and researcher. His research focuses on how technology, and the internet in particular, interacts with individuals and institutions and with education and career.

PREFACE

The book aims to provide a number of provocative yet insightful perspectives on contemporary debates in education through examining a variety of viewpoints on important educational matters. The book is designed to challenge current thinking on a number of topics, some of which could be deemed as controversial. It also aims to think about the bigger picture on how education should meet some of the challenges of the 21st century. The debates featured in this book are wide-ranging and centre on Special Education Needs and Disability (SEND), sexuality in education, self-harming, mental health, parental choice and the quasi-marketisation of education, younger learners not in education, employment and training (NEETs), creativity in the curriculum, extremism and radicalisation of young people, eradicating child poverty in schools, building resilient communities through the curriculum, and finally how education should rise to the challenges of the digital world.

Each chapter will be linked to the central question, 'What is the nature and purpose of education?' Chapters challenge the reader to think about who should benefit from education. Should it be the individual, society or the economy? And who decides what should happen in education?

The purpose of education is also linked to who teaches, how they teach and what they teach; these will be explored throughout the book. Additionally, education is viewed in the broadest sense from the non-formal to the formal and also from a variety of contexts (for example, lifelong learning, primary, HE). In contemporary Britain, a variety of stakeholders (students, teachers, policy makers, researchers, community workers, health practitioners, social workers and so forth) have a vested interest in what education should 'look like' and for whom. By challenging assumptions through sensitive debate, this book aims to provide some insight into the most important social institution in modern society: education. You are invited to join the debate!

ACKNOWLEDGEMENTS

First of all, I would like to thank each author who took time to contribute to this book. They have given us a real insight to the contemporary debates in education that shape our lives. Secondly, I would like to acknowledge our places of work as they supported us in writing our chapters. Thirdly, we must acknowledge those individuals for whom education has not been a successful endeavour. We will always strive for positive change and by bringing some of the debates into the open, we are one step closer.

I would also like to thank the reviewers whose comments helped shape the book. Also, to the students at the University of Derby and Sophie Harward, in particular, whose drawing is featured in the book (Figure 9.1). Thanks also goes to the commissioning editor Annamarie Kino – without her support this book would not have been possible.

1 Introduction

The nature and purpose of education in contemporary society

Jennifer Marshall

This chapter explores:

- what is education;
- who is it for;
- what is the purpose of education?

> **✏ Activity: What is education?**
>
> Before beginning this chapter, how would you define or describe what education is? Draw a mind map of all the words you associate with education. Is education different to schooling or training? Is your definition of education different depending on whether you are a student, parent, teacher or policy maker? Also, consider what it means to be educated.

What is education?

Around the world, students, parents, teachers and policymakers involved in educational matters should be encouraged to challenge traditional ideas on what the aims of education should be and how they are best achieved. While education policy and practice seem to be in an ever-constant sea of change, have the goals of education changed over time and are they appropriate for today's society?

Before looking into the purposes or aims of education, it is important to consider briefly, what is education? This is one of the main questions students are asked on Education Studies degrees around the UK and elsewhere, and as such many core texts deal with this topic (see Curtis et al., 2014; Arthur & Davies, 2010; Bates & Lewis, 2009). Education means different things to different people according to the context in which they experience it. It is not the aim of this chapter to delve into this debate in particular, but to point out that a teacher of ten- to eleven-year-olds may say that education is schooling while a mentor teaching an apprentice how to wire a socket may say education is training. A summary of some possible answers to the question is given in Figure 1.1. For the purpose of this book, education is diverse – from the informal to the formal, as a process (for example, learning another language, developing confidence) and a product (receiving a qualification at the end of a course). Despite its

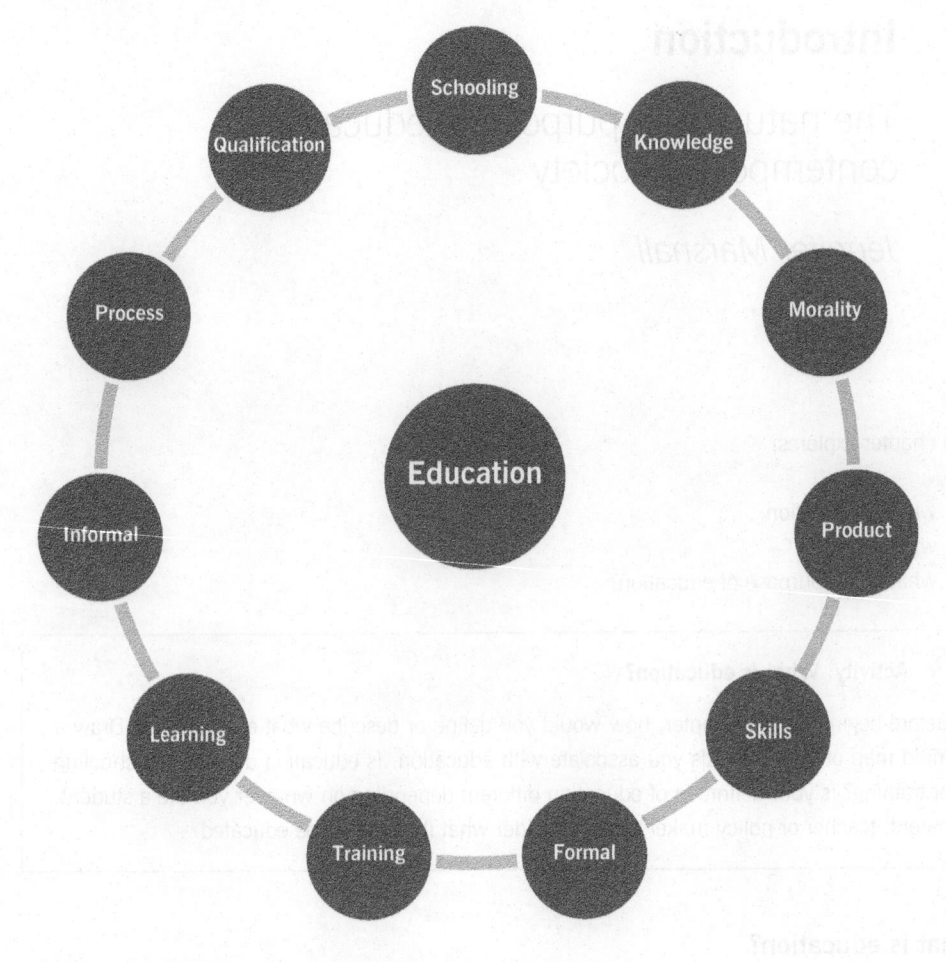

Figure 1.1 What is education?

diversity, education is fundamentally seen as essential for human development for both individuals and societies and has the potential to empower, change lives, bring about greater opportunities and enrich those who experience it. These ideas of education are what lie at the very heart of this book.

What is the purpose of education?

Since education comes in many forms, what is it supposed to achieve? Smith (2015) believes, 'Education is deliberate. We act with a purpose – to develop understanding and judgement, and enable action.' Like the nature of education, the purpose of education varies according to context as well. In the UK, the schools minister, Nick Gibb, in his address to the education reform summit asked, 'Today, though, I would like to take a step back from the details of our reforms and turn to a broader question: what is the purpose of education?' (DfE, 2015b).

> ✎ **Activity: What is the purpose of education?**
>
> As a student, lecturer or practitioner, how would you answer this question? What is the UK government's view on this as well as other countries'? How are educational aims manifested in practice?

There are a variety of perspectives on such an important question; the purpose of education is highly contested and much debated in the academic discourse. This question has been debated for centuries (Kant, 1803[2007]; Dewey, 1938; Plato, 1955; Rousseau, see Darling 1994; Aristotle, see Hummel 1999[1993]; Locke, 2013). Early philosophers on education emphasised the role of education as a moral enterprise and centred on concepts such as ethics and democracy. Key questions related to whether education is for the benefit of the individual or society. More recently, the economic advantages of education (Schultz, 1961) have been prominent and are clearly seen in education policy (DBIS, 2010; DfE, 2010; DBIS, 2015). The answer proffered by the DfE (2015) is:

> Education is the engine of our economy, it is the foundation of our culture, and it's an essential preparation for adult life. Delivering on our commitment to social justice requires us to place these 3 objectives at the heart of our education system.
>
> We all have a responsibility to educate the next generation of informed citizens, introducing them to the best that has been thought and said, and instilling in them a love of knowledge and culture for their own sake. But education is also about the practical business of ensuring that young people receive the preparation they need to secure a good job and a fulfilling career, and have the resilience and moral character to overcome challenges and succeed.

Education as engine for economic growth

Policy makers have, in recent years, focussed more heavily on the role of education in the economic wellbeing of the nation. However, Wood (2011) believes that schooling has a long history of preparing learners for the world of work; schools have always been concerned with teaching literacy and numeracy, both of which are needed for employment. Links between education and economic productivity are not really new. Schultz (1961) played a fundamental role in recognising the economic value that people can have when they invest in acquiring skills and knowledge through education. Human capital is the idea that people, through education, are seen as an important resource and have economic value much like physical capital (money, raw materials, buildings and so forth). This idea is essential to the economy and '[i]n general, it is supported by many national leaders because it promises economic growth and development' (Spring, 2009, p. 16). However, the link between education and economic performance has not been proved (Easterly, 2002; Wood, 2011; Allen, 2011). If this is the case, then why do policy makers place so much importance on this particular aim?

Human capital and education are important in the knowledge economy. The OECD (1996, p. 7) defined the knowledge-based economies as 'economies which are directly based on the production, distribution and use of knowledge and information'. Changes in technology have led to greater investments in high-technology industries which require highly skilled workers who are creative and innovative. The role education plays in the digital world will be discussed in Chapter 12. However, Leadbeater (1999) believes that,

> The knowledge driven economy is not just a new set of high-tech industries such as software and biotechnology, which have built on a science base. Nor is it just a set of new technologies: information technology and the Internet, for example. The knowledge driven economy is about a set of new sources of competitive advantage, particularly the ability to innovate, create new products and exploit new markets, which apply to all industries, high-tech and low-tech, manufacturing and services, retailing and agriculture. In all industries the key to competitiveness increasingly turns on how people combine, marshal and commercialise their know-how.

Countries are continually seeking a competitive advantage in the world economy through education. In *The Importance of Teaching* white paper, which led to a number of education reforms (shift to a knowledge-based curriculum, introduction of the English Baccalaureate, creation of teaching schools and the Troops into Teachers programme), the UK's prime minister (DfE, 2010) wrote,

> So much of the education debate in this country is backward looking: have standards fallen? Have exams got easier? These debates will continue, but what really matters is how we're doing compared with our international competitors. That is what will define our economic growth and our country's future. The truth is, at the moment we are standing still while others race past.

✎ Activity: What are the key educational debates?

Reflect on the quote above. What are the key educational debates currently facing the education system? Are these debates concerned with falling standards and the examination system? Is education in the UK 'standing still'?

The World Bank (2009) is actively involved in 'Education for the Knowledge Economy (EKE) [which] refers to the World Bank's work with developing countries to cultivate the highly skilled, flexible human capital needed to compete in global markets – an endeavor that affects a country's entire education system'. Therefore, the World Bank assists countries in the following areas:

- secondary education that lays the foundation of a healthy, skilled, labor force capable of learning new skills as needed
- tertiary education that creates the intellectual capacity to produce and utilize knowledge
- lifelong learning that promotes education throughout the life cycle and helps countries adapt to changing market demands
- science, technology, and innovation capacity that continually assesses, adapts, and applies new technologies
- information and communications technology (ICT) that offers access to learning to people who most need it (such as out-of-school youth and children with disabilities) and that improves the quality of teaching and learning outcomes.

(World Bank, 2009)

Linked to the economy is neo-liberalism. The ideas of neo-liberalism have come to dominate educational goals since the 1980s (Davies & Bansel, 2007). Neo-liberalism stems from the political belief that a free-market economy and market forces will lead to greater parental choice, increased efficiency within schools and competition between schools. The effect of this is supposed to improve the quality of education provision (Marshall, 2014). The marketisation of education will be discussed further in Chapter 4.

Education as socialisation for society

> **Activity: Socialisation**
>
> What does the word socialisation mean? How do families and schools contribute to the socialisation of individuals and society?

Education is central to the socialisation of both individuals and society. Firstly, it is important to understand what is meant by socialisation.

> Socialization is the process through which people are taught to be proficient members of a society. It describes the ways that people come to understand societal norms and expectations, to accept society's beliefs, and to be aware of societal values.
>
> (Little, 2014)

Schooling, in particular, teaches children and young people about acceptable behaviour and how to live as well as get along with others.

One of the first sociologists to consider the relationship between education and society was the French sociologist Emile Durkheim (1858–1917) who considered schooling to be central in the socialisation process and to social cohesion. Durkheim argued that the purpose of education is to develop children's physical, intellectual and moral capabilities so they are able to meet the demands of the society in which they live in (Durkheim, 1956). For Durkheim, the moral values were the foundation of society (Sadnovik, 2011). Durkheim believed schooling was pivotal in maintaining social order and consensus among society. Teaching moral values to young people was crucial to this. When conflict occurs, it is because there has been a breakdown in this consensus, meaning individuals or groups have failed to share the same values.

Criticisms of Durkheim centre on the assumption that consensus benefits all members of society and education functions for the greater good. However, this ignores the fact that individuals have different needs, and values are not universally shared. Nowadays, societies, big or small, are ethnically, culturally, linguistically and economically diverse. Diversity has recently been seen as a positive force rather than a source of potential conflict (for example, Equality Act 2010). We also need to question whether we can and should all subscribe to the same values. Moreover, in the rhetoric of consensus, '[i]nequality, in terms of income or wealth, is actually seen as something which itself performs a function of encouraging us to better ourselves and, in the process, benefits the society as a whole' (Bartlett & Burton, 2012, p. 18). Inequality as a source of motivation is not something most educators ascribe to. Many argue that our current system perpetuates existing inequities by failing to reach the most disadvantaged pupils (for example, Bourdieu, 1974). In fact, the Centre for Social Justice (2014) has cited educational failure as a major cause of deprivation in communities across the UK. From a perspective of fairness and social justice, one of the primary goals of education should be to reduce serious disadvantage rather than create it. Issues of child poverty and schooling will be discussed in Chapter 2.

Many children who experience early failure in education go on to be what are known as NEETs, which stands for young people aged 16–24 who are Not in Education, Employment or Training. The UK government identifies a person as NEET if they are either unemployed or economically inactive and are either looking for work or are inactive for reasons other than being a student or a carer at home. Recent government statistics state that '857,000 people aged 16–24 were NEET in the third quarter of 2016, representing 11.9% of the age group' (Mirza-Davies & Brown, 2016). This equates to around 853,000 young people. This is above the Organisation for Economic Cooperation and Development's (OECD) average. In a longitudinal study of young people in England, the Department for Education (DfE, 2011) identified that those eligible for free school meals, those who have been excluded or suspended from school, those with their own child and those who have a disability are more likely to be NEET. Other factors that can affect the chances of becoming NEET are living in areas of social deprivation, parental factors (unemployment, little or no education and attitude) and growing up in care (Public Health England, 2014). The charity Impetus-PEF (2014, p. 4) believe,

> A young person who experiences a period NEET will, on average, lose up to £50,000 in earnings over their working life when compared to a peer who doesn't experience a period NEET. They will lose up to £225,000 over the same period when compared to a peer who has never been NEET and who has graduated from university. The long-term scarring of a period NEET to a young person's future life is dramatic. If we do not prevent the 120,000 of today's 13-year-olds who are at risk of becoming NEET from doing so, they collectively stand to lose £6.4 billion.

While the economic consequences are clear from the above data, what about the social disadvantage NEETs face? Public Health England (PHE, 2014) report that being a NEET has a damaging effect on young peoples' physical and mental health. It can also result in unhealthy behaviours and involvement in crime. The reality is that many NEETs face multiple sources of disadvantage and a key question remains as to how best to support them. The issues surrounding NEETs will be discussed in Chapter 6.

United Kingdom goals

The overarching goals of primary education in the UK are set out in the Education Act 2002 which states that every state-funded school must offer a curriculum that is balanced and broadly based which:

- promotes the spiritual, moral, cultural, mental and physical development of pupils at the school and of society, and
- prepares pupils at the school for the opportunities, responsibilities and experiences of later life (DfE, 2014a).

In addition, all state schools are required to teach religious education to pupils at every key stage, and sex education to pupils in secondary education (DfE, 2014a). Looking at these aims, it is clear that the goals are to develop both the individual and society. While it does not explicitly mention the economy, one can assume, partly, by preparing pupils for later opportunities in life that this entails individuals securing employment and taking their place in the workforce.

> **Activity: How to achieve the stated aims?**
>
> How should schools encourage the spiritual, moral, cultural, mental and physical development of pupils? What would you put in the curriculum to achieve these? More importantly, is it the responsibility of schools to do this? Are teachers equipped with the skills to deal with learners' mental health issues? Whose culture is being taught?

Mental health development of children as a goal

There has been a recent surge in the UK in the number of young people suffering from mental health issues, which include eating disorders, depression and self-harm (to be discussed in Chapter 9). According to the charity Young Minds (2016):

- One in four (26 per cent) young people in the UK experience suicidal thoughts.
- ChildLine (UK) has revealed that it held 34,517 counselling sessions in 2013/14 with children who talked about suicide – a 116 per cent increase since 2010/11.
- Among teenagers, rates of depression and anxiety have increased by 70 per cent in the past 25 years, particularly since the mid 1980s.
- The number of children and young people who have presented to A&E with a psychiatric condition has more than doubled since 2009 (8,358 in 2010/11; 17,278 in 2013/14).
- Of children who have been bullied, 55 per cent later developed depression as adults.
- Of children and young people under the age of 18 detained under s.136, 45 per cent were taken into police custody in 2012/13.

With figures so alarming, the Department for Education appointed its 'first ever mental health champion for schools to raise awareness and reduce the stigma around young people's mental health' in August 2015 (DfE, 2015a). Groups vulnerable to mental health issues include young offenders, looked after children, LGBT (lesbian, gay, bisexual and transsexual), BAME (Black, Asian, and minority ethnic), those with disabilities (discussed in Chapter 8), homeless youth, young people in gangs, and unemployed young people (Young Minds, 2016). Particular issues surrounding the LGBT community are discussed in Chapter 7.

Goals of education in Kenya

In comparison, the official educational goals of Kenya, first written by the government in 1964 on independence from colonial rule and later revised in 2002 (Mwaka et al., 2013, pp. 150–151) are:

1. To foster nationalism, patriotism and promote national unity: Kenya's people belong to different ethnic groups, races and religions but these differences need not divide them. They must be able to live and interact as Kenyans. It is a paramount duty of education to help the youth acquire this sense of nationhood by removing conflicts and by promoting positive attitudes of mutual respect which enable them to live together in harmony, and foster patriotism in order to make a positive contribution to the life of the nation.
2. To promote the social, economic, technological and industrial needs for national development: Education should prepare the youth of the country to play an effective and productive role in the life of the nation.
    a. Social needs: Education in Kenya must prepare children for the changes in attitude and relationships which are necessary for the smooth process of a rapidly developing modern economy. There is bound to be a silent social revolution following in the wake of rapid modernisation. Education should assist our youth to adapt to this change.
    b. Economic needs: Education in Kenya should produce citizens with skills, knowledge, expertise and personal qualities that are required to support a growing economy. Kenya is building up a modern and independent economy which is in need of adequate domestic manpower.
    c. Technological and industrial needs: Education in Kenya should provide the learners with the necessary skills and attitudes for industrial development. Kenya recognises the rapid industrial and technological changes taking place especially in the developed world. We can only be part of this development if our education system deliberately focusses on knowledge, skills and attitudes that will help prepare the youth for these changing global trends.
3. To promote individual development and self-fulfilment: Education should provide opportunities for the fullest development of individual talents and personality. It should help its recipients to develop their potential interests and abilities. A vital aspect of individual development is character building.
4. To promote sound moral and religious values: Education should provide for the development of knowledge, skills and attitudes that will enhance acquisition of sound moral values and help children to grow up into self-disciplined, self-reliant and integrated citizens.
5. To promote social equality and responsibility: Education should promote social equality and foster a sense of social responsibility within an education system which provides equal education opportunities for all. It should give all learners varied and challenging opportunities for collective activities and corporate social services irrespective of gender, ability or geographical environment.
6. To promote respect for and development of Kenya's rich and varied cultures: Education should instil in the youth of Kenya an understanding of past and present cultures and their valid place in the contemporary society. The learners should be able to blend the best of traditional values with the changed requirements that must follow rapid development in order to build a stable and modern society.
7. To promote international consciousness and foster positive attitudes towards other nations: Kenya is part of the international community. It is part of the complicated and

interdependent network of people and nations. Education should therefore lead the youth of the country to accept membership in this international community with all the obligations and responsibilities, rights and benefits that this membership entails.

8. To promote positive attitudes towards good health and environmental protection: Education should inculcate in the youth the value for good health in order to avoid indulging in activities that will lead to physical or mental ill health. It should foster positive attitudes towards environmental development and conservation. It should lead the youth to appreciate the need for a healthy environment.

> **Activity: Kenyan goals**
>
> Critically reflect on the goals of education in Kenya. Are these goals beneficial to individuals, societies or the nation as whole? What are the limitations? How are these different to the UK? How are these similar? Be prepared to give an explanation for your answer.

Nationalism and education

Education has continually played a key role in nation building and nationalism. Formal schooling, in particular, is central to instilling ideas, values, beliefs and norms of national culture (Marshall, 2014). It is important in fostering community cohesion and creating a shared sense of identity and belonging. Philosophers such as Jean-Jacques Rousseau believed one of the aims of education was to create future citizens of a nation (Wiborg, 2000). Others like Dewey, recognised how important schooling was to a creating a robust democracy (Dewey, 1916). However, citizenship education did not formally become a part of the National Curriculum as a non-statutory, cross-curricular subject until the 1988 Education Reform Act. It then became separate and statutory in 2002 for Key Stages 3 and 4. In 2014, the British government published a report for schools on how to promote British values in UK schools as part of the spiritual, moral, social and cultural (SMSC) development of pupils (DfE, 2014b).

> **Activity: Fundamental British values**
>
> What values do you think are fundamentally British and why? Are these different to French values, for instance? How would you teach these values?

Fundamental British values

The notion of teaching British values was born out of the UK government's response to terrorism/extremism in the wake of the 7 July bombings in 2005 and first set out in the Prevent Strategy (HM Government, 2011) (extremism, radicalisation and education will be discussed in Chapter 3). The guidance states, 'Schools should promote the fundamental British values of democracy, the rule of law, individual liberty, and mutual respect and tolerance of those with different faiths and beliefs' (DfE, 2014b, p. 5). Schools are required to develop a strategy for embedding these values and pupils are expected to demonstrate:

- a knowledge and understanding of how citizens can influence decision-making through the democratic process;
- an appreciation that living under the rule of law protects individual citizens and is essential for their wellbeing and safety;
- an understanding that there is a separation of power between the executive and the judiciary, and that while some public bodies such as the police and the army can be held to account through Parliament, others such as the courts maintain independence;
- an understanding that the freedom to choose and hold other faiths and beliefs is protected in law; an acceptance that other people having different faiths or beliefs to oneself (or having none) should be accepted and tolerated, and should not be the cause of prejudicial or discriminatory behaviour;
- an understanding of the importance of identifying and combatting discrimination.

(DfE, 2014b, pp. 5–6)

Schools have the freedom to promote these values in a number of ways and this is now part of Ofsted's inspection framework (Ofsted, 2015). However, there have been a number of criticisms with the British values agenda. Firstly, whose values are these and does everyone subscribe to the same set? Easton (2014) examines whether teaching British values is a good thing and asks, 'Would promoting the rule of law make it more difficult for schools to teach about civil disobedience?' He also questions whether democracy is the best form of government, 'And when it comes to mutual respect and tolerance of those with different faiths and beliefs, how respectful and tolerant should one be?' The sociologist Frank Furedi (2014) also believes that nobody can really answer the question, what does it mean to be British? If everyone has differing views on this, how can it be taught?

> **Activity: The Cranbourne Primary School**
>
> Have a look at the Cranbourne Primary School website at: www.cranbourne.herts.sch.uk/promoting-british-values/ How does this school promote British values?

Aims of higher education

> **Activity: Purpose of higher education**
>
> Before reading the next section, why do individuals go to university? What is learnt on degree courses? The Browne Review (DBIS, 2010, p. 14) believes higher education (HE) matters because:
>
> > It helps to create the knowledge, skills and values that underpin a civilised society. Higher education institutions (HEIs) generate and diffuse ideas, safeguard knowledge, catalyse innovation, inspire creativity, enliven culture, stimulate regional economies and strengthen civil society. They bridge the past and future; the local and the global.
>
> To what extent do you agree with this?

Since their inception in medieval times, universities have a long tradition in discovering 'truth' and 'knowledge' through scientific discovery and research. Is this still the case today? Wood (2011, p. 23) argues that

> Universities in the UK are changing. The old ideas of their being seats of learning where the battle for truth is fought out and a critical approach to the world adopted is fading. As with schooling, the state is looking to universities to fill the skills gap and the number of vocational courses is increasing. They are becoming more job focussed.

What should the higher education (HE) landscape look like today? Should the core purpose be knowledge production or preparing people for the world of work? Moreover, who should pay for it?

In the UK, tuition fees for higher education courses increased from around £3,000 a year in 2004 to a current cap of £9,000 as a result of recommendations set out in the Browne Review in 2010 (DBIS, 2010). The average student will typically graduate from a three-year undergraduate course in the UK with debts roughly between £35,000 and £40,000 (Boursnell, 2015). Research from the OECD (2012, p. 28) suggests that '[p]eople with higher (tertiary) education can expect to earn 55% more on average in OECD countries than a person without tertiary education'. However, is this personal investment in higher education a good one and what kinds of rate of return do students get? According to the 2015 Student Academic Experience Survey conducted by the Higher Education Policy Institute (HEPI) and the Higher Education Academy (HEA), 29 per cent of undergraduates feel they are getting 'poor' or 'very poor' value for money (Buckley et al., 2015). In light of this, recent discussions have centred on the number of contact hours, the quality of teaching and employability in particular.

While the number of hours students can expect in terms of attending scheduled teaching and learning activities or contact time (for example, lectures, seminars, tutorials) varies between courses, the average student can expect to spend around 12 hours per week during term time and those students who have fewer than ten hours of contact time per week are the least satisfied (Buckley et al., 2015). However, a focus solely on contact hours as a proxy for student satisfaction can be misleading as it does not give any indication of the quality of that experience.

The quality of higher education provision in the UK is very much subject to intense debate. The UK government has recently announced plans to implement a Teaching Excellence Framework (TEF) which hopes to raise standards in higher education (DBIS, 2015). Underpinning the framework is the idea that,

> Students expect better value for money; employers need access to a pipeline of graduates with the skills they need; and the taxpayer needs to see a broad range of economic and social benefits generated by the public investment in our higher education system.
> (DBIS, 2015, p. 18)

The TEF will also put teaching on a par with research and encourage better monitoring of the retention and progress of students from disadvantaged backgrounds. As it has yet to be implemented, doubts remain as to whether the TEF can really boost economic productivity, increase social mobility and improve overall standards in HE.

The real goals of education

In spite of the academic discourse, what do we really want learners to achieve as a result of participating in early childhood education, primary and secondary schooling, college or university? Littky and Grabelle (2004, p. 1) write about the 'real goals of education', which are for children to:

- be lifelong learners;
- be passionate;
- be ready to take risks;
- be able to problem-solve and think critically;
- be able to look at things differently;
- be able to work independently and with others;
- be creative;
- care and want to give back to their community;
- persevere;
- have integrity and self-respect;
- have moral courage;
- be able to use the world around them well;
- speak well, write well, read well, and work well with numbers;
- truly enjoy their life and their work.

> **Activity: The real goals of education**
>
> Take a moment to reflect on the 'real goals of education'. Do you agree with these goals? How are schools, colleges and universities able to achieve these and should they? Imagine a situation where you have a learner from a disadvantaged background. The only meal they receive is in school. They are hungry, tired and their home life is difficult and chaotic. Are these goals suitable for their needs?

Creativity as a real goal of education can be seen in one of the stated aims of the new National Curriculum launched in 2014 (DfE, 2014a). Sir Ken Robinson, a leader in creativity and innovation in education and business, believes creativity is the essential skill for the 21st century but that most schools are actually killing rather than fostering it (Robinson, 2011; Robinson & Aronica, 2015). Creativity is a central part of critical thinking and finding new ways of doing things. Some would argue this is important for economic productivity. However, Wyse (2014) believes that creativity is being severely neglected in the new curriculum, which could potentially harm the UK's reputation for creative teaching and learning. Creativity in the UK will be explored further in Chapter 5.

It could be argued that a number of the 'real' goals of education such as 'be ready to take risks' and 'persevere' link to the concept of resilience. Chapter 11 looks at how education can impact and influence individual and societal resilience by exploring what it means to be resilient. Is resilience about responding to and recovering from major emergencies (for example, earthquakes, terrorist attacks) or helping individuals to maximise their life chances through being safe, healthy and overcoming the negative effects of adversity at home or in the workplace? Whatever your views on resilience, should education take a role in building it?

What should we teach?

The purpose of education is also linked to who teaches, how they teach and what they teach. Once the goals of education are established, how we achieve them is linked to the curriculum and the content of what we teach. In other words, the curriculum is a realisation of our goals in practice. This book will take a wide view of what curriculum means and will look at different meanings of the term curriculum. UNESCO (2016) presents a typology of the curriculum as intended, implemented, achieved and hidden:

- Intended curriculum – what societies envisage important teaching and learning constitutes. It is usually presented in official documents; it may be also called the 'written' and/or 'official' curriculum.
- Implemented curriculum – at classroom level this intended curriculum may be altered through a range of complex classroom interactions and what is actually delivered can be considered the 'implemented' curriculum.
- Achieved or learned – what learners really learn (i.e. what can be assessed and demonstrated as learning outcomes/learner competencies) constitutes the 'achieved' or 'learned' curriculum.
- Hidden curriculum – points to the unintended development of personal values and beliefs of learners, teachers and communities; unexpected impact of a curriculum; unforeseen aspects of a learning process.

The curriculum is not just a list of subjects to be taught but must include the goals of what it should achieve. Having discussed these at length in this chapter, what do you think they should be?

Conclusion

In recent years, education has become the panacea for all society's ills. It is impossible for it to be the remedy for many social and economic problems so it is imperative to think carefully about which issues are a priority. The goals of education must be selected according to our most urgent needs. What do we need education for? Is the purpose to prepare future workers, increase productivity and encourage economic growth? Should it focus primarily on instilling societal values to ensure community cohesion and if so, which values? Is it about ensuring national unity, citizenship and the preservation of democracy in the face of increased terrorist activities? Or should our efforts concentrate on ensuring individuals are mentally healthy and resilient members of society? Education should serve to minimise individual and societal disadvantage, and by engaging in the contemporary debates discussed in this book you are invited to decide exactly how this should be achieved.

Suggested reading

Bartlett, S. & Burton, D. (2016) *Introduction to Education Studies*, 4th edn. London: Sage.

This is an essential text on any Education Studies degree and looks at all aspects of education from a variety of perspectives. Its in-depth content gives you an overview on the historical, psychological, sociological and political dimensions of education.

References

Allen, R. (2011) The economics of education, in Dufour, G. & Curtis, W. (eds), *Studying Education: An Introduction to Key Disciplines in Education Studies*. Maidenhead: Open University/McGraw Hill.

Arthur, J. & Davies, I. (eds) (2010) *The Routledge Education Studies Textbook*. Abingdon: Routledge.

Bartlett, S. & Burton, D. (2012) *Introduction to Education Studies*, 3rd edn. London: Sage.

Bates, J. & Lewis, S. (2009) *The Study of Education: An Introduction*. London: Continuum.

Bourdieu, P. (1974) School as a conservative force: Scholastic and cultural inequalities, in J. Eggleston (ed.), *Contemporary Research in the Sociology of Education*, pp. 32–46. London: Methuen.

Boursnell, P. (2015) *How Much Debt Will You Actually Get into by Going to University?* Available at: http://university.which.co.uk/advice/student-finance/how-much-debt-will-i-actually-get-into-by-going-to-university

Buckley, A., Soilemetzidis, I. & Hillman, N. (2015) *The 2015 Student Academic Experience Survey*. Available at: www.hepi.ac.uk/2015/06/04/2015-academic-experience-survey/

Centre for Social Justice (2014) *Closing the Divide: Tackling Educational Inequality in England*. Available at: http://centreforsocialjustice.org.uk/UserStorage/pdf/Pdf%20reports/Closing-the-Divide.pdf

Curtis, W., Ward, S., Sharp, J. & Hankin, L. (2014) *Education Studies: An Issues-Based Approach*, 3rd edn. Exeter: Learning Matters.

Darling, J. (1994) *Child-Centred Education and its Critics*. London: Paul Chapman.

Davies, B. & Bansel, P. (2007) Neoliberalism and education. *International Journal of Qualitative Studies in Education*, 20(3), 247–259.

DBIS (2010) *Securing a Sustainable Future for Higher Education: An Independent Review of Higher Education Funding and Student Finance* [Browne Review]. Available at: https://www.gov.uk/government/publications/the-browne-report-higher-education-funding-and-student-finance

DBIS (2015) *Fulfilling our Potential: Teaching Excellence, Social Mobility and Student Choice*. Available at: https://www.gov.uk/government/consultations/higher-education-teaching-excellence-social-mobility-and-student-choice

Delebarre, J. (2016) *NEET: Young People Not in Education, Employment or Training*. Available at: http://researchbriefings.parliament.uk/ResearchBriefing/Summary/SN06705

Dewey, J. (1916) *Democracy and Education*. New York: Macmillan.

Dewey, J. (1938) *Experience and Education*. New York: Simon and Schuster

DfE (2010) *The Importance of Teaching Schools White Paper*. Available at: https://www.gov.uk/government/publications/the-importance-of-teaching-the-schools-white-paper-2010

DfE (2011) *Youth Cohort Study and Longitudinal Study of Young People in England: The Activities and Experiences of 19 Year Olds: England 2010*. Available at: https://www.gov.uk/government/statistics/youth-cohort-study-and-longitudinal-study-of-young-people-in-england-the-activities-and-experiences-of-19-year-olds-2010

DfE (2014a) *National Curriculum in England: Framework for Key Stages 1 to 4*. Available at: https://www.gov.uk/government/publications/national-curriculum-in-england-framework-for-key-stages-1-to-4/the-national-curriculum-in-england-framework-for-key-stages-1-to-4

DfE (2014b) *Promoting Fundamental British Values as Part of SMSC in Schools*. Available at: https://www.gov.uk/government/uploads/system/uploads/attachment_data/file/380595/SMSC_Guidance_Maintained_Schools.pdf

DfE (2015) *Speech: The purpose of education*. Available at: https://www.gov.uk/government/speeches/the-purpose-of-education

Durkheim, E. (1956) *Education and Sociology*. Translated by S. D. Cox. Chicago: The Free Press.

Easterly, W. (2002) *The Elusive Quest for Growth*. Cambridge, MA: MIT Press.

Easton, M. (2014) Should teachers 'promote' British values? Available at: www.bbc.co.uk/news/uk-27784747

Furedi, F. (2014) The question no one can answer: what does it mean to be British? Available at: www.spiked-online.com/newsite/article/the-question-no-one-can-answer-what-does-it-mean-to-be-british/16271#.Vt7xxPmLSUI

HM Government (2011) *Prevent Strategy*. Available at: https://www.gov.uk/government/uploads/system/uploads/attachment_data/file/97976/prevent-strategy-review.pdf

Hummel, C. (1999/1993) Aristotle. *Prospects*, 23(1/2), 39–51.

Impetus-PEF (2014) *Makes NEETs History in 2014*. Available at: http://impetus-pef.org.uk/wp-content/uploads/2013/12/Make-NEETs-History-Report_ImpetusPEF_January-2014.pdf

Kant, I. (1803/2007) Lectures on pedagogy. In: Zöller, G. and Louden, R. B. (eds) *Anthropology, History, and Education*, The Cambridge Edition of the Works of Immanuel Kant in Translation. Cambridge: Cambridge University Press.

Leadbeater, C. (1999) *New Measures for the New Economy*. Available at: www.oecd.org/sti/ind/1947910.pdf

Littky, D. & Grabelle, S. (2004) *The Big Picture: Education is Everyone's Business*. Alexandria, Virginia: ASCD.

Little, W. (2014) *Introduction to Sociology: 1st Canadian Edition*. Available at: https://opentextbc.ca/introductiontosociology/

Locke, J. (2013) *Some Thoughts Concerning Education*, Mineola: Dover Publications.

Marshall, J. (2014) *An Introduction to Comparative and International Education*. London: Sage.

Mirza-Davies, J. & Brown, J. (2016) *NEET: Young People Not in Education, Employment or Training*. Available at: http://researchbriefings.parliament.uk/ResearchBriefing/Summary/SN06705#fullreport

Mwaka, M., Kafwa, V., Musamas, J. & Wambua, B. (2013) The national goals of education in Kenya: Interrogating the achievement of national unity. *Journal of Education and Practice*, 4(4), 149–156.

OECD (1996) *The Knowledge Based Economy*. Available at: www.oecd.org/sti/sci-tech/1913021.pdf

OECD (2012) How much more do tertiary graduates earn? *Education at a Glance 2012: Highlights*. Available at: www.oecd-ilibrary.org/docserver/download/9612041ec010.pdf?expires=1458575002&id=id&accname=guest&checksum=5416E8DBD9EADB2400904371AF18443D

Ofsted (2015) *School Inspection Handbook*. Available at: https://www.gov.uk/government/publications/school-inspection-handbook-from-september-2015

Plato (1955) *The Republic*. London: Penguin.

Public Health England (2014) *Local Action on Health Inequalities: Reducing the Number of Young People not in Employment, Education or Training (NEET)*. Available at: https://www.gov.uk/government/uploads/system/uploads/attachment_data/file/356062/Review3_NEETs_health_inequalities.pdf

Robinson, K. (2011) *Out of Our Minds: Learning to be Creative*, 2nd edn. West Sussex: Capstone.

Robinson, K. & Aronica, L. (2015) *Creative Schools: Revolutionizing Education from the Ground Up*. London: Allen Lane.

Sadnovik, A. (ed.) (2011) *Sociology of Education: A Critical Reader*, 2nd edn. Abingdon: Routledge.

Schultz, T. (1961) Investment in human capital. *The American Economic Review*, 51(1), 1–17.

Smith, M. K. (2015). *What is Education? A Definition and Discussion*. Available at: http://infed.org/mobi/what-is-education-a-definition-and-discussion/

Spring, J. (2009) *Globalization of Education*. New York: Taylor & Francis.

UNESCO (2016) *Different Meanings of Curriculum*. Available at: www.unesco.org/new/en/education/themes/strengthening-education-systems/quality-framework/technical-notes/different-meaning-of-curriculum/

Wiborg, S. (2000) Political and cultural nationalism in education: The ideas of Rousseau and Herder concerning national education. *Comparative Education*, 36(2), 235–243.

Wood, K. (2011) *Education: The Basics*. Abingdon: Routledge

World Bank (2009) *Education for the Knowledge Economy*. Available at: http://web.worldbank.org/WBSITE/EXTERNAL/TOPICS/EXTEDUCATION/0,,contentMDK:20161496~menuPK:540092~pagePK:148956~piPK:216618~theSitePK:282386,00.html

Wyse, D. (2014) *Creativity and the Curriculum (Inaugural Professorial Lecture)*. London: Institute of Education Press.

Young Minds (2016) *Mental Health Statistics*. Available at: www.youngminds.org.uk/about/whats_the_problem/mental_health_statistics?gclid=CjOKEQjwlLm3BRDjnML3h9ic_vkBEiQABa5oeWOchUurAL-lxo1k-P9LMa4brcP-fDb3v__maEgHQztoaAoDj8P8HAQ

2 Child poverty

Trends, causes and responses

Ihsan Caillau-Foster

This chapter explores:

- the meaning of child poverty;
- the consequences of child poverty;
- the causes of child poverty;
- the responses to child poverty.

> **Activity: Defining terms**
>
> What do you think is meant by the term 'child poverty'? Read the following definitions for both terms and compare your explanation with the different organisations' and authors' meanings.

Defining child poverty

Child poverty is a concept that is extensively and freely used by everyone from policy makers to stakeholders, and yet it is highly contested. Some organisations, such as the Joseph Rowntree Foundation (JRF) (2000), calculate child poverty using a subjective child deprivation index that accounts for the views of adults on what they believe are necessities of life and compares them to other measures (such as standards of living, social exclusion, poverty line, household average income, budget standards).

Alternatively, other organisations believe the percentage of population living in poverty can be scientifically determined using different scientific formulas such as the General Linear Models (both ANOVA and logistic regression) (see JRF, 2000, p. 78), the Human Development Index (HDI), or the Multidimensional Poverty Index (MPI). For the United Nations Children's Emergency Fund (UNICEF, 2013), for instance, relative poverty (i.e. people's way of life and income is much worse than the general population) as opposed to absolute poverty (i.e. experiencing extreme poverty due to lack of basic necessities for survival) is 50 per cent of the average income for the country in which children live. Somewhat different to the above, UNICEF offers an alternative, and perhaps more comprehensive, discourse to the meaning of child poverty. Poverty, the organisation seems to believe, is the consequence of the absence of 'desirable' and 'basic necessities of modern life'.

Perhaps realising that children and adults in developed and developing countries may differ in what they view as desirable and basic necessities of modern life, the United Nations introduced two definitions for child poverty. In the developed or wealthy countries' context, a child is deemed in poverty if they lack two or more of the following:

1. Three meals a day
2. At least one meal a day with meat, chicken or fish (or a vegetarian equivalent)
3. Fresh fruit and vegetables every day
4. Books suitable for the child's age and knowledge level (not including schoolbooks)
5. Outdoor leisure equipment (bicycle, roller-skates, etc.)
6. Regular leisure activities (swimming, playing an instrument, participating in youth organizations etc.)
7. Indoor games (at least one per child, including educational baby toys, building blocks, board games, computer games etc.)
8. Money to participate in school trips and events
9. A quiet place with enough room and light to do homework
10. An Internet connection
11. Some new clothes (i.e. not all second-hand)
12. Two pairs of properly fitting shoes (including at least one pair of all-weather shoes)
13. The opportunity, from time to time, to invite friends home to play and eat
14. The opportunity to celebrate special occasions such as birthdays, name days, religious events, etc.

(UNICEF Innocenti Research Centre, 2012, p. 2)

> **Activity: Measuring poverty**
>
> Looking at UNICEF's 14 items describing children's poverty, do you think you or someone you know may lack two or more of the above? What are your views on the items? Do you think they are good measures of 'child poverty'? Do you think some points need to be included or omitted? Explain.

Unlike its counterparts, UNICEF has incorporated what it regarded as 'necessities' that influence children's lives such as food, shelter, clothing, fuel, recreational and social activities, customs and obligations.

For the underdeveloped countries, the United Nation's Administrative Committee on Coordination Economic and Social Council (ECOSOC, 1998, p. 2) defines poverty as a:

> violation of human dignity. It means lack of basic capacity to participate effectively in society. It means not having enough to feed and clothe a family, not having a school or a clinic to go to, not having the land on which to grow one's food or a job to earn one's living, nor having access to credit. It means insecurity, powerlessness and exclusion of individuals, households and communities. It means susceptibility to violence and it often implies living in marginal and fragile environments, not having access to clean water and sanitation.

The European Union calculates poverty as the ratio of number of individuals whose household income falls below the poverty line, taken as half the average income of a country's population (OECD, 2012). The European Commission preserved its 1975 European Council's description of 'child poverty'. It correlates poverty to inadequate income and resources that prevent them from having an acceptable standard of living similar to others in their society. Because of their poverty, the Council of the European Union (2004) wrote, individuals may experience 'unemployment, low income, poor housing, inadequate health care and barriers to lifelong learning, culture, sport and recreation' (p. 8). Also, individuals may find themselves 'excluded and marginalised from participating in activities (economic, social and cultural) that are the norm for other people and their access to fundamental rights may be restricted' (Council of the European Union, 2004, p. 8). Professor Peter B. Townsend (1979), a British sociologist and the cofounder of the Child Poverty Action Group, similarly associates poverty with the absence or loss of 'resources (that) are so seriously below those commanded by the average individual or family that they are, in effect, excluded from ordinary living patterns, customs and activities' (p. 31).

For the UK, the definition of 'child poverty' is evolving and in need of revisiting to ensure it is in line with the present time. In 2010, the Labour government deemed a child in 'relative poverty' or 'relative low income' if his/her household's income was less than 60 per cent of the average household income (Lansley, 2012). In 2015, however, the Conservative government abandoned the earlier definition and introduced 'life chances' measures in four areas: children living in workless households in England; children living in long-term workless households in England; the educational attainment of children in England at the end of Key Stage 4; and the educational attainment of disadvantaged children in England at the end of Key Stage 4. These indicators somehow differ to what some research organisations such as the Joseph Rowntree Foundation use to measure poverty, such as whether the household is receiving Income Support, income-based Jobseekers Allowance, income-related Employment and Support Allowance, Child Tax Credit, council tax benefits or Working Tax Credit, Universal Credit and Housing Benefits, and residential property value as a socio-economic status indicator.

> **Activity: Debating definitions**
>
> Summarise the different definitions presented above. Identify the key words that stand out. Do you agree with the United Nations that poverty needs to account for the country's economic status? Explain your answer.

What definition would you use to describe child poverty? As evident from the above, childhood poverty cannot be equally defined. Poverty, one can argue, does not only relate to material shortage but also poverty of opportunities (such as time and access to leisurely and educational activities), family relationships (such as the presence of full-time parents/carers) and poverty of ambitions and aspirations.

Overall trends in child poverty in the UK

The UK's Department for Work and Pension's (2015) figures show that from 2013 to 2014, there were 3.7 million children living in poverty – three in every ten children in the UK. Despite the department's figures showing that the percentage of children having a relatively low income is 'the lowest since the 1980s' (p. 5), other statistical data from various charities show the fight to eradicating child poverty is far from over. According to the Trussell Trust (2014) which runs 420 foodbanks around the country, families in need of food and support are growing. In the first half of 2014–15, some 492,641 people were offered three days' food and support, including 176,565 children between April and September 2014, compared to 355,982 during same period in the previous year. This is a 38 per cent increase from the same period in the previous year. Likewise, Save the Children (2014) has reported that more than 1.6 million children are living in severe poverty in the UK. The charity believes this number could reach 5 million by 2020 due to recession, flat wages, cuts to benefits and rising cost of living. The Department for Work and Pensions (2015) also has reported that the increase in child poverty is rising among employed and unemployed families. Out of the 3.5 million children living in poverty, 63 per cent live in families with someone in employment.

> **Activity: Factors affecting poverty**
>
> From the figures presented above, why do you think poverty continues to sweep the UK, one of the richest countries in the world? List all the factors that you think contribute to child poverty in the UK, and outside the UK. Compare your factors with the section below.

Factors affecting child poverty

Individuals' beliefs, attitudes and behaviours

In the late 1950s, the anthropologist Oscar Lewis (1959) introduced the 'culture of poverty' theory as he studied the urban poor in Mexico and Puerto Rico. He suggested that largely people become, and remain, poor because of their beliefs, attitudes and behaviours. He added individuals who are born into a 'culture of poverty' and unable or unwilling to better themselves. He believes the culture of poverty is self-perpetuating. It is passed on from one generation to another. By the time children are six to seven years of age, he believes, they would have adopted their subculture's values and attitudes; they will not venture outside their norms to help enhance their lifestyles. Poverty, to Lewis, is primarily an individual failing.

Lewis (1971, cited in Stack, 1974) argues the above viewpoint is shared by those who want 'to believe that raising the income of the poor would not change their life styles or values, but merely funnel greater sums of money into bottomless, self-destructing pits' (p. 23). Clearly, the 'culture of poverty' has a racist and classist connotation that puts the sole responsibility on individuals to overcome poverty. This view differs to the previous perspectives offered earlier in this chapter that define poverty as the result of society's economic and political structure.

Lewis's (1971) perspective disregards the notion that while many low-income families may have the will and desire to work, there are other barriers outside their control that dictate otherwise, such as the onset of illness and disability of either themselves or others in the household. Not only that, but personal and/or household circumstances such as size of the household, low level of education and skills, parental separation or divorce, death, ill health, disability, caring responsibilities etc. can influence significantly their income level and their decision to find employment and access support.

Political factors

Over the years, many political parties in the UK have abandoned and then taken on new social policies. One of the most concerning for years, however, was the old social benefit system that seemed to teach dependency and reprimand betterment. Studies done by the Centre for Social Justice (2009, 2015) have found that families time and time again have lost their out-of-work benefits as soon as they were employed, regardless of how much they were earning. This, the Centre for Social Justice (2015) found, consequently decentivised many households from seeking employment. The welfare system was, concluded the Centre for Social Justice, clearly not working: if anything it celebrated social failure and it 'undermin(ed) social stability and personal responsibility ... Often it fought against the best interests of those in low income, not for them' (2015, p. 4).

Since 2016, the Conservative government has overhauled the above system and replaced it with the Universal Credit (UC). The aim is twofold: first, to simplify the welfare system and replace the six benefits and tax credits with a single monthly payment paid out to those with low income or who are out of work. Second, it encourages those who are on low incomes or out of work to take on employment and earn rather than live off benefits (Gov, 2016). Those who undertake work will be able to retain their income and increase their work incentives. Whether this new reform will drive efficiency and get the persistently unemployed into work, remains to be seen.

Economic factors

Since the financial crisis in 2008, the United Kingdom has been undergoing a considerable fiscal consolidation. Some of its austerity measures included the largest reduction to state spending since the Second World War, including cuts to social security, schools, further and higher education, defence, home office, justice, transport and housing, public sector jobs, investment spending, and public service spending to offset the ongoing public borrowing.

A number of reforms introduced included the loss of, for example, the £150.1 million grants dedicated to pregnant mothers due to the abolition of the Health in Pregnancy Grant (worth £190 per child) which was paid to 790,000 families with children (Family and Parenting Institute, 2010, p. 2). Also, the Sure Start Maternity Grant, which was originally payable per child, has been reduced to only the first child; this affected some 131,000 families (p. 4).

Not only that, but also policy reforms have affected working families. For example, the number of hours needed to claim Working Tax Credits have been increased from 16 to 24 (Family and Parenting Institute, 2010, p. 2). Refusal to engage will cost individuals £3,810 per annum of their tax credit entitlement (p. 2). This change has affected approximately 205,000 families with children. Adding to this, employed parents have also been hit by the reduction in the childcare element of the tax credit which has taken away some £381 million of support families received, affecting 489,000 families (p. 9).

On top of all the above cuts and reforms, the cost of living, as measured by the Retail Price Index, has increased by a total of 19.8 per cent between 2010 and 2014 (UNISON, 2015). The increase in the cost of everyday consumables, cuts in the welfare system and the loss of public and private sector jobs have all conspired to put a strain on already impoverished income-poor families. According to the national charity Children Society's (2013), the level of welfare support has fallen well below the level needed to lift children living in employed and unemployed households out of poverty. In fact, End Child Poverty Coalition (2015) found one in five families (nearly one 1.5 million families) with 2.5 million children were cutting back on food and heating due to benefit increases below inflation.

Unfortunately, the fiscal consolidation especially in our welfare system is forecasted to carry on for many years until the country has reduced its deficit and structural borrowing. In addition to the welfare cuts and rise of cost of living, the Joseph Rowntree Foundation (2014) warns that families in poverty have to contend with other factors such as the 'special' cost in spending incurred due to their circumstances (for example, the unemployed spend more time at home hence will spend more of their income on paying heating bills). As well as this, low-income families have to cope with the 'poverty premium' (the idea that 'the poor pay more'; see Caplovitz, 1967). For instance, paying for energy through expensive prepayment meters, or paying for excruciatingly expensive house and car insurance that takes into account risk factors such as home address and employment status.

> **Activity: Consequences of poverty**
>
> What consequences do you think poverty can have on children and their families?

Consequences of child poverty

The duration, severity and extent of poverty can have many negative consequences on individuals experiencing poverty, including their physical and mental health, financial income, behaviour, family and personal relationships and self-esteem. Some consequences can have short-term effects, but others can have medium, or lifetime, or even intergenerational effects (Joseph Rowntree Foundation, 2008). The next section will explore some of these effects.

Financial

Hirsch (2013) estimated that the financial cost of child poverty has soared between 2008 and 2013 from £25 to £29 billion. This increase has been the result of (a) tax receipts lost to government (a rise from £3.3 to £3.5 billion) due to loss of household earnings by those who grew in poverty, as well as (b) benefits spending (an increase from £2 to 2.4 billion) on out-of-work benefits to families growing up in poverty. And, also, the result of (c), the loss incurred (from £8 to 8.5 billion) in private post-tax earnings by adults who had grown up in poverty. While the above figures seem to be revealing the extent of the monetary cost of poverty, they need to be approached with caution. For instance, they exclude the NHS's healthcare cost associated with inequality. Child obesity alone has been estimated by the Department of Health (2011) to cost approximately £4.2 billion a year; it is predicted by 2050 this will be more than double.

Mental and physical health

The effects of poverty on health have been studied and recorded over the years with some (see for example, Bradshaw et al., 2016) identifying low birth weight as being affected by mother's poverty, health, ethnicity and health-related behaviour, such as smoking. Not only that but maternal health can also affect children's immunity to disease, behaviour and emotional development (Bradshaw, 2007). Bradshaw et al. (2016) found that children born into poverty also have more chances of having poor dental health and being born early. Infant mortality, claims HM Treasury (2004), is in fact higher among families in poverty.

The account is similar in childhood with children living in poverty more likely to be absent (1.6 times higher than their more affluent peers) from school due to short- and long-term illness and hospitalisation (DfE, 2013). Studies have found that low-income families in general consume fewer nutrients and fresh fruits and vegetables than average-income families. They are also prone to follow a poor or unhealthy high-sugar, high-sodium diet and suffer from health problems related to malnutrition (Bradshaw et al., 2016).

Not merely that, but research found that hunger in children can inhibit their cognitive functioning due to an inadequate supply of glucose to the brain (Benton, 2001, cited in Farthing, 2014). As a result, these children become lethargic and unable to concentrate. Likewise, food insecurity (inconsistent access to adequate food) can have significant effects on children's health and can cause developmental delays (Fabian Commission, 2015), iron-deficiency anemia and common illnesses such as stomach aches, headaches and colds at preschool age. One study (see Dowler et al., 2001) even said it contributed to childhood obesity.

In addition to the above risks to health, the Marmot Review (Marmot, 2010) found that individuals living in the poorest neighbourhoods will on average die seven years earlier than those living in the richest areas, and they are nearly three times as likely to suffer mental health problems than their more affluent peers.

Low educational attainment

On top of the financial and health complications, educational attainment can also affect children living in poverty. In a study funded by the Department for Education (2012), data showed that pupils in maintained schools, including academies and City Technology Colleges, who are eligible for Free School Meals (FSM) continue to underperform in comparison to non-FSM eligible pupils. It reported that only one in three children receiving FSM achieved 5 A*–C at GCSE in 2010 compared with the national average of approximately 60 per cent.

Likewise, in a later study funded by the Department for Education (2015b), statistical evidence showed that only 64 per cent of FSM-eligible pupils achieved Level 4+ in Reading, Writing and Mathematics in 2013/2014 in comparison to 82 per cent who are not FSM eligible. Similar trends were found for FSM-eligible pupil attainment at GCSE by another DfE-funded research project (2015a). The statistical data (see Figure 2.1) found 33.5 per cent of pupils eligible for FSM achieved at least 5 A*–C GCSEs (or equivalent) grades including English and mathematics compared to 60.5 per cent of all other pupils (a gap of 27.0 percentage points).

Clearly from the above, student progression is more significantly different in mathematics (23 per cent) than English (15 per cent) (DfE, 2015a). The Department for Education's (2015a) data

Child poverty: Trends, causes and responses 23

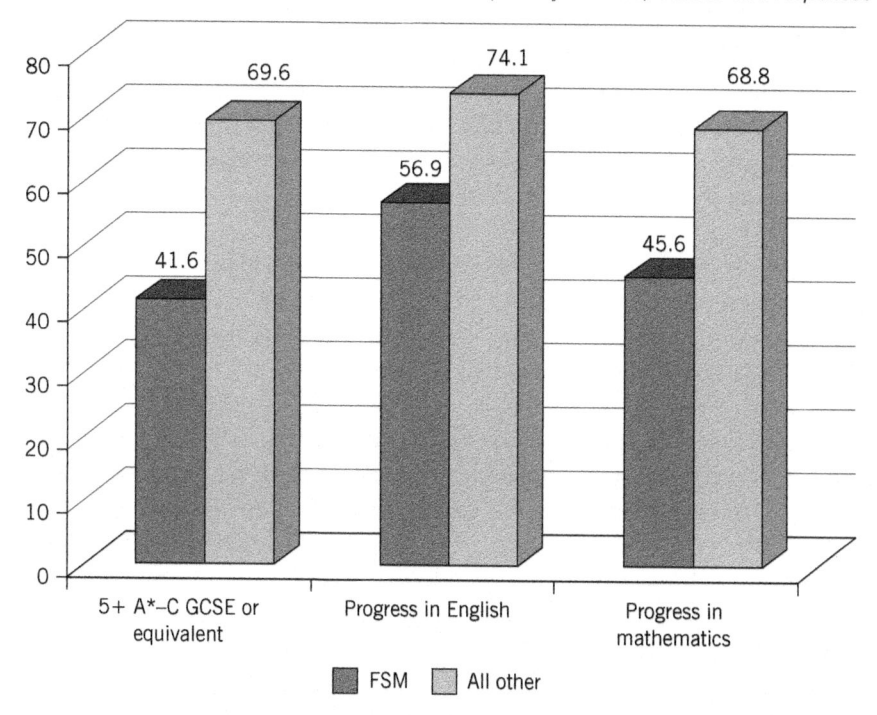

```
                    74.1
80   69.6                          68.8
         
70                                 
              56.9
60                                 
                              45.6
50   41.6
                                   
40                                 
                                   
30                                 
                                   
20                                 
                                   
10                                 
                                   
 0                                 
   5+ A*–C GCSE or  Progress in   Progress in
    equivalent      English       mathematics
         ■ FSM      □ All other
```

Figure 2.1 Attainment at Key Stage 4 by FSM eligibility, percentage of pupils achieving each indicator, England, 2013/2014 (adapted from DfE, 2015a, p. 11)

also showed (see Figure 2.1) that 36.5 per cent of disadvantaged pupils achieved at least 5 A*–C GCSEs (or equivalent) grades including English and mathematics compared to 64.0 per cent of all other pupils, a gap of 27.4 percentage points.

> **Activity: Addressing poverty**
>
> The Department for Work and Pensions and the Department for Education (2012) estimate that between 2011 and 2021, the number of under-16-year-olds will increase by 1.3 million. Also, by 2050, it forecasts there will be one person of pension age to every two people of working age. For this reason, they recommend, 'These demographic and economic challenges we face mean we simply cannot afford to waste the potential of children growing up in poverty. Not only do we need to act to tackle causes of child poverty, but we need to act now' (p. 20).

With the above forecasted figures, what strategies would you recommend to help address child poverty?

Read the next section and compare your suggestions to the government's policies and practices.

Addressing child poverty

Unfortunately, there is no single response that will succeed on its own to address child poverty. According to the UNCRC (the United Nations Convention on the Rights of the Child, 2009), all children have basic rights (adopted in November 1989, and enforced in September 1990, in accordance with Article 49) to four broad clusters:

1. Child survival including access to water, nutrition, sanitation and health care services.
2. Child protection from violence, exploitation, abuse and neglect.
3. Child development including education and psychological development.
4. Child participation in community decisions that affect their lives.

To help implement the legal and moral responsibilities to all children, the UK has applied a plethora of cross-cutting policy targets and initiatives to enhance children's life chances, such as the 1999 and 2011 government strategy to halve child poverty by 2020, the introduction of the Child Poverty Act 2010, the 2014 Child Poverty Strategy, the Universal Infant Free School Meals (UIFSM), Healthy Start (replaced the Welfare Food Scheme in 2006) for pregnant women and young children, and the 2015 Welfare Reform and Work Bill. Though some policies have been implemented, many have been criticised and abandoned, such as the Child Poverty Act 2010 and the Government's pledge to fund an extra £2,300 per school per year for hot meals to help with the transition to the Universal Infant Free School Meals (UIFSM).

It would be difficult to examine all the poverty-reduction initiatives within the framework of this chapter. Instead, five important policies have been selected and will be explored in the next sub-section.

Family intervention programmes

Evidence from the Department for Education (2014) showed that owing to several family intervention programmes and initiatives, on average there was a 50 per cent reduction in the proportion of families involved in crime and antisocial behavior; 53 per cent decrease in families with school-aged children who are either truanting, excluded or behaving badly at school; 34 per cent fall in the number of families with health risks including mental or physical health and drug or alcohol problems; and a 14 per cent decrease in the proportion of families who were 'workless'. Two of the most successful family programmes are described below.

Troubled Families Programme

A major social justice initiative introduced in 2011 by the UK government is the Troubled Families Programme to help improve the lives of 120,000 'troubled families' in England who are: involved or at risk of crime and antisocial or criminal behaviour, with mental and or physical health problems, unemployed, and/or have a child or more who has been truant, excluded or misbehaving in school. In a study carried out by the Department for Communities and Local Government (2014), data findings showed that from 2012 to 2013, of the 97,000 families engaged in the initiative, almost 53,000 families have made significant progress including returning their children to school, reducing crime and antisocial behavior and returning to work. Clearly, this programme has turned some families' lives around. Additional research, however, is needed to explore whether its effect on families is long term.

Sure Start

Another successful family intervention is Sure Start. Building on the successes and learning of the Head Start programme in the US and Australia and Ontario's Early Years Plan, Sure Start was introduced in 1998 to alleviate some of the effects of poverty in some areas. It was overseen by the Department for Children, Schools and Families and the Department for Work and Pensions and involved volunteers and practitioners from education, health and social care, for pregnant women, their partners and their children aged up to five years. Support provided to families included midwifery home visits, outreach community activities, nutrition, parental classes etc. The reviews of Sure Start have been mixed with some such as the University of Durham (cited in Merrell, 2010) claiming it was ineffective at improving results in early schooling from 2001 to 2008. Others, such as the National Evaluation of Sure Start Research Team (2008, 2010), disputed these findings, maintaining that Sure Start's impact has been very positive on families. Follow-up research assessing Sure Start's impact on families continue.

> **Activity: Effects of family intervention programmes**
>
> What do you think are the factors that are likely to impede the long-term successes of Troubled Families Programme and Sure Start? List and explain with reference to some literature.

Academies

Academy schools, initially known as City Academies, were built on the successes of the US charter schools and Swedish *friskolor*. They were initiated by the UK Labour government in 2002 as a driver to improve educational attainment and low expectations in failing schools in deprived areas. Unlike other state schools, they have the right to choose how to deliver their school curriculum, their staffs' selection, pay and conditions, and the length of school term and school day.

There are two types of academy schools: sponsored and converter academies. On the one hand, the sponsored academies replaced underperforming schools to improve the educational performance and aspirations of pupils. On the other hand, the converter academies were introduced to replace well-performing schools. The choice to convert to academy status varies for each converted school, but it is mainly to enjoy the benefit of increased autonomy the academy status brings.

The overall effects of academies in addressing pupil performance and aspirations, especially in poor environments, are inconclusive. On the one hand, the National Audit Office's (2014) review found some evidence that sponsored secondary academies have a positive effect on students' academic achievement. For example, GCSE results in English and mathematics have improved in secondary academies including for those eligible for FSMs and with special educational needs (Hutchings et al., 2014). On the other hand, Worth (2015) found there was no significant difference in GCSE performance between converter academies and maintained schools. This research also concluded that the attainment gap between pupils eligible for FSM and those who are not is merely half a GCSE grade per pupil (6 per cent of the existing gap).

> ✎ **Activity: Perspectives on academies**
>
> In 2016, the Education Secretary, Nicky Morgan, gave a speech at the National Union of Teachers' (NUT) conference describing her department's plan to convert every state school into an academy. Yet several days later, she abandoned her plan. Commenting on the Secretary's u-turn, Christine Blower, the General Secretary of the National Union of Teachers, highlighted several disadvantages to academies.
>
> Read the excerpt from both Nicky Morgan and Christine Blower's speech (Department for Education, 2016; and NUT, 2016), and comment on their arguments on the strengths and weaknesses of academies. Refer to some literature to support your arguments.

Pupil Premium Grant (PPG)

The Pupil Premium was introduced in the UK in 2011 to raise the attainment of disadvantaged pupils eligible for FSM and to close the gap with their peers. It takes the form of additional funding that is directly granted to schools to help assist pupils (from Reception to Year 6) eligible for FSM and who have been looked after continuously for more than six months (Education Funding Agency, 2015). The amount paid out to schools has increased over the years to total £1,320 per primary pupil and £935 per secondary pupil per financial year (Sutton Trust and Education Endowment Foundation, 2015).

Schools receiving Pupil Premium are encouraged by the government to use the Teaching and Learning Toolkit to assess whether they have met their 34 measurable learning gains. Also, to prove their effects on individual pupils, schools are required to submit school's results for those pupils before their Ofsted inspection visit. Moreover, the most improved schools are urged to compete for the Pupil Premium Award. Prizes range from £250,000 for national winners and £100,000 for regional winners, and hundreds of other smaller awards.

Insights from primary and secondary teachers have emphasised there is 'no doubt' the attainment of less advantaged pupils has improved. The GCSE results, however, tell a different story. The Sutton Trust and Education Endowment Foundation (2015) found the GCSE scores between Pupil Premium and non-Pupil Premium pupils are barely closing. They warn, however, that this finding needs to be considered with caution as the threshold measure only changes when a student achieves a C rather than a D grade but not if they achieve an E rather than F or an A rather than a B grade. If one does, nevertheless, look at the pupils' grades across several subjects (English, mathematics, three subjects from science, computer science, history, geography and languages, plus three other subjects) each year, they argue, one will find the gap is closing fast for children achieving a Level 4B or better in Key State 2 tests at age 11.

Free School Meals (FSM) and Universal Infant Free School Meals (UIFM)

Free School Meals (FSM) is not a novel idea. It was introduced in 1879 in Manchester and Bradford for 'destitute and badly nourished children'. Later, the London School Board, the Salvation

Army and other philanthropic organisations began to provide subsidised or free school dinners. The overwhelming perspective among politicians and educators was that if hungry children are to learn, then they will need to be fed first. Several years later, the Education (Provision of Meals) Act of 1906 permitted, but did not oblige, local authorities to provide school meals. Later in the Second World War, the school meals service was expanded and over 1.6 million free and subsidised meals were served daily to a third of the school population (Education Funding Agency, 2015). Unfortunately, due to the financial cost it was incurring on the government's budget and public spending, free school meals were stopped in the 1980s under Margaret Thatcher's Conservative government. Fortunately, in 2013 free school meals became a statutory benefit to school-aged children in Reception and Years 1 and 2 whose families are eligible for social benefits. It was not until September 2014, however that *all* infant school pupils in Reception, Year 1 and Year 2 in England became entitled to Universal Infant Free School Meals (UIFM), a free hot meal at lunchtime every day.

In addition to ensuring all children have access to free meals and are not stigmatised, the UIFM is expected to allow families with school-aged children in relative poverty previously eligible for FSM to increase their hours of work without losing their FSM benefits. The fate of the new programme, however, remains unclear, with many schools struggling to cope with the additional staffing and rooming the initiative has incurred on already strained budgets.

Activity: The value of Universal Infant Free School Meals (UIFM)

Ofsted's *School Inspection Handbook* (2015) states that inspectors 'will take particular account of the progress made by disadvantaged pupils by the end of the key stage compared with that made nationally by other pupils with similar starting points and the extent to which any gaps in this progress, and consequently in attainment, are closing'. It also adds that inspectors will compare the progress and attainment of the school's disadvantaged pupils with the national figures for the progress and attainment of non-disadvantaged pupils.

What are your views on Ofsted's comparison of attainment and progress scores between schools and pupils? How do you think Ofsted's report on these contribute to (a) the pupils, (b) the school?

Extended services in schools

Though the term 'Full Service Extended Schools' seems to be merely 13 years old, in fact it is an old idea that can be traced back to the 1920s when many British schools offered additional activities to meet pupils and their families' needs. When the first national initiatives were instigated in the country in 2002/03, a large majority of schools were already offering extended services to the community.

Since its launch, many traditional schools, especially those in disadvantaged areas, were offered funding so they could transform themselves into community schools to help develop pupils' educational skills and enhance their work prospects (DfE, 2004). To help pave its way, the government passed the Education Act 2000 which gave the governing bodies the power to directly provide community services such as health and social care and childcare as well as community facilities such as a youth club. Also, it published an Extended Schools Guidance document to provide schools with practical advice for those thinking about extending their services (DfE, 2010).

Although the evidence on the success of the extended services in schools is inconclusive, findings from the DfE (2010) show it has met its main objective of targeting children and adults who are economically, socially and educationally disadvantaged. There is somewhat robust indication that extended services can help improve the status quo of many families. The report concludes that the service does and can help retain and engage children in school, and it can inspire them 'onto productive pathways after school' (p. 15). Extended services can also help build family resilience (discussed in Chapter 12), develop parenting skills and encourage adults to pursue additional learning and employment pathways. Not only that, but it will also ultimately influence their children's learning and life chances.

> **Activity: Developing extended services in schools**
>
> If you had been tasked to develop extended services for your previous school, what would have been your priorities? What type/s of services would you provide and for whom? How would you ensure these are being met?

Conclusion

As shown above, the term 'child poverty' is difficult to define, difficult to understand, difficult to measure and difficult to intervene. It could take some decades before the full effect of a poverty reduction policy or programme can be evidenced. Sure Start is one example of the many programmes whose impact continues to be assessed to our day. Politicians and practitioners clearly realise the importance of investigating its developmental trends across the life span to assert its effects in addressing the underlying causes of poverty.

From this chapter, you would have also realised that the various policy interventions and programmes in the UK seem to be underpinned by the UK's definition of poverty and its effects. These policies have been introduced with the primary aim of providing some additional support to families with children, including social security, early childcare intervention, free school hot meals and pre-natal and parental guidance and help. All these are delivered by schools, children's centres, government officials and charitable organisations. While some of their effects on eradicating child poverty and enhancing attainment are yet unclear, for now they are the only ones we have that appear to be a cost-effective investment.

> **Case study 2.1: The case of Jade and her children**
>
> Jade is expecting a new baby. She is 25 years of age, and already she is a mother of three children. Jade suffers with postnatal depression and drug addiction.

Jade's addiction spans several years. Because of her dependency on drugs as a teenager, she rarely had any money to spend on food. Hence, she relied on the local foodbank to survive. Food insecurity is nothing new to Jade. She has experienced hunger ever since she was a young child. When she was merely four years of age, she and her sister used to be sent off to rummage through fast-food restaurant bins in search for food. Occasionally, they would also steal food for their peers' lunchboxes at school. Jade's experiences with food insecurity have been coupled with long-term physical and mental abuse and neglect by her father and his string of girlfriends.

At the age of six, Jade was taken into care after she was found trembling on the street. Later, however, she was returned to her father. At ten, she ran away after her father and one of his girlfriends tried to sell her for drugs. After that, Jade was placed in the foster care system but repeatedly ran away. Finally, at the age of 17, she found her safe haven on the street. From then onwards, she worked as a prostitute.

Feeling the urge to settle down and raise a family, Jade got married. Sadly, however, none of her relationships lasted and her depression and drug addiction grew over the years so that she is now unable to wake up to her children's calls.

Neglected, hungry and unloved, every day Jade's children leave in haste in the early hours of the morning in the hope they can secure several bowls of cereals and milk before their peers at the school's breakfast club. Their physical ill health has not gone unnoticed by the school staff. The headteacher has already reported the children to social services after Jade has failed to return his calls. The concern was particularly raised after one of Jade's younger boys was caught stealing boxes of cereals from the breakfast club's kitchen shelf.

- What do you think about Lewis's view that families become and remain in poverty because of their beliefs, attitudes and behaviours? What factors do you think contributed to Jade and her children's circumstances?
- Jade's children have relied on their school's breakfast club for food. Look up on the internet how many breakfast clubs there are in the UK and who finances them. Why do you think there are so many breakfast clubs?
- After having read this chapter, what do you think (a) families, (b) governments, (c) schools, and (d) communities should be doing to support families such as Jade's?

Suggested reading

Bradshaw, J. (ed.) (2016) *The Well-Being of Children in the UK*. Bristol: Policy Press.
Dowler, E., Turner, S. and Dobson, B. (2001) *Poverty Bites: Food, Health and Poor Families*. London: CPAG.
Pe Symaco, L. (ed.) (2014) *Education, Poverty, Malnutrition and Famine*. London: Bloomsbury.

References

Bradshaw, J., Dale, V. and Bloor, K. (2016) Physical health. In Bradshaw, J. (ed.) (2016) *The Well-Being of Children in the UK*. Bristol: Policy Press.
Bradshaw, T. K. (2007) Theories of poverty and anti-poverty programs in community development. *Journal of Community Development*, 38(1), 7–25.
Caplovitz, D. (1967) *The Poor Pay More: Consumer Practices of Low-Income Families*. New York: A Free Press.
Centre for Social Justice (2009) *Breakthrough Britain: Dynamic Benefits, Towards Welfare that Works*. Available at: www.centreforsocialjustice.org.uk/UserStorage/pdf/Pdf%20Exec%20summaries/CSJ%20Dynamic%20Benefits%20exec.pdf

Centre for Social Justice (2015) *Breakthrough Britain 2015, An Overview*. Available at: www.centreforsocialjustice.org.uk/UserStorage/pdf/Pdf%20reports/CSJJ2470_BB_2015_WEB.pdf

Children's Society (2013) *A Good Childhood for Every Child? Child Poverty in the UK*. Available at: www.childrenssociety.org.uk/sites/default/files/tcs/2013_child_poverty_briefing_1.pdf

Council of the European Union (2004) *Joint Report by the Commission and the Council on Social Inclusion*. Available at: http://ec.europa.eu/employment_social/soc-prot/soc-incl/final_joint_inclusion_report_2003_en.pdf

Department for Communities and Local Government (2014) *Understanding Troubled Families*. London: Department for Communities and Local Government. Available at: www.gov.uk/government/uploads/system/uploads/attachment_data/file/336430/Understanding_Troubled_Families_web_format.pdf

Department for Education (DfE) (2010) *Extended Services in Practice – A Summary of Evaluation Evidence for Head Teachers*. Available at: www.gov.uk/government/uploads/system/uploads/attachment_data/file/182456/DFE-RR155.pdf

Department for Education (DfE) (2012) *GCSE and Equivalent Attainment by Pupil Characteristics in England, 2010/11*. Available at: www.gov.uk/government/statistics/gcse-and-equivalent-attainment-by-pupil-characteristics-2012-to-2013

Department for Education (DfE) (2013) *Pupil Absence in Schools in England, including Pupil Characteristics: 2011/12*, Available at: www.gov.uk/government/uploads/system/uploads/attachment_data/file/221799/sfr10-2013.pdf

Department for Education (DfE) (2014) *Monitoring and Evaluation of Family Intervention Services and Projects between February 2007 and March 2011*. Available at: www.gov.uk/government/uploads/system/uploads/attachment_data/file/184031/DFE-RR174.pdf

Department for Education (DfE) (2015a) *Statistical First Release: GCSE and Equivalent Attainment by Pupil Characteristics, 2013 to 2014 (revised)*. Available at: www.gov.uk/government/uploads/system/uploads/attachment_data/file/399005/SFR06_2015_Text.pdf

Department for Education (DfE) (2015b) *Statistical First Release: National Curriculum Assessment at Key Stage 2 in England, 2014 (revised). National tables: SFR 50/2014*, Available at: www.gov.uk/government/uploads/system/uploads/attachment_data/file/428838/SFR50_2014_Text.pdf

Department for Education (DfE) (2016) *Nicky Morgan speech at the NAHT annual conference 2016*. Available at: www.gov.uk/government/speeches/nicky-morgan-speech-at-the-naht-annual-conference-2016

Department for Education and Skills (DfES) (2004) *Evaluation of the Extended Schools Pathfinder Projects*. Available at: www.ncl.ac.uk/cflat/documents/2k.pdf

Department for Work and Pensions and the Department for Education (2012) *Child Poverty in the UK: The Report on the 2010 Target*. Presented to Parliament pursuant to section 1(1) of the Child Poverty Act 2010, June 2012. London: The Stationery Office, Available at: www.gov.uk/government/uploads/system/uploads/attachment_data/file/192213/child_poverty_in_the_uk_the_report_on_the_2010_target.pdf

Department for Work and Pensions (2015) *Households below Average Income, an Analysis of the Income Distribution 1994/95–2013/14, Tables 4a and 4b. 201, 5*. Available at: www.gov.uk/government/uploads/system/uploads/attachment_data/file/437246/households-below-average-income-1994-95-to-2013-14.pdf

Department of Health (2011) *Obesity: General Information*. Available at: www.dh.gov.uk/en/Publichealth/Obesity/DH_078098

Dowler, E, Turner, S. and Dobson, B. (2001) *Poverty Bites: Food, Health and Poor Families*. London: CPAG

ECOSOC (United Nations Economic and Social Council) (1998) *Statement of Commitment for Action to Eradicate Poverty Adopted by Administrative Committee on Coordination, May 20, 1998*. ECOSOC. Available at: www.unesco.org/most/acc4pov.htm

Education Funding Agency (2015) *Guidance Universal Infant Free School Meals (UIFSM): Conditions of Grant 2015 to 2016*. Available at: www.gov.uk/government/publications/universal-infant-free-school-meals-uifsm-funding-allocations-2015-to-2016/universal-infant-free-school-meals-uifsm-conditions-of-grant-2015-to-2016

End Child Poverty Coalition (2015) *Short Changed: The True Cost of Cuts to Children's Benefits*. Available at: www.endchildpoverty.org.uk/wp-content/uploads/2015/07/PDF_Short_Changed_fullreport.pdf

Fabian Commission on Food and Poverty (2015) *Hungry for Change*. London: The Fabian Society. Available at: www.fabians.org.uk/wp-content/uploads/2015/10/Hungry-for-Change-web-27.10.pdf

Family and Parenting Institute (2010) *Families in an Age of Austerity: How Tax and Benefit Reform Will Affect UK Families*. Available at: www.familyandchildcaretrust.org/sites/default/files/files/2.5.2%20Download%20part%20one%20Families%20in%20the%20Age%20of%20Austerity%20the%20report.pdf

Farthing, R. (2014) School, poverty and hunger in the UK. In L. Pe Symaco (ed.), *Education, Poverty, Malnutrition and Famine*. London: Bloomsbury

Gov (2016) *Universal Credit*. Available at: www.gov.uk/universal-credit/overview

Hirsch, D. (2013) *An Estimate of the Cost of Poverty in 2013*. Loughborough: Centre for Research in Social Policy. Available at: www.cpag.org.uk/sites/default/files/Cost%20of%20child%20poverty%20research%20update%20(2013).pdf

HM Treasury (2004) *Child Poverty Review*. London: The Stationery Office.

Hutchings, M., Francis, B. and De Vries, R. (2014) *Chain Effects: The Impact of Academy Chains on Low-Income Students*. London: Sutton Trust.

Joseph Rowntree Foundation (2000) *Poverty and Social Exclusion in Britain*. York: Joseph Rowntree Foundation. Available at: http://hdr.undp.org/en/content/multidimensional-poverty-index-mpi

Joseph Rowntree Foundation (2008) *The Costs of Child Poverty for Individuals and Society: A Literature Review*. Available at: www.jrf.org.uk/sites/default/files/jrf/migrated/files/2301-child-poverty-costs.pdf

Joseph Rowntree Foundation (2014) *Poverty and the Cost of Living*. Available at: www.jrf.org.uk/report/poverty-and-cost-living

Lansley, S. (2012) *The Cost of Inequality*. London: Gibson Square Books.

Lewis, O. (1959) *Five Families: Mexican Case Studies in the Culture of Poverty*. New York: Basic Books.

Lewis, H. (1971) Culture and poverty? What does it matter? In Leacock, E. B. (ed.), *The Culture of Poverty: A Critique*. New York: Simon & Schuster.

Marmot, M. (2010) *Fair Society, Healthy Lives* [The Marmot Review]. Available at: www.instituteofhealthequity.org/projects/fair-society-healthy-lives-the-marmot-review

Merrell, C. (2010) Early years' initiatives, such as Sure Start, are failing the poor, eight-year study shows. Available at: www.dur.ac.uk/news/newsitem/?itemno=11251

National Audit Office (2014) *Academies and Maintained Schools: Oversight and Intervention* (HC 721). Available at: www.nao.org.uk/wp-content/uploads/2014/10/Academies-and-maintained-schools-Oversight-and-intervention.pdf

National Evaluation of Sure Start Research Team (2008) *The Impact of Sure Start Local Programmes on Three Year Olds and Their Families*. Available at: www.ness.bbk.ac.uk/impact/documents/42.pdf

National Evaluation of Sure Start Research Team (2010) *The Impact of 14 Local Programmes on Five Year Olds and Their Families*. Available at: www.gov.uk/government/uploads/system/uploads/attachment_data/file/182026/DFE-RR067.pdf

NUT (2016) Nicky Morgan suggested 'u turn' on forced academies. Available at: www.teachers.org.uk/news-events/press-releases-england/nicky-morgan-suggested-u-turn-on-forced-academies

OECD (2012) *Poverty Rate*. Available at: https://data.oecd.org/inequality/poverty-rate.htm

Ofsted (2015) *School Inspection Handbook*. Available at: www.gov.uk/government/publications/school-inspection-handbook-from-september-2015

Save the Children Fund (2014) *A Fair Start for Every Child: Why We Must Act Now to Tackle Child Poverty in the UK*. London: Save the Children. Available at: www.savethechildren.org.uk/sites/default/files/images/A_Fair_Start_for_Every_Child.pdf

Stack, C. (1974) *All Our Kin: Strategies for Survival in a Black Community*. New York: Harper and Row.

Sutton Trust and Education Endowment Foundation (2015) *The Pupil Premium, Next Steps*. Available at: www.suttontrust.com/wp-content/uploads/2015/06/Pupil-Premium-Summit-Report-FINAL-EDIT.pdf

Townsend, P. (1979) *Poverty in the United Kingdom*. London: Penguin.

Trussell Trust (2014) *Low Income and Welfare Problems*. Available at: www.trusselltrust.org/wp-content/uploads/sites/2/2015/06/Low-income-and-welfare-problems-lead-to-40-percent-rise-in-foodbank-use.pdf

UNICEF (2013) *Child Well-Being in Rich Countries, A Comparative Overview*. Innocenti Report Card 11, Florence. Available at: www.unicef-irc.org/publications/pdf/rc11_eng.pdf

UNICEF Innocenti Research Centre (2012) *Measuring Children's Poverty: New League Tables of Child Poverty in the World's Rich Countries*. Innocenti Research Centre, Report Card 10. Available at: www.unicef-irc.org/publications/pdf/rc10_eng.pdf

UNISON (2015) *The Cost of Living Outline*. Available at: www.unison.org.uk/content/uploads/2015/08/Cost-of-livingv2.docx

United Nations Convention on the Rights of the Child (2009) *Convention on the Rights of the Child*. London: UNICEF. Available at: www.unicef.org.uk/Documents/Publication-pdfs/UNCRC_PRESS200910web.pdf

Worth, J. (2015) *Analysis of Academy School Performance in GCSEs 2014, Final Report*. Available at: www.nfer.ac.uk/publications/LGGA03/LGGA03.pdf

3 Terrorism, extremism and radicalisation

Ihsan Caillau-Foster

This chapter explores:

- the meaning and causes of 'terrorism', 'radicalisation' and 'extremism';
- the British government's policies and strategies to counter the attack on our 'British values';
- the role of school staff and the larger community in preventing radicalisation and extremism.

Introduction

Unemployment, neglect, abuse, poverty, malnutrition, domestic and political conflicts, and natural disasters have created a climate of chaos and unpredictability in our world. It is perhaps no wonder that many of our children are experiencing psychological (Leahy, 2015; Tatar and Amram, 2008; Schlenger et al., 2002), cognitive and/or behavioural (Hodgins et al., 2007) problems. Frustrated with their situations, some of our children have been reported to have engaged in delinquent and juvenile offences in their communities (UN, 2003; Kim and Kim, 2008; Benekos and Merlo, 2015). The media is scattered with examples of children who have turned into murderers, from 11-year-old Daniel Bartlam's murder of his mother, to ten-year-olds Robert Thompson and Jon Venables's kidnap of a two-year-old child, to the case of Connor Doran, Smith Evans and Brandon Doran's (aged 14 to 17) attack on a 53-year-old homeless man, and of course 15-year-old Will Cornick, who stabbed his teacher in her own classroom. But the 'incidents' of aggression, we are finding, are no longer directed against their immediate families and communities. They have become more calculating, zealous and global, with partners spread all over the world. Some are turning to international terrorist organisations who provide our at-risk youth with 'a sense of dignity, purpose, obligation, and belonging' (Hussain, 2014).

For over 20 years, school-aged children from the underdeveloped world have been recruited to the ranks of militaries, militias, gangs and terrorist organisations to act as informants, fundraisers or hosts. But, according to the USA's Homeland Security Institute (2009, p. 4), children as young as 11 from the Western developed world are now being used as porters, suicide bombers, snipers, smugglers and executioners. The majority of extremist networks seem to be operating all over the world, and certainly in the United Kingdom including in London, Bristol, Birmingham, Exeter and Manchester.

Defining terrorism

The word 'terror' stems from the Latin verb *terrere*, meaning frighten, scare, startle or terrify. The suffix 'ism' originates from the Greek, and was then borrowed by Latin and French. 'Ism' is used as a productive suffix in the formation of nouns denoting action or practice, state or condition. Together, 'terror' plus 'ism' convert to 'causing fear'. The typology definition for terrorism is debatable. This is understandable, given the different types of terrorists' motives and behaviours. For some, terrorism is driven by idealist ideological beliefs or entrepreneurial determination.

The first act of terrorism was committed by the Sicarri, led by the descendants of Judas of Galilee in the first century to oust their Roman rulers from Judea. The meaning of 'terrorism' since then has evolved. Under the UK's Terrorism Act 2000 (TACT) it is described as (a) an action that endangers or causes serious violence to a person/ people; (b) causing serious damage to property, or (c) seriously interfering or disrupting an electronic system. It is designed to influence the government or to intimidate the public and is made for the purpose of advancing a political, religious or ideological cause.

The above definitions perceive the act of terrorism as involving violence against civilians, and its goal is not political gain but to inspire and change a faction in society's behaviour and views (Laqueur, 1999). The historical accounts allude to the fact that terrorism at times was seen as necessary to influence status quo and realise goals (Sandler and Enders, 2004).

The saying, 'One person's terrorist is another person's freedom fighter' underscores the controversy in the term 'terrorism'. While some believe terrorists are the defenders of order and liberty, others believe they are criminals and immoral. For example, terrorist groups such as Hezbollah in Lebanon, Hamas in Palestine, Liberation Tigers of Tamil Eelam (LTTE) in Sri Lanka, White Supremacy in the United States of America, the Revolutionary Armed forces of Colombia (FARC) and the Provisional Irish Republican Army (Provos) in the United Kingdom might admit their violent approach is extreme, but they (and their supporters) may defend their behaviour claiming it equates their tyrants' transgressions. Clearly, this argument compounds the complexity of settling on one definition for 'terrorism'.

> **Activity: Defining terrorists**
>
> Some argue, 'One person's terrorist is another person's freedom fighter.' Do you agree or disagree with this? Explain.

Extremism and its traits

To help understand terrorism, it is important to comprehend the origins of terrorism. To do so, we must first comprehend the core trait of all terrorist activities, i.e. extremism. Extremism is the precursor to terrorism, a system of belief that terrorists adopt to justify or rationalise their aggressive criminal behaviour. It is worthwhile noting that only those who *act* on their extremist beliefs, such as Sinn Féin and the Irish Republican Army (IRA), are classified as 'terrorists'. Both the terms extremist and extremism are not defined by the UK's legislation. The Home Office (2016) describes extremism as 'vocal or active opposition to fundamental British values, including democracy, the rule of law, individual liberty and mutual respect and tolerance of different faiths and beliefs' (p. 9).

Underlying all acts of terrorism is an ideology, a belief system dominated by intolerance to others' views. The extremist will hold negative permanent views about their opponents that differ to their own. They will also adopt their own political ideas and, despite their ramifications, will antagonise others. They will even justify their violent acts ethically and morally.

What is radicalisation then? The best definition is offered by the Quilliam Foundation (2014), which describes it as 'the process by which individuals and/or groups come to adopt extremist ideologies' (p. 7). There is a difference, the Foundation states, between 'radicalisation' and 'violent radicalisation', with the latter 'engaging in violent activities' and the former engaging in 'radicalised non-violent thinking' (p. 6).

With these definitions, let us now look at the following case studies and try to establish each terrorist's motives and reasons for their violent behaviour.

The making of extremists and terrorists

Causes of terrorism

Understanding the origin of terrorism, including the needs of terrorists, is one way we can better understand the perpetrators, manage risk and help advocate change. Several counter-terrorism policy makers in the UK and elsewhere, write Neumann (2008) and Kundnani (2015), have taken into account the different underlying factors that fuel terrorism to help develop a holistic counter-terrorism policy response, and understand 'what goes on before the bomb goes off' (Neumann, 2008, p. 4).

The motives of terrorists have been debated since the beginning of time. Some have claimed that terrorists simply turn to violence because of their religious beliefs, a persuasive ideology or their own circumstances, including discrimination, injustice, poverty, unemployment, mental health, oppression or grievance against a country's unfair foreign policy. Economists made the behavioural assumptions that individuals only take part in an activity if they believe the profit outweighs the cost (Gupta, 2005). This 'rational choice' hypothesis was earlier used to analyse market behaviour, but it is now utilised to explain human actions, including criminal behaviour. Humans may 'agree' to be radicalised and/or join a terrorist organisation, argues Gupta, if they see a personal benefit that outweighs their losses. Some profitable gains that drive some terrorists may include monetary rewards, political grievance, acceptance, defence against retributions etc. While one may feel anger and the need to act aggressively against the oppressors, others may not. Southers (2013, p. xiii) cautions, 'it is often impossible to know who will exit the radicalization pathway as a violent extremist until they do so'. If we are to understand why individuals join a terrorist organisation, Gupta (2005) argues, we will need to explore each terrorist as a separate independent entity with his/her own life experiences and motives.

There is no one factor that can draw an individual or groups into terrorism. The following section outlines some of the debates surrounding the causes of terrorism.

1. The nurture versus nature debate

The question whether terrorists are born evil or nurtured by society (including but not necessarily solely by parents) continues. Thomas Hobbes (1588–1679), an English philosopher, believes primitive human life is 'solitary, poor, nasty, brutish, and short'. He felt that the 'natural' state of man was akin to being corrupt, or evil, and it is the society that uncleans them.

In contrast to Hobbes, John Locke (1632–1734), another English philosopher and physician, argued that children are born blank slates, but they do have natural inclinations including personalities and opinions. He believed that early education could critically shape their development. Locke encouraged parents to watch their children to help them understand their individual inclinations. With this, he believed, they can then improve their offspring's temperament and conduct. Locke warned parents that some children may be more disposed than others to fall from the path of reason. He argued that all men are the result of their education. If we are to use this trajectory, one could argue that terrorists have evolved into human beasts as a result of education. But if so, can one then assume that all children raised by terrorists or living in a war- or gang-like community become terrorists?

> **Activity: Philosophical underpinning of human nature**
>
> Do you agree with John Locke's belief that children are blank slates? Do you believe adults such as those featured in the case studies at the end of this chapter are the result of their parents' education, or something else? Explain.

2. Mental health and illness

From interviews with female terrorists in Italy, Neuberger and Valentini (1996) concluded that female terrorism is related to childhood maladjustments such as oppressive fathers and submissive mothers. Maladjusted girls, who identify with their weak mothers, they found, tended to leap into men's violent world. They fight for the weak and oppressed and they reverse their gender role, and triumph in the knowledge that men will tremble from their acts of terrorism. No research has confirmed these assumptions nor that terrorists necessarily suffer from major mental ill-health. Earlier studies conducted by McCauley and Segal (1987), Crenshaw (1990), and Horgan (2003) found that rarely do terrorists have mental illnesses such as schizophrenia, major depression or Antisocial Personality Disorder (APD). Instead, other factors interplayed to influence terrorists.

In a study conducted by Bhui *et al.* (2014) involving a survey and interviews with over 600 men and women between the ages of 18 to 45 of Muslim heritage in London and Bradford, evidence showed that the poorer the social capital (trust in others and feelings of safety), the higher the risk of becoming radicalised. Data also found that 2.4 per cent of research participants showed some sympathy for violent protest and terrorist acts (especially from those under 20, in full-time education, born in the UK, speaking English at home, and earning over £75,000 a year).

3. Information and communication technologies

The use of information and communication technologies (ICTs) has increased in unparalleled proportion. According to the International Telecommunication Union (ITU, 2015), around 2 billion people use the internet in developing countries compared to 1.2 billion in developed countries. This, one may argue, is a positive thing; it brings individuals together and helps share information. Nevertheless, evidence shows it has become a significant medium for indoctrination and inciting, disseminating and celebrating violent acts, and intolerance.

According to the European Commission against Racism and Intolerance (ECRI, 2015), 'hate speech through the social media is rapidly increasing and has the potential to reach a much larger audience than extremist print media were able to reach previously' (p. 7). Over the years, international terrorist organisations have made use of this medium; they have even developed their own websites. Among other things, they publish military guidebooks on how to use social networks without being detected, how to maintain anonymity and encryption of cellular devices and personal computers, how to perfect their battle tactics and how to manufacture explosives. In addition, they host home-recorded documentaries by their 'martyrs' and leaders, publish hate speech, advise as to the detonation of Improvised Explosive Devices (IED) against enemy vehicles, show ritual beheadings of foreign and native captives, and even computer simulations (CBRNE, 2011).

Not only this, but the terrorists have grown technologically savvy. They have developed their own hacking divisions (for example, Islamic State Hacking Division, IS Hacking Division and ISIS Cyber Army, and Cyber Caliphate). Over the past few years, cybercriminal terrorists have conducted continuous cyberwar attacks on websites and Twitter accounts, the US army, the French *Charlie Hebdo* newspaper and the French television channel, TV5 Monde, and the US's Office of Personnel Management. Unlike the French government, which has been granted the power to interrupt any internet public communication service that encourages terrorism, the UK still cannot force compulsory filtering of terrorist or violent sites. Hate speech, beheadings and killings continue to be aired on various websites.

> **Activity: Media censorship**
>
> In your view, do you think we can censor internet based materials in the absence of national boundaries? What role do you think education can play in addressing extremism?

4. Religion

In addition to technology, some perceive radical religious beliefs have been a possible catalyst for terrorism; but according to Southers (2013), this alone does not legitimise extremism. Many other factors, such as the ones we shall explore later, may interplay to 'create conditions in which someone might cross the line from extremist rhetoric to violent action. This is the radicalisation pathway' (Southers, 2013, p. xiii). Recent examples of terrorism and extremism fuelled by religious convictions include Al-Qaeda which masterminded the attacks on the World Trade Centre in America in 2001; Al Shabab in Somalia; and Daesh (Al-Dawla Al-Islamiya Fil Iraq Wa Al-Sham) fighting to establish a 'caliphate', a state governed in accordance with Islamic law.

5. Charismatic terrorist leaders

According to the Home Office (2011), charismatic leaders with persuasive narratives such as Abu Hamza Al-Masri (born Mustafa Kamel Mustafa) and Adolf Hitler play a vital role in radicalising and recruiting violent extremists. Captivated by their rhetoric, the study concluded, their impressionable fans will then do whatever it takes to establish themselves as worthy companions and fighters for the cause. These findings conflict with other earlier studies (see, for example, Sageman, 2004) that found extremist groups can also develop through socialisation with like-minded people.

6. Socio-political and economic structural factors

Is one's socio-economic status a facilitator for violent radicalisation and ultimately terrorism? Views on this vary. In the 1980s, for example, research by Russell and Miller (1983) and Clark (1983) found the typical terrorist, such as Osama Bin Laden, was someone from the middle- or upper-middle-class strata with some college education. Other studies, however, by Weinberg and Eubank (1987) who studied Italian women terrorists, postulate that if they are female, they tend to be in their twenties and white-collar workers. Ferracuti (Ferracuti and Bruno, 1981; Ferracuti 1982) and Sageman (2004) disagree. They believe there are no notable differences in the terrorists' socio-economic and/or educational background.

Yet in a more recent study conducted by Sprinzak and Denny (2003), 35 Middle Eastern Asian extremists (21 Hamas and its armed miltary wing Izz a-Din al Qassan, Islamic Jihad, and Hezbollah, and 14 secular terrorists from Fatah and its military wing, PFLP and DFLP) were interviewed. The data revealed that families' political involvement influenced their children. If families were politically active, they tended to socialise their sons and support their involvement at an early age. The large majority of both secular and Islamist group members interviewed (70 per cent secular and 80 per cent Islamist) reported no one from their family was involved with the organisation when they joined. In most cases, where a father or older sibling was an actual member, the sons were more likely to join. The study also found that education level and age among the interviewees varied. Some were in their teens while others were older and some had some form of education, while some had none. The social environment, mainly peer pressure and enhancing social standing, seemed to be the main reasons for joining a terrorist organisation. Imprisonment, anger and hatred were also cited as additional reasons.

Many writers (see, for example, Crenshaw, 2000; Bongar, 2007) do not agree with the above terrorist profiling. Rees *et al.* (2002) and Krueger and Maleckova (2002) believe the earlier characteristics of terrorists have changed, with terrorists coming from a varied demographic range such as women, men, teenagers, blue and white collar, middle class, rich or impoverished backgrounds. This clearly contradicts the typography of a terrorist offered by Hubbard (1971) and Ferracuti and Bruno (1981) which included the following characteristics: shy, with poor social achievement, religious parents, a basic education, adherence to norms, from a single-parent family, with a weapon fetish, extroverted, hostile, suspicious, and defensive. The latter characteristics – poor education, obsession with weapons, suspicious – one can argue, may help explain the Oklahoma bomber Timothy James McVeigh and the French farm worker Gregoire Moutaux, but not the others.

The characteristics and hypothesis above, believes Victoroff (2005), are invalid. Undoubtedly, they cannot be proven and hence relied on to shed accurate light on the terrorists' identities and motives for several reasons. The sample size is small hence rendering it ungeneralizable. Perhaps a larger and more exhaustive longitudinal study may help obtain more generalizable data.

7. State sponsorship

Rather than wage war in one's homeland, some countries (for example, the USA in support of the Contras in Nicaragua and Mujahidin fighters in Afghanistan; and Saudi Arabia) prefer to sponsor terrorism outside their homeland (Richardson, 2005). This tactic, argues Richardson, has 'potential for a high pay-off' (p. 194). State sponsored terrorism (a) does not incur significant financial or domestic human costs, (b) helps achieve the country's foreign policy objectives, and (c) it is difficult to prove the sponsors' involvement and hence implicate them. In addition to financing terrorism, sometimes training and a safe haven is offered to the sponsored terrorist groups. The relationship between the sponsors and the sponsored terrorists, Richardson (2005) claims, tends to vary from very tight to very loose control.

Counter-extremism policies and practices

> **Activity: Policies and practices on counter-terrorism**
>
> According to former prime minister David Cameron (HM Government, 2015), extremism is 'really a symptom; ideology is the root cause' (p. 5).
> What policies and practices do you believe would help counter extremism?

To help prevent and combat extremism and terrorism, several strategies have been adopted by many countries such as the UK, for example: military resistance, negotiation, economic interventions, and anti-terror policies and programmes including educational campaigns, multi-agency interventions with the community, schools, police, military, and judicial and legal.

Military resistance campaigns

From the 1990s to the present (2016), the UK, along with several of its allies, has been involved in several wars against terrorism such as the Gulf War (1991), Operation Desert Fox (1998), Kosovo War (1998–99), Sierra Leone Civil War (2000–02), War in Afghanistan (2001–14), Iraq War (2003–09), Libyan War (2011) and the ongoing military intervention against ISIL (2014–present). The question whether violence should be met with violence has been researched by Stephan and Chenoweth (2008). After comparing the results of 285 nonviolent and violent resistance campaigns from 1900 to 2006, they found that major nonviolent campaigns (conducted by social, economic, psychological and political means) have succeeded 55 per cent of the time, compared to 26 per cent for violent resistance campaigns. Stephan and Chenoweth (2008) concluded that violence is ineffective in overthrowing oppressors and helping the oppressed. Nonviolent methods, Abrahms (2006) argues, tend to improve the chances of political parties with terrorist connections being legitimately accepted domestically and internationally. They also inspire resistance and pressure on the oppressors to disarm and/or change their tactics.

Economic measures

Starving terrorists and their supporters of funding is a strategy that has been adopted by the UK. In fact, the UK Parliament introduced the Terrorist Asset-Freezing Act 2010 for that very purpose. Any individual or group suspected of involvement in terrorist activity would be investigated and financial restrictions placed on them. On a global scale, the United Nations has and will continue to apply economic sanctions against regimes sponsoring terrorism, for example, the Islamic Republic of Iran, North Korea, Colombia and so on.

Intelligence and Secret Service

The UK relies on its Secret Intelligence Service (SIS) and its several sections such as MI5 (Military Intelligence, Section 5) that deals with threats inside the UK, and MI6 (Military Intelligence, Section 6) that combats overseas threats. These and several others units (MI1 to MI15) were established under the Security Service Act to supply the government with foreign intelligence. The Secret Service's role is governed by intrusive powers, principally under the Regulation of Investigatory Powers Act 2000. It works covertly in the UK and overseas to build foreign contacts and gather intelligence to help protect the UK's people, economy and interests. Theresa May, then a senior Cabinet minister, declared in a keynote address (Home Office, 2014) that since 2007 there had been 753 arrests for terror-related activities, 212 individuals charged with offences, 148 successfully prosecuted, 138 locked up and 13 suspects extradited overseas.

The United Kingdom's anti-terror policies and programmes

In addition to the above, to prevent, undermine and eliminate extremism and radicalisation, the British government has introduced several interventions and counter-extremism policies. It has also commissioned research by the DfE on teaching approaches that help to build resilience to extremism among young people. Also, it has offered training such as the Home Office's Workshop to Raise Awareness of Prevent (WRAP). Moreover, it published guidance literature (e.g. Protecting Children from Radicalisation: The Prevent Duty) for educational institutions to thwart extremists and to prevent the radicalisation of children and young people.

Not only that but it has also given schools additional responsibilities to assess the risk of radicalisation and incorporate a response to the threat of it in their school. They have also been encouraged to ensure that fundamental British values are promoted in the school curriculum. Schools have also been advised to ensure their staff have been WRAP-trained.

Activity: Addressing terrorism

In your opinion, is the fight against terrorism the job of the UK's counter-terrorist (CT) forces and/or schools? Discuss your views.

Having explored the different debates and research on the causes of terrorism, the next section will explore the various interventions to counter terrorism.

Counter-terrorism interventions

Contest strategy

Developed by the Home Office in 2003, Contest was introduced to protect the UK from internal and external terrorism. The delivery of the strategy is organised around four principles or four Ps: Pursue, Prevent, Protect and Prepare (Home Office, 2010b). Some of the key developments brought about by Contest include changes to the legislative system including enhanced sentencing of individuals connected with terrorism, new foreign travel restrictions, notification and monitoring of convicted terrorists released from prison, and new powers for HM Treasury to take action against terrorist financing and money laundering, including asset freezing. Not only that, but through work with further and higher education institutions, schools, industries and communities including prison services, the Home Office's programmes have been introduced to destabilise propagandists for violence.

1. Pursuing terrorists and those who sponsor them

To stop terrorist attacks, Pursue has been allocated seven priorities (as opposed to three in 2006), including 'increasing covert detection and investigation capability and capacity; improving the effectiveness of the UK prosecution process; developing more effective non-prosecution actions; improving capability to disrupt terrorist activities overseas; strengthening the coherence between our counter-terrorism work and counter-insurgency and capacity building overseas; and enhancing inter-agency coordination on this workstream' (Home Office, 2010b, p. 9). It is worthwhile mentioning that many countries have different legislation on international arrest warrants and two-way rendition treaties (Hopkins and Norton-Taylor, 2016). This, report Hopkins and Norton-Taylor, has caused friction in the past between various countries and it has been proven counter-productive in establishing a cohesive global effort to combat global terrorism.

2. Preventing terrorism

Prevention deals with addressing radicalisation factors in the UK and internationally, including inequalities and discrimination as well as changing the environment. Under the Prevent strand of the government's counter-terrorism strategy, and under Section 26 of the Counter-Terrorism and Security Act 2015 in England, from 2015 schools, further education and higher education institutions in the UK were required by law to follow the Prevent Strategy to avert their pupils and others from being drawn into supporting and/or becoming terrorists. This is referred as the 'Prevent Duty'.

To work towards meeting their obligations, the Department of Education (2015) has published non-statutory advice for schools (including governors, leaders and school staff) and childcare providers inducting them to their Prevent role and responsibilities. For example, as part of the school staff's role, they are required to (a) impart and teach British values to their students, and (b) to identify and refer those who are at risk of radicalisation. On the one hand, this approach has received praise by ministers for being a true partnership approach (Casciani, 2014). On the other hand, it was criticised, for example, by the United Nation's special rapporteur (Gayle, 2016) for its abdication of responsibility.

To meet the aims of the Prevent Strategy, school staff have been offered training by the police and local education authorities. An assessment of the value of school staff training by education charity Think Global (2016) has yielded several findings. Their straw-ball survey of 100 teacher members on the support needed for teachers in their duties to safeguard children against the risk of extremism, found teachers lacked confidence in their training, especially to do with 'proactive safeguarding'. Teachers found that creating a safe space in school for children to discuss global issues connected to extremism and radicalisation was unclear. The teachers, did, however, report that they have more confidence in spotting the danger signs and taking action, engaging in 'reactive safeguarding'.

Since the introduction of the Prevent Strategy, several concerns have been raised including those by the House of Commons Communities and Local Government Committee's report (2010). The concerns were that counter-terrorism did not go hand in hand with community cohesion work. The report noted that Prevent is 'unlikely to ever be accepted in its current form by those it is most important to engage' (p. 18). It also commented that it singled out the Muslim community as untrustworthy. It also provoked resentment from other minority groups for its spending on the Muslim community rather than on their own. Also, some voiced their anger for (a) campaigning for inter-faith dialogue in the context of extremism and terrorism; and (b) disregarding the threats of other non-Islamic factions such as the Far Right or Northern Irish sectarian organisations.

Since Prevent's introduction, the National Union of Teachers (NUT) (cited in TES, 2016) has expressed concern about the surge in student referrals. At its annual conference in Brighton in 2016, the NUT voiced its trepidation that the strategy has affected home–school relations and put 'people ... under pressure and feel they have to behave in ways that aren't necessarily required' (p. 1). According to data gathered by Full Fact charity (2015) under the Freedom of Information Act, the National Police Chief's Council's (NPCC) data shows an increase year on year on Prevent referrals from police, more than those from education and other 'statutory partners' put together. And, they warned that:

> Grooming by extremist groups happens mainly on social media sites, not on school promises. Schools' best contribution to countering any behaviour that could be a problem is by encouraging discussion. Some aspects of Prevent inhibit this and it is for this reason that we need a review of the strategy to find the right, and best way to protect children and young people.
>
> (Full Fact, 2015, p. 2)

The problem with the Prevent Strategy, writes Frank Furedi (2016), a sociologist and commentator, is that it endorses 'technical and security-related solutions rather than facing up to the challenge of educating and socialising young people' (p. 2). The NUT (2016) has called for the government to develop alternative strategies to prevent, safeguard and identify risks to children and young people.

The counter-terrorism and law enforcement agencies are short on human and monetary resources. Communities have a large role in protecting their members from radicalisation. They can support individuals before they engage in violent acts of terrorism. Communities, however, cannot stand alone; they need to work alongside other agencies to help reduce the risk of radicalisation and subsequent terrorism. Southers (2013) suggests that rather than remain silent, community effort should be dedicated to assisting policy makers and members of the community to identify possible changes and hostility in individuals, factors hindering progress. If we are to undermine extremism, rather than ask communities to act as police and refer potential extremists through the Prevent programme, we need to forge a strong partnership between the community, law enforcement and the security service. Profiling individuals due to their religious or ethnic heritage is not the answer. Profiling, Southers (2013) argues, will breed victimisation and subsequently opportunities for extremists to recruit among the 'marginalised' persecuted groups. Profiling, as we have already seen, may be unreliable.

3. The Protect strand

To reduce vulnerability, both domestically and internationally, many initiatives were introduced in the UK including strengthening border security (including the use of biometrics), protecting key utilities, reducing transport risk and protecting people in crowded places such as at airports, train stations, on the Underground and so forth.

In addition to the disruption, time and inconvenience caused by airport security, the use of biometric passports (also known as e-passports) and automatic face recognition systems has been criticised for unfairly placing a burden (monetary and staffing) on businesses and individuals such as airlines and airports to act as first-line counter-terrorist agents. Compounding this are the ethical and social issues surrounding the use of e-passports and surveillance cameras in public places. The argument 'if you have nothing to hide, you have nothing to fear' has been used in an attempt to counter the concerns of many people regarding their right to privacy. The question remains, are we turning into an Orwellian society where everyone is a suspect until proven innocent? Indeed, technological convergence of mobile telephony and banking systems offer the security services easy access to individuals' movements and spending habits far more quickly than ever before.

4. Preparing for the consequences

This strand relates to ensuring the UK is prepared for post-terrorist attack. This includes identifying risks and assessing impact, building capabilities to respond, and continuously exercising to ensure response to incidents will be appropriate and swift. In other words, this implies that the security services accept that an attack is a matter of when not if. The aim of this approach is to ensure that all relevant stakeholders (the emergency services, police, local government, transport, utilities etc.) are well briefed and well prepared to manage the aftermath of an attack when it does happen.

Counter-extremism legislation

In our multicultural context, it has become evident that the antagonistic public debate on issues such as political orientation, immigration, migration and integration of minorities is causing racism, xenophobia and extremist views bordering on radicalisation to fester in society. Rhetoric from certain right-wing commentators and groups is unhelpful and is threatening to destabilise our country's tolerance and cohesion. While there is a consensus that racist or radical speeches are not tolerated in Europe, there is little agreement on how to address the issue. Concerns about limiting individuals' freedom of expression have mostly derailed changes in policy on hate speeches and terrorist websites. In the UK, several policies to protect freedom of expression and prohibit discrimination and intolerance (Equality Act 2010) have been adopted over the last two centuries, including the European Convention on Human Rights (ECHR) (Articles 9 and 10 are similar to ICCPR's Articles 18 and 19) and the International Covenant on Civil and Political Rights' (ICCPR) human rights treaty. In addition, the UK has introduced its own anti-hate speech statutes such as the Public Order Act 1986 that forbids expressions of racial hatred due to colour, race nationality (including citizenship) or ethnic or national origins; the Criminal Justice and Public Order Act 1994 (added Section 4A to the Public Order Act 1986); the Football Offences Act 1991 (amended by the Football Offences and Disorder Act 1999); the Racial and Religious Hatred Act 2006 (amended Part 3A of the Public Act

1986); the Criminal Justice and Immigration Act 2008 (amended Part 3 of the Public Order Act 1986); and the Crime and Courts Act 2013 that prohibits stirring up racial hatred and indecent or racist chanting at any venues, including designated football matches.

> **Activity: Comparing counter-terrorism legislation**
>
> Look up online (a) the United Nation's Right to Freedom of Speech, Articles 18 to 20 (www.ohchr.org/en/professionalinterest/pages/ccpr.aspx); (b) the UK's anti-speech legislation (such as the Public Order Act 1986 (Part 3); the Criminal Justice and Public Order Act 1994; the Racial and Religious Hatred Act 2006; the Criminal Justice and Immigration Act 2008; and the Football Offences Act (www.legislation.gov.uk/).
>
> Compare and contrast the UN and the UK's legislations. What are their strengths and weaknesses? Do you agree with them? Explain your view.

The Acts preserving the human right of freedom of speech and reprimanding hate speeches seem to conflict. On one hand, the freedom of speech seems to promise us the right to express our views and on the other the anti-speech law is impeding our right to free speech. Organisations such as the European Commission against Racism and Intolerance (ECRI, 2015) have criticised this very fact. Anti-speech statutes, the ECRI argued, such as that of the UK's, conflict with the human right to freedom of speech. The ECRI fears anti-speech laws smother political opposition and 'criminalise legitimate expressions of grievances to perceived discrimination and social exclusion' (2015, p. 9).

The freedom of expression, as set out in Article 19 of the ICCPR and Article 10 of the ECHR, emphasises that the right to this freedom carries with it the responsibility to protect others' rights, including defamation, insult, or violent threats by others for their beliefs or convictions (Foreign and Commonwealth Office, 2014). The government, under the Racial and Religious Hatred Act 2006, has the right to warrant the arrest or withdrawal of any material that is threatening or intended to stir up hatred.

> **Activity: The UK government's rights and responsibilities**
>
> Under the Humans Right Treaty, the UK government has the right to decide whether and how to protect people's rights to practise and observe their convictions and beliefs. For instance, it can ban and dispose of any communication (audio and/or visual) material that is threatening or is intending to stir up religious hatred. What are your views on this?

Curbing the threat of cybercrime and terrorism

Jonathan Russell (cited in Vaughan, 2015), the political liaison officer at the counter-extremism thinktank Quilliam Foundation, said that the problem should be treated not as a 'national security threat' but as a safeguarding issue (p. 16). This is particularly important when addressing online activity. The internet, he believes, is the 'new battleground' in the war against radicalisation. He calls schools to police web activity. He added, 'We need to use technology to the best of our ability to reduce vulnerability and increase resilience' (p. 16). To help curb the threats from the internet and related technology, including organised crime, the Home Office published two cybercrime strategy documents in 2009 and 2010. Not only that, but it also assigned law enforcement agencies, including the National Crime Agency (formerly the Serious Organised Crime Agency e-crime unit), the National Cyber Crime Unit, the Medicines and Healthcare Regulatory Agency (MHRA), HM Revenue & Customs, and the Child Exploitation and Online Protection (CEOP) Centre. In addition, cross-government collaboration has taken place with the Office of Cyber Security and Information Assurance (OCSIA) and cybercrime awareness resource Get Safe Online to help protect the public from cyber criminals. The Home Office (2010a) recognises cybercrime is not only financially but is also non-financially driven, targeting children and young people and luring them to some form of exploitations including psychological and physical harm such as hate crime, harassment and political extremism.

Internationally, anti-cybercrime organisations have developed, including the recent 2015 Sawab Centre, an online message and engagement programme supported by a 63-country Global Coalition Against Daesh, and co-founded by the US Secretary of State for Public Diplomacy and Public Affairs and the United Arab Emirates. The Centre's role is to intercept and block terrorist propaganda, recruitment campaigns, fundraising and intimidating and terrorising messages. The Centre has a Twitter presence with over 68,000 followers from all over the world. Meanwhile Europol has launched the European Union Internet Referral Unit (EU IRU) which monitors terrorist propaganda and reports to service providers.

British naturalisation and British values

The official narrative over the past few years has steadily emphasised that extremism resulting in terrorism is caused by the community's (including teachers) failure to honour and uphold British values. The government has hence demanded that immigrants to the UK pass a new citizenship test and pledge an oath of allegiance to British values before they are naturalised as British citizens. Clearly, the idea is that if immigrants have an investment in the country through making the oath, they will less likely turn against it. It is unrealistic to assess the value of this oath-based approach in the attempt to reduce radicalisation and extremism for the reasons we have already discussed above.

This argument connecting terrorism to the loss of British values and identity has been supported by several ministers in the UK, including Tony Blair, Gordon Brown and other Labour party politicians such as Jacqui Smith and Hazel Blears (Kundnani, 2015). Summing up the shared views of many politicians, David Cameron argued in his 'muscular liberalism' speech to the Munich Security Conference (Gov, 2011) that an important 'reason so many young Muslim (terrorists) are drawn to (terrorism) comes down to a question of identity' (p. 3).

> **Activity: Pledging an oath of allegiance**
>
> Do you think swearing an oath of allegiance to British values will be sufficient to overturn deep-rooted radical views? Explain your answer with reference to the names and profile of terrorists mentioned in this chapter and in the news.

Rehabilitation of terrorists

Professor Rohan Gunaratna (2015) suggests that while many strategies are needed to mitigate the threat by rehabilitating the 'infected' terrorists and immunising vulnerable communities from radicalisation, breaking the cycle can only be accomplished by the rehabilitation of insurgents and community engagement of their potential and actual supporters. In the life of an insurgent, the most important opportunity government has to transform him/ her is when he/she is in custody. Unless guerrillas and terrorists in custody are transformed, when released they will harbour the same violent ideas and propagate and infect others with their views. They will continue to pose an enduring threat to public safety and security.

In addition to posing a direct and indirect security threat, the released men and women will form part of the guerrilla and terrorist iconography. They will earn the status of hero, worthy of respect and emulation by the next generation of violent and radical recruits. To help address this, the re-orientation and rehabilitation of insurgents to help integrate them into the large community is not a novel thing. Rehabilitation programmes are adopted in several countries such as Nigeria, Saudi Arabia, Iraq, Sri Lanka, Afghanistan, the USA and the UK. In Saudi Arabia, for instance, they teach history to terrorists in custody (Gunaratna, 2011). In Nigeria, repentant Boko Haram terrorists are assigned to camps called 'Operation Safe Haven' where they receive vocational training (Nwankpa, 2014). In Sri Lanka, rehabilitated terrorists study professional training courses including mechanical skills, information technology, agriculture, animal husbandry, beauty therapy, food processing, construction etc. They also receive psychological, religious, spiritual and cultural support. Of all 12,000 rehabilitated terrorists, more than 230 are reported to have been qualified to pursue a higher education degree while 35 are already studying at university (Embassy of Sri Lanka, 2014).

In the UK, radicalised young people are referred to the government's counter-radicalisation scheme (more on this later in the chapter). According to White (2014), out of 150 terrorist offenders in the UK, 110 who are currently in prison or on parole are resisting rehabilitation.

> **Activity: Debating the rehabilitating of terrorists measures**
>
> Do you agree with Professor Gunaratna (above) that terrorists can be rehabilitated and converted to abandon terrorism? Explain your position.

The Quilliam Foundation (Benotman and Malki, 2016) recommends that children who have been radicalised by terrorist ideologies to take arms and fight must be supervised and reintegrated by a newly created EU body called 'Commission to Protect Future Generations from Radical Violence'. Information gathering about at-risk children and sharing good practice in the interests of children and in line with international human rights would be this body's priority. It also recommends that a support network is inaugurated and managed by local NGOs and funded by individual European states to help engage community members including practitioners (such as social workers, psychologists, career advisors, teachers, mentors etc.) to ensure effective and sustainable reintegration.

Conclusion

This chapter has identified the complexity in defining 'radicalisation', 'extremism' and 'terrorism'. Through the different case studies (below), it has illustrated the difficulty in distinguishing between the radical and violent radical. The chapter has also listed some of the known factors contributing to the formation of terrorists. Different interventions were described including anti-terrorist legislation and the surveillance and reporting of children and staff who are perceived to be at risk of radicalisation.

As has been apparent in this chapter, the role of education has been included not only in safeguarding and preventing youths' radicalisation but also in the rehabilitation of terrorists. Vocational training and humanities courses (e.g. religious studies, history, philosophy and literature) are some of the subject specialisations offered in many countries to help repentant terrorists reflect and scrutinise their perspective and contribute socially and economically in society. The lack of opportunities and exposure to different viewpoints are, as was made evident in this chapter, not the only things that radicalise our youth or lure them into terrorism. There are several pull factors that need to be accounted for such as community cohesion and a platform to debate different viewpoints if we are to counter terrorism and radicalisation. If we want our children to achieve a sense of belonging and embrace social justice, then the whole community will need to encourage them to debate radical and alternative ideologies, and discuss openly, without any ramifications, the critical and pertinent issues affecting their lives. After all, isn't that what our British values are all about?

Read the following four real-life stories of different people from different corners of the world who led a somewhat ordinary life before they drifted into terrorism.

Case study 3.1: Gregoire Moutaux

Gregoire Moutaux, a 25-year-old French farm worker was arrested, detained and charged at the Yahodyn border crossing between Ukraine and Poland on 7 June 2016. He was armed with five machine guns, two rocket-propelled grenade launchers, 125 kilograms of TNT, 100 detonators and other arms. He also had 20 balaclavas, possibly for his accomplices.

His employer described him as 'an exemplary employee', and the Mayor of Nant-Le Petit in France where Gregoire lives described him as 'polite lad, intelligent and pleasant to his neighbours. Always happy to lend a hand to help you' (Ladepeche, 2016). And yet this pleasant Frenchman was a 'far-right nationalist' planning 15 mass attacks on the Euro 2016 football championship. He objected to his country being taken over by immigrants. Unknown to many, he was under police surveillance for months. He is a confirmed Islamophobic and anti-Semite who wanted to target mosques, synagogues and the large crowds building up around Euro 2016 with the aim of causing as much loss of life as possible.

Case study 3.2: Mohammed Hamzah Khan

On 4 October 2014, a 19-year-old United States engineering student by the name of Mohammed Hamzah Khan, along with his two siblings, a 17-year-old sister and 16-year-old brother, were detained by the FBI Joint Terrorism Task Force at O'Hare International Airport in Chicago on their way to join Daesh (Al-Dawla Al-Islamiya Fil Iraq Wa Al-Sham) fighters in Syria. Mohammed was charged with attempting to 'provide material support' to Daesh. Surprisingly, Mohammed was never suspected as a terrorist.

Mohammed was an improbable radical until his arrest. One of the Khans' neighbours described him as 'very polite ... seems normal'. A fellow mosque-goer portrayed him as 'the last person that you'd think that would happen to'. Mohammed's parents, immigrants from India, were also shocked. They had not noticed anything untoward about their son, apart from his excessive phone use. His parents admitted to raising their children in a protective environment. However, apart from this, they claimed their children behaved 'like any other normal American family'. Mohammed's mother alleged that her children were victims of extremist propagandists who are using 'brainwashing recruiting' tactics.

Case study 3.3: Maryam Sharipova

On Sunday 28 March 2010, Maryam Sharipova, a 27-year-old Russian teacher from the remote village of Balakhani in the Republic of Dagestan, arrived in central Moscow, some 1,800 kilometres away from her home, and blew herself up in the Metro, killing herself and 26 others. This was followed by another bomb not far from the first station, detonated by 18-year-old Dzhennet Abdullaeva. Jointly, the two suicide bombs killed over 40 and injured more than 100 in the northern Caucasus in Russia. Maryam's parents were, like Mohammed's, stunned that their children could do something like that. Describing his daughter, Maryam's father said, 'She wasn't the kind of person who could do this. She was self-confident, someone who defined clear goals, and who wanted to achieve them.' Her father portrayed her as a self-disciplined and mature, bright girl who studied mathematics at their state university. She was from a middle-class, educated, non-delinquent family. She was the first person from her district to acquire a Master's degree in mathematics and a second degree in psychology. Four years before she decimated herself, she had begun working as the village school teacher.

> **Case study 3.4: Timothy James McVeigh**
>
> On 19 April 1995, Timothy James McVeigh, a 27-year-old American-born resident of Pendleton, New York, was convicted and executed for the detonation of a truck bomb in Oklahoma City. Timothy was born to a father who worked at a local Harrison Radiator plant and a mother who was a travel agent. After his parents' divorce, he lived with his father who worked long shifts and saw little of his son. As a teenager, he became captivated with computers and guns. His computing skills earned him acclamation in his school. Timothy later joined the army where he excelled in his disciplined lifestyle along with his fellow army recruits. His peers were impressed; one told journalists Michel and Herbeck, 'he was more or less, to me, the epitome of infantry. You know, the extremist, "follow me," kind of guy'. Along with thousands of other American soldiers, Timothy was sent to the Persian Gulf to fight against the invasion of Saddam Hussein's troops. After the war, he was awarded several medals for his heroic act of shooting with his cannon, from a distance of nearly 2,000 yards, an Iraqi soldier who was firing a machine gun.
>
> 'When he came back, he seemed broken,' Timothy's aunt claimed. 'When we talked about it, he said it was terrible there. He was on the front line and had seen death and caused death' (CNN, 2007). Without a college degree and in the midst of a recession, McVeigh found obtaining a good job outside of military life difficult and eventually settled for a security guard position, which he found tiring and tedious. Several years later, Timothy parked his rental truck packed with 4,800 pounds of explosives just outside the Oklahoma federal building, killing 168 people including 19 children who were in the daycare centre at that time.

Clearly, the individuals above seem, in the first instance, average people who are no different to anyone else's next-door neighbours. They were ambitious, compassionate, loving. They seemed 'normal' and yet they committed crimes against humanity.

> **Discussion**
>
> Having read all four case studies, what do you think they have in common?

Suggested reading

Bongar, B. and Brown, L. M. (eds) (2007) *Psychology of Terrorism*. Oxford: Oxford University Press.
McDonald, K. (2013) *Our Violent World: Terrorism in Society*. London: Palgrave Macmillan.
Southers, E. (2013) *Homegrown Violent Extremism*. London: Elsevier.
Tore Bjorgo, T. (ed.) (2005) *Root Causes of Terrorism: Myths, Reality and Ways Forward*. London and New York: Routledge.

References

Abrahms, M. (2006) Why terrorism does not work. *International Security*, 31 (2): 42–78.
Benekos, P. J. and Merlo, A. V. (2005) Juvenile offenders and the death penalty: How far have standards of decency evolved? *Youth Violence and Juvenile Justice*, 3 (4): 316–333.

Benotman, N. and Malik, N. (2016) *The Children of Islamic State*. London: Quilliam Foundation. Available at: https://f.hypotheses.org/wp-content/blogs.dir/2725/files/2016/04/the-children-of-islamic-state.pdf

Bhui, K., Warfa, N. and Jones, E. (2014) Is violent radicalisation associated with poverty, migration, poor self-reported health and common mental disorders? *PLOS ONE*, 9 (3): 1–10.

Bongar, B. (2007) The psychology of terrorism: Defining the need and describing the goals. In Bongar, B. and Brown, L. M. (eds) (2007) *Psychology of Terrorism*. Oxford: Oxford University Press, pp. 3–12.

Casciani, D. (2014) Analysis: The Prevent Strategy and its problems. BBC News online, 26 August. Available at: www.bbc.co.uk/news/uk-28939555

CBRNE (2011) Osama Bin Laden – the end. *CRBE Terrorism Newsletter* 38, 360–597.

Clark, R. (1983) Patterns in the lives of ETA members. *Terrorism*, 6: 423–454.

CNN (2007) *Terror on Trial: Who was Timothy McVeigh?* Available at: http://edition.cnn.com/2007/US/law/12/17/court.archive.mcveigh2/

Crenshaw, M. (1990) Questions to be answered, research to be done, knowledge to be applied. In W. Reich (ed.), *Origins of Terrorism: Psychologies, Ideologies, Theologies, States of Mind*. Cambridge: Cambridge University Press, pp. 247–260.

Crenshaw, M. (2000) The causes of terrorism, past and present. In Kegley, C. (ed.), *The New Global Terrorism*. Upper Saddle River, NJ: Pearson, pp. 92–105.

Department for Education (2015) *The Prevent Duty, Departmental Advice for Schools and Childcare Providers*. Available at: www.gov.uk/government/uploads/system/uploads/attachment_data/file/439598/prevent-duty-departmental-advice-v6.pdf

ECRI (2015) *Annual Report on ECRI's Activities*. Strasbourg: Council of Europe.

Embassy of Sri Lanka (2014) *Rehabilitation of Ex-LTTE Cadres Nearing Completion*. Available at: http://slembassyusa.org/news/rehabilitation-of-ex-ltte-cadres-nearing-completion/

Ferracuti, F. (1982) A sociopsychiatric interpretation of terrorism. *Annals of the American Academy of Political and Social Science*, 463: 129–140.

Ferracuti, F. and Bruno, F. (1981) Psychiatric aspects of terrorism in Italy. In Barak-Glantz, I. L. and Huff, C. R. (eds), *The Mad, the Bad and the Different: Essays in Honor of Simon Dinitz*. Lexington, MA: Lexington Books.

Foreign and Commonwealth Office (2014) *Hate Speech, Freedom of Expression and Freedom of Religion: A Dialogue*. Available at: www.gov.uk/government/publications/hate-speech-freedom-of-expression-and-freedom-of-religion-a-dialogue

Full Fact (2015) 'Deradicalisation' referrals: young and increasing? Available at: https://fullfact.org/news/deradicalisation-referrals-young-and-increasing/

Furedi, F. (2016) We need to talk about terrorism. *Spiked Online*. Available at: www.spiked-online.com/newsite/article/we-need-to-talk-about-terrorism/17959#.V0dxZ77QX3Y

Gayle, D. (2016) Prevent Strategy 'could end up promoting extremism': UN Special Rapporteur criticises UK government's counter-terrorism programme and snooper's charter. *Guardian*, 21 April. Available at: www.theguardian.com/politics/2016/apr/21/government-prevent-strategy-promoting-extremism-mainakiai

Gov (2011) PM's speech to Munich Security Conference. Available at: www.gov.uk/government/speeches/pms-speech-at-munich-security-conference

Gunaratna, R. (2011) Terrorist rehabilitation: A neglected secret CT weapon. *CTX Journal*, 1: 1. Available at: https://globalecco.org/en_GB/ctx-v1n1/terrorist-rehabilitation

Gunaratna, R. (2015) *The Global Jihad Movement: A Handbook*. Maryland: Rowman and Littlefield.

Gupta, D. K. (2005) Exploring roots of terrorism. In Bjorgo, T. (ed.), *Root Causes of Terrorism: Myths, Reality, and Ways Forward*. London and New York: Routledge.

HM Government (2015) *CONTEST: The United Kingdom's Strategy for Countering Terrorism: Annual Report for 2014*. Available at: www.gov.uk/government/uploads/system/uploads/attachment_data/file/415708/contest_annual_report_for_2014.pdf

Hodgins, S., Alderton, J., Cree, A., Aboud, A. and Mak, T. (2007) Aggressive behaviour, victimisation, and crime among severely mentally ill patients requiring hospitalisation. *British Journal of Psychiatry*, 191: 343–350.

Home Office (2010a) *Cyber Crime Strategy*. Available at: www.gov.uk/government/uploads/system/uploads/attachment_data/file/228826/7842.pdf

Home Office (2010b) *Pursue Prevent Protect Prepare: The United Kingdom's Strategy for Countering International Terrorism*. Available at: www.gov.uk/government/uploads/system/uploads/attachment_data/file/228907/7833.pdf

Home Office (2011) *Understanding Vulnerability and Resilience in Individuals to the Influence of Al Qa'ida Violent Extremism: A Rapid Evidence Assessment to Inform Policy and Practice in Preventing Violent Extremism.* Office for Security and Counter-Terrorism, Available at: www.gov.uk/government/uploads/system/uploads/attachment_data/file/116723/occ98.pdf

Home Office (2014) *Home Secretary Theresa May on Counter-Terrorism.* Available at: www.gov.uk/government/speeches/home-secretary-theresa-may-on-counter-terrorism

Home Office (2016) *Prevent Duty Guidance.* Available at: www.gov.uk/government/publications/prevent-duty-guidance

Hopkins, N. and Norton-Taylor, R. (2016) Blair government's rendition policy led to rift between UK spy agencies. *Guardian*, 31 May. Available at: www.theguardian.com/uk-news/2016/may/31/revealed-britain-rendition-policy-rift-between-spy-agencies-mi6-mi5

Horgan, J. (2003) The search for the terrorist personality. In Silke, A. (ed.) *Terrorists, Victims and Society.* Chichester: Wiley.

House of Commons Communities and Local Government Committee (2010) *Preventing Violent Extremism: Sixth Report of Session 2009–2010.* Available at: www.publications.parliament.uk/pa/cm200910/cmselect/cmcomloc/65/65.pdf

Hubbard, D. G. (1971) The Skyjacker: *His Flights of Fantasy.* New York: Macmillan.

Hussain, R. (2014) *Countering Violent Extremism and Terrorist Recruiting in the Digital Age.* U.S. Department of State. Available at: http://m.state.gov/md234988.htm

ITU (2015) *ITU Facts and Figures.* Available at: www.itu.int/en/ITU-D/Statistics/Pages/facts/default.aspx

Kim, H. and Kim, H. (2008) *Juvenile Delinquency and Youth Crime.* New York: Nova Science Publishers, Inc.

Krueger, A. B. and Maleckova, J. (2002) *Education, Poverty, Political Violence, and Terrorism: Is there a Connection?* Working Paper No. w9074, National Bureau of Economic Research. Available at: http://papersnber.org/papers/w9074

Kundnani, A. (2015) *A Decade Lost: Rethinking Radicalisation and Extremism.* London: Claystone. Available at: www.claystone.org.uk/wp-content/uploads/2015/01/Claystone-rethinking-radicalisation.pdf

Ladepeche (2016) Euro: Le mystérieux profil du français accusé de préparer des attentats. Available at www.ladepeche.fr/article/2016/06/07/2360491-euro-mysterieux-profil-francais-accuse-preparer-attentats.html

Laqueur, W. (1999) *The New Terrorism: Fanaticism and the Arms of Mass Destruction.* Oxford: Oxford University Press.

Leahy, R. L. (2015) *Emotional Schema Therapy.* New York: Guilford Press.

McCauley, C. and Segal, M. (1987) Social psychology of terrorist groups. In C. Hendrick (ed.), *Review of Personality and Social Psychology, volume 9.* Beverly Hills, CA: Sage, pp. 231–256.

Neumann, P. (2008) *Perspectives on Radicalisation and Political Violence: Papers from the First International Conference on Radicalisation and Political Violence*, London, 17–18 January 2008. London: International Centre for the Study of Radicalisation and Political Violence. Available at: http://icsr.info/wp-content/uploads/2012/10/1234516938ICSRPerspectivesonRadicalisation.pdf

Neuburger, L. C. and Valentini, T. (1996) *Women and Terrorism* (trans Hughes, L.). London: Palgrave Macmillan.

NUT (2016) *Prevent Strategy.* Available at: https://www.teachers.org.uk/news-events/conference-2016/prevent-strategy

Nwankpa, M. (2014) The politics of amnesty in Nigeria: A comparative analysis of the Boko Haram and Niger Delta insurgencies. *Journal of Terrorism Research*, 5 (1): 67–77.

Quilliam Foundation (2014) *Islamic State: The Changing Face of Modern Jihadism.* London: Quilliam Foundation. Available at: www.quilliamfoundation.org/wp/wp-content/uploads/publications/free/islamic-state-the-changing-face-of-modern-jihadism.pdf

Rees, M., August, M., Baghdadi, G., Hamad, J., Klein, A., MacLeod, S. and Mustafa, N. (2002) Why suicide bombing is now all the rage. *Time*, 15 April, 33–39.

Richardson, L. (2005) State sponsorship – a root cause of terrorism? In Tore Bjorgo, T. (ed.), *Root Causes of Terrorism: Myths, Reality and Ways Forward.* London and New York: Routledge, pp. 188–197.

Russell, C. and Miller, B. (1983) Profile of a Terrorist. Reprinted in *Perspectives on Terrorism.* Wilmington, Delaware: Scholarly Resources Inc.

Sageman, M. (2004) *Understanding Terror Networks.* Philadelphia: University of Pennsylvania Press.

Sandler, T. and Enders, W. (2004) An economic perspective on transnational terrorism. *European Journal of Political Economy*, 20: 301–316.

Schlenger, W. E., Caddell, J. M., Ebert, L., Jordan, B. K., Rourke, K. M., Wilson, D., Thalji, L., Dennis, J. M., Fairbank, J. A. and Kulka, R. A. (2002) Psychological reactions to terrorist attacks: Findings from the national study of Americans' reactions to September 11. *JAMA* 288 (5): 581–588.

Southers, E. (2013) *Homegrown Violent Extremism*. London: Elsevier.

Sprinzak, E. and Denny, L. (2003) The terrorists in their own words: Interviews with 5 incarcerated Middle Eastern terrorists. *Terrorism and Political Violence*, 15 (1): 171–181.

Stephan, M. J. and Chenoweth, E. (2008) Why civil resistance works: The strategic logic of nonviolent conflict. *International Security*, 33 (1): 7–44.

Tatar, M. and Amram, S. (2008) Israeli adolescents' help-seeking behaviors in relation to terrorist attacks: the perceptions of students, school counselors and teachers. *British Journal of Guidance and Counselling*, 36: 51–70.

TES (2016) Exclusive: School anti-terror referrals surge amid 'climate of fear'. Available at: www.tes.com/news/school-news/breaking-news/exclusive-school-anti-terror-referrals-surge-amid-climate-fear

Think Global (2016) *Think Global Schools Survey: 'Prevent' Needs to Include Proactive Approach*. Available at: http://think-global.org.uk/think-global-schools-survey-prevent-needs-include-proactive-approach/

United Nations (UN) (2003) *Report on the World Social Situation, 2003. Social Vulnerability: Sources and Challenges*. Available at: www.un.org/esa/socdev/rwss/docs/2003/fullreport.pdf

US Homeland Security Institute (2009) *Recruitment and Radicalisation of School-Aged Youth by International Terrorist Groups, Final Report*. U.S. Department of Education, Office of Safe and Drug-Free School. Available at: http://homelandsecurity.org/docs/reports/Radicalization_School-Aged_Youth.pdf

Vaughan, R. (2015) Treat extremism like anorexia, says terrorism expert. *Times Educational Supplement* (TES), 2 October.

Victoroff, J. (2005) The mind of the terrorist: A review and critique of psychological approaches. *The Journal of Conflict Resolution*, 49 (1): 3–42.

Weinberg, L. and Eubank, W. L. (1987) Italian women terrorists. *Terrorism: An International Journal*, 9: 241–262.

White, M. (2014) Jailed terrorists refuse to change beliefs. *Sky News*. Available at: http://news.sky.com/story/1189231/jailed-terrorists-refuse-to-change-beliefs

4 The marketization of education

Trevor Cotterill

This chapter explores:

- the process of marketization or 'quasi-marketization';
- the notion of choice for individuals within education;
- the debate surrounding accountability within a market economy.

> ✎ **Activity: Are there any similarities between shopping and education?**
>
> - When planning a shopping trip for your weekly groceries, what factors contribute to where you shop?
> - When a parent is thinking about sending their child to a new school, or a student is planning to go to university, what factors contribute to their choice?
> - Are there any similarities between shopping and education?

Marketization in education

Much has been written about the marketization of Higher Education in England, with the emphasis on student choice of university, fees and league tables, but this chapter examines market forces within the wider sector of education. The changes in the HE environment are routinely identified and named by adding the suffix '-ization' to a specific concept, for example, marketization, privatization, globalization, internationalization or marketingization. Marketization is the gradual introduction of the Economic Market logic into HE (Nedbalová et al., 2014). Slaughter and Rhoades (2009) discuss the importance of academic capitalism where university patent and copyright policies, faculty ownership over courseware and teaching materials, entrepreneurial practices, university boards of trustees and brands, logos and trademarks demonstrate how the emergence of market-like behaviour transforms research into products, faculty into capitalists and students into consumers. The impetus for these changes is academic capitalism with the pursuit [by the university] of market and market-like activities to generate external revenue. However, McCaig (2015) suggests that a result of marketization in HE has been the expansion of social mobility and widening participation.

> ✎ **Activity: Choosing a university**
>
> What key factors would you/did you identify as informing your choice of a place at university? What messages are universities trying to get across to would-be students? How do these relate to the market (such as employability prospects) and to the academic standing of the university and course? Are they related in any way?

Until recently the thinking surrounding schooling in England tended to focus upon issues such as pedagogy, allocation of resources and league tables (Allen and Burgess, 2011). Now, through 'quasi-marketization', issues such as competition, deregulation and parental choice have become a dominant discourse. The education system in England is developing along a 'quasi-market' route which sees parents being viewed as 'consumers', provided with information about schools in order to make choices or 'preferences' for their children (West et al., 2011). Economists describe a 'quasi-market' as one which is underpinned of necessity, by government regulation and finance (Lucas and Mace, 1999). To make a market work in education, performance indicators are needed so that consumers (students and parents) can make informed choices about where they can receive the best services. The introduction of market principles and greater autonomy for schools comes with the increased internal and external accountability for these performance indicators, which include Ofsted reports, the publication of league tables and the impact of a 'Tripadvisor' approach to the ratings of schools on social media.

Successive governments point to generous public spending on education but this has also seen the development of the 'business state' (Devine et al., 2009) whereby despite increases in public expenditure the underlying theme remains that 'the market knows best'. This is where changes always have a market principle, putting employers in charge of government-funding bodies, replacing the public servant with people from business. This includes privatizing parts of the public sector, private finance initiatives, growth in the numbers of managers and consultants drawn from the business community. Behind every development in education over the past few years, there has been a drive towards this marketized view of education (Lawson and Spours, 2011) with education reduced to competing schools, colleges and profit-making organizations. For example, in the FE sector, colleges compete in a quasi-market in a culture of targets, bureaucracy, inspection, targets and regulation – with the voice of the professional increasingly marginalized.

> ✎ **Activity: Choosing a Further Education college**
>
> - What key factors would you/did you identify as informing your choice of a place at a Further Education college, studying a vocational course?
> - What messages are colleges trying to get across to would-be students? How do these relate to the market (such as employability prospects) and to the academic standing of the college and course? Are they related in any way?

This marketization, or rather 'quasi-marketization', of education refers to privatization of the education industry in the process of providing educative services. Economic advantage is the main driving force for the emergence of this style of education. An instance involves the period 1998, where the government published a report comparing the GCSE and Standard Assessment Tests of schools, giving parents a choice between different competing schools (Bates, 2011; Friedman, 2003). This meant that schools performing well attracted a high number of parents, resulting in increased revenues from fees. However, does this approach meet the objective of providing the best educative services and an equal opportunity for students?

It is cardinal to the whole notion of an economic market that both producers and consumers have access to reliable information about price, availability and quality of the product on offer. Equally important, however, is the risk that, unless it is carefully controlled, competition leads to rationalization and an actual reduction in diversity and consumer choice. The publication of test results has produced a 'quasi-market' of winners and losers within the school system. The concepts of economics as a motivator to marketization of education are highly criticized by Lauder (2006), who argued that economic factors have replaced the learning aspects of education to more material-oriented learning processes, whereby schools concentrate on how they can achieve customer satisfaction as opposed to impartation of knowledge and skills. As long ago as the 1990s, Lauder was arguing that marketization of education arose due to the emergence of the class system. Parents from rich backgrounds saw the need for taking their children to private schools, because they offered higher quality education over state schools (Lauder et al., 1999). This aspect caused a rift between the rich and the poor in the educative process in terms of acquisition of knowledge. Bates *et al.* (2011) and Kishan (2008) observe that parents with low incomes struggle to send their children to private schools, and this accelerates the process of social segregation. The European Research Institute of Education conducted research on the marketization of education in Europe. It found that the state had lost its ability to regulate the education system in Europe as a result (Kishan, 2008).

Another aspect of the marketization of education is the changing needs of the society that the education system needed to address. This issue is vague in its description, because education is age-old, and issues affecting the society are the same. Lauder (2006) agrees with this notion and notes that the education system concerns itself with the impartation of skills necessary for an individual to survive in the world. This was the objective of the education system in former centuries, the needs of the society are always the same, but how to solve such needs differ. The main needs of the society are survival in a fierce competitive environment; an education system that offers mechanisms and skills to survive in such an environment is welcomed. Government schools also offer such skills and those who argue that this style of education emerged due to changes in the needs of the populace are misguided. The schooling system has evolved to an extent that business organizations have a commercial presence in schools, and this is evidenced by the commercial advertisements on teaching materials. On this notion, educative services are seen as a business opportunity.

To Friedman (2003), marketization of education arose due to the need for allowing greater access to education and movement within the system. He notes that the combination of marketization, liberalization and privatization in the education sector ensures that development, prosperity and cooperation is achieved in the world, because information is shared freely. Without marketization of education, Friedman states that government institutions can interfere with the process of the free flow of information (Friedman, 2003; Bates, 2011). Lauder (2006) argues against this system of education and maintains that the marketization of education is a replacement of instructive thoughts with economic thoughts, and that instead of preparing students for social and personal development, the education system concerns itself with aspects of client satisfaction, cost effectiveness and competitiveness. Bridgehouse (2006) asserts that marketization of education has resulted in the neglect of children with special educational needs by schools due to a focus on how to minimize costs, thus because schools aim at profit making they see the need for hiring specialized staff as costly.

> **Activity: Choosing a secondary school**
>
> - What key factors would you/did you identify as informing your choice of a place at secondary school?
> - Which type of school (e.g. academy, grammar or free school) would/did you choose and what did/would inform your choice?
> - What criteria do these types of school compete on?

Education as a profitable market

Education is becoming itself a new profitable market. As economic globalization takes hold across the world, there is an increase in economic competition, resulting in instability, high unemployment rates, heavy pressure on public expenditures and a continuous pursuit of competitiveness. Also, industry and services have been entering the era of new technologies, especially information and communication technologies. Therefore, education is asked to attach less importance to knowledge, which is nowadays, in our fast-moving societies and economies, a perishable product (Cresson, 1998), and to put more emphasis on those skills that can guarantee flexibility and adaptability of the workforce. The really important thing in school is not more to learn, but to 'learn to learn', to be able to adapt quickly to the fast-changing technological environment and to the rapid rotation of the labour force in industry and services. Flexibility and unpredictability mean also that education systems themselves have to develop their capacity of adaptation, by becoming more autonomous, more competitive and less dependent on central regulation. The most decentralized (education) systems are also the most flexible, the quickest to adapt and hence have the greatest propensity to develop new forms of partnership (CEC, 1995).

In schools the neoliberal dream of fully self-regulating markets, disembodied from all politics and social life, finds its clearest expression in the regimented conformity of target-driven schooling, a constant drilling for high-stakes tests. The new public management that has emerged demands standardized provision, the development of a set of performance indicators to produce numerical data and a subsequent 'league table' of 'weak' and 'outstanding' schools. Education becomes valued solely for its extrinsic worth (qualifications, certificates etc.) and might more accurately be called 'certification'.

Playfair (2015) sees a number of key processes in the marketization of education, such as commodification, choice and competition. This is the mantra of those who uphold that education needs to be seen as a business. Commodification sees education as a commodity, something which can be consumed and traded, with education, previously having been seen as lifelong social interactions and developmental processes, becoming a tradable thing with tangible exchange value. Relationships change with students and parents becoming consumers, demanding that education 'delivers' outcomes for them, and they also themselves become commodities, to be selected by providers based on their likelihood of success. Teachers become the agents of 'delivery' and the institutions they work in 'perform' better or worse on a numerical scale. To be tradable, every aspect of learning needs to quantified and given a value, including grades, points and qualifications. This promotes a hierarchy of worth and inevitably changes people's perceptions of their own worth and that of others.

Is it about choice?

Another key factor of marketization is the focus on choice, but these choices may not be equitable. As consumers we sense that there is always something better to aspire to. We seek to benefit from the inequality, or 'diversity', of what is on offer by grasping something distinctive and valuable which not everyone can have. However, the market actually limits our options and only allows us to strive for certain things. It leaves inequalities unchallenged and in fact tends to widen them. Whether it's the global economic outcomes, the Programme for International Student Assessment (PISA) scores, or national league tables of various kinds, publication of such data leads to comparison and competition. If there is an increasing pressure to make better choices, achieve higher grades, enter the highest achieving schools or Russell Group university, then most students will inevitably be 'losers'. Thus, good schools will attract more students and less good schools will be motivated to improve by the competition for students from the good schools. The less popular schools might get some support to improve or be rebranded and relaunched with new leadership under 'forced conversions' for example. The possibility of decline, failure or closure sharpens everyone's focus on doing better.

When we are shopping we like to be able to choose between different products, check prices and value for money and make our own judgement about what's best for us. However, do we really want to shop around and choose between different educational offers for ourselves or our children? The debate is about education as a public service, and as with our other public services, we want education to respond to our needs and aspirations and ultimately to be accountable to us – all of us. However, with choice comes the sustainability of courses. The small sixth-form centre in a local comprehensive may not be able to offer such a wide range of courses as the local FE college, but could still offer a setting which suits a number of students and thus be in demand. Being able to measure demand is very important in a market system. Choosing a school or college is generally a single-outcome decision; each consumer will only choose one at a time. Both the school application system and the post-16 free-for-all allow for multiple applications. Consumers make several applications but will ultimately choose only one, so perhaps conversion rates are a better way to measure the success of a market-led system.

An ideal market requires well-informed consumers who are in a position to make choices between products based on accurate information about the things that matter to them. If public services like education are really to operate in a market, consumers, whether parents or students, need to be well informed about the alternatives available before they exercise their choice. It also means trusting and understanding the data in a wide range of 'objective' published data and statistical claims, but this can reinforce the prior advantages of some consumers. Providers with good reputations will tend to attract the kinds of students who are most likely to further enhance their attractiveness in an upward spiral of positive feedback. Other providers can easily fall into a downward spiral. However, as well as looking at students as consumers, they are also commodities; it is the provider who is the consumer vying to pick the 'best' students, as in the case of HEIs.

> **✎ Activity: Welcome to our school**
>
> Imagine that a school is rebranding, or that permission has been granted to start a new school in your local area and you are in charge of marketing the school to prospective parents.
>
> - What are the key messages you would want to get across?
> - How would you market the school?
> - What performance indicators might you use to promote the school?

The market and accountability in education

Market accountability has sought to make available a range of information by which consumers (parents) could hold English schools accountable. Information is available to parents in a variety of forms including the results of national tests and external exams taken at 11, 16 and 18, widely reported and commented upon in the media and reports of school inspections by Ofsted. Comprehensive information is available to parents about every school (DfE, 2016). Collectively, these different sources of information impact upon a school's reputation and inform consumer choice (West et al,, 2011). Sanctions in relation to market accountability centre on the possibility of parental exit, and school closure is possible if consumer demand declines significantly, but a more likely result is that of a reduction in funding.

Figlio and Loeb (2011) suggest that accountability in education is a broad concept that could be addressed in many ways. These include political processes such as the publication of Green Papers to assure democratic accountability, the use of market-based accountability to inform parents and pupils or peer-based systems to increase the professional accountability of teachers. Accountability in education is aimed at increasing student achievement, and involves evaluation and responsibility for all those involved. Education is the imparting of knowledge through a variety of means and Sahlberg (2010) suggests that we need to rethink accountability in a knowledge society. The advantage of such a system, with its trend towards competition and test-based accountability on predetermined knowledge, is that it may do much to improve performance of educational systems, but increased competition may not benefit the social capital of schools and the communities they serve.

Keddie (2012) examines a key theme in this discussion on accountability, that of autonomy. On the one hand, she argues, it could be that schools have greater autonomy with respect to resource allocation, the linking of funding to student numbers and greater parental choice. The increase of academies (accelerated with the Academies Act 2010) and free schools (from 2011) are clear examples of the government's prioritizing of market-oriented school reforms, the premise that parental choice, school diversity and competition between schools for their 'market' share of students will drive up school performance and outcomes. But do parents have that much of a choice? Only days after the government planned to make all schools in England academies (May 2016), it was dropped and new legislation was proposed to include sweeping powers for the DfE to force schools in 'underperforming' local authorities to convert to academy status. The DfE said it expected the rate of academy conversions to increase, bolstered by the Education and Adoption Act that came into force in March 2016, giving the department extra powers to intervene in 'coasting' schools and have them taken over by academy sponsors. Those councils with successful track records will be able to continue to maintain their local schools, including the contentious plan of removing the right of parents to be represented on academy boards of governors and radical proposals allowing head teachers to award staff qualifications. However, the new Education Secretary Justine Greening, speaking to the Education Select Committee in September 2016, announced she was abandoning her predecessor's plan, which would have allowed academy trusts to operate without any parent governors either in individual schools or on the board of trustees. Still, under existing academy rules, chains are not required to have parent governors in individual schools.

Case study 4.1: The rise of the academies

The rise of academies has produced a system whereby an underperforming school can be forced to become an academy, so-called 'forced conversions' whereby an academy order is issued because they are 'eligible for intervention'. The Education and Adoption Act 2016 has effectively removed the right to consultation over whether a school should become an academy and over the identity of the sponsor, except in a limited number of circumstances. However before a school becomes an academy the sponsor must communicate to parents the sponsor's plans to 'improve the school'.

The decision to apply for voluntary academy status is taken by the governors. In the case of foundation schools with a foundation, and voluntary schools, the governing body may only apply for academy status with the agreement of any existing trust and those entitled to appoint any foundation governors.

Having registered their interest in academy status with the DfE, the governors simply have to vote in favour of a resolution to convert to academy status. The decision can be made by a simple majority of those present at the meeting. The application goes to the Secretary of State for Education but in practice will be considered by the Regional Schools Commissioner and the Head Teacher Board.

Once the academy application is approved, an 'academy order' is issued which gives the school the legal right to start the conversion process, apply for the conversion grant, establish new governance arrangements, register the academy trust and so on. Once all the legal arrangements are in place, the academy trust signs the funding agreement with the Secretary of State or her representative and the academy conversion process is complete. The whole transfer process can take as little as three to four months from start to finish.

- What reasons may there be for either a forced or voluntary conversion?
- If you were a parent of a child at a school in either of these situations, what information would you want to be given as to why a school may wish, or be forced to become, an academy?

There is much debate about how academies are performing. The DfE (2014) state that schools under the floor standard alongside a history of under-performance, face being taken over by a sponsor with a track record of improving weak schools, a so-called academy order, but critics suggest that GCSE exam results in 2014 were lower than those for schools under local authority control. Adams and Weale (2014) stated that six out of nine of England's largest chains of academy schools only passed the government's minimum GCSE targets (40 per cent) through success in other equivalent qualifications that are soon to be disqualified or downgraded in national league tables. Thus, an important measure of accountability, that of performance tables, can be manipulated by the addition or removal of vocational qualifications, or a change in the marking criteria such as that seen in the 2014 summer exams with the number asking for a review of marks increasing 48 per cent from 2013, with more than one in five challenges for both GCSEs and A-levels leading to new grades. (Adams and Weale, 2014).

Free schools extend the idea of the academies programme; they are also independent, state-funded and not governed by the LEA but are established and run by parents, teachers, charities, businesses and other groups and are not bound to the National Curriculum or by national union agreements (Hatcher, 2011). Supporters argue that they offer more choice to parents, while opponents suggest that they are taking resources away from established schools. There may have been a move towards greater autonomy, but equally, as far as state schools are concerned, there has been a move to a prescriptive National Curriculum and assessment framework where student performance is audited and converted to a public ranking of schools in the form of league tables with school 'effectiveness' policed and regulated through Ofsted inspections (Glatter, 2012; Lawson et al., 2013). However Wilby (2016), writing in the *Guardian* with respect to academies, states that at least it can be argued that parents are able to opt for a different provider and thus in effect the Tories are marketizing schools, even if as yet the providers are unable to make a profit.

Conclusion

People like the market choice around where to shop and how to shop and this choice is welcomed and empowering for consumers. When they read about the impact of shopping habits on supermarket share, perhaps the focus is still on 'Where can I get value for money?' The market listens and shops engage in publicity campaigns, with reduced prices and an emphasis on the shopping experience. This has led to many traders diversifying or focusing on what they do best. If we were to take that analogy to education, do we want a return to the 'corner shop' where we know the shopkeeper, but have little choice? Or do we want to search around for a shop/shops that meet our needs? It is clear that there are a range of schools to chose from, including state-funded, faith schools, academies, free schools and UTCs, each vying for your custom. Inevitably, there will be winners and losers, as in any market-driven commodity. I suggest that although there appears to be a wide choice on offer, here the similarity ends. Catchment areas, fees, the cost of housing and the numbers of students 'allowed in', may suggest, as Theresa May points out, that 'the truth is that we already have selection in our school system'. What price choice if this is driven by a system presided over by individuals with little or no experience in the 'market' of education?

Case study 4.2: The new kid on the block?

In September 2016, Prime Minister Theresa May gave a speech at the Tory Party conference, in which she stated 'For too long we have tolerated a system that contains an arbitrary rule preventing selective schools from being established – sacrificing children's potential because of dogma and ideology. The truth is that we already have selection in our school system – and its selection by house price, selection by wealth. That is simply unfair.' She advocated that new selective schools will be allowed to open and that existing schools will be able to become grammars. 'This is about being unapologetic for our belief in social mobility and making this country a true meritocracy – a country that works for everyone.' We know that grammar schools are hugely popular, and she set out why she believed they were part of her plan to build 'a truly diverse system which taken as a whole can give every child the support they need to go as far as their talents can take them' (Prime Minister's Office, 2016).

The Education Secretary, Justine Greening, has also argued that poorer children who went to grammar schools progressed twice as fast at grammars as children from wealthier backgrounds. Grammars for them were about closing the attainment gap, so the question is how can we make sure grammar schools are more open for those disadvantaged children, so that they can really turbo-charge their education (Walker and Elgot, 2016)?

Research suggests grammar schools have just 3 per cent of pupils from very poor backgrounds – those on the Pupil Premium who are basically from families in receipt of certain benefits or earning less than £16,000 a year. Nationally, 14 per cent of pupils are in this category. Hence the new requirement for any new selective school/grammar to take a proportion of disadvantaged pupils, establish a 'high quality, non-selective free school', set up or sponsor a primary feeder school in a deprived area or sponsor an underperforming academy. Speaking on the Andrew Marr programme (BBC) on 2 October 2016, Theresa May stated that it was about ensuring we have good school places for every child and not a return to the binary system of grammar schools and secondary modern of the 1950s. She emphasized that she would require new or expanding grammars to take a proportion of pupils from lower-income households to ensure that selective education is not reserved for those with the means to move into a catchment area or pay for tuition to pass the test.

However, there are a number of people who have been quick to criticize this vision of creating a 'revised' player in the education market, with some suggesting that 'inclusive grammars' are an oxymoron like 'fun run', with many successful adults carrying the emotional scars of failing the 11-plus. A report by Cribb et al. (2013) for the Sutton Trust suggests claims that the opening up of academic selection will increase social mobility and raise the attainment of children from poorer backgrounds are not borne out by evidence. Indeed, at Prime Minister's Question Time (14 September 2016), Jeremy Corbyn (the leader of the Opposition), stated that a selective education would never bring about equality but lead to a 'second-class schooling for many'.

- If you were producing a report on 'Why there should not be a return to grammar schools', who would you consult, what types of data would you wish to examine, and what counter-arguments might you propose?

Suggested reading

Benn, M. & Downs, J. (2015) *The Truth About Our Schools: Exposing the Myths, Exploring the Evidence.* London: Routledge.

Debunking the ideology of marketization, and exposing the half-truths that pass for objective reporting, Benn and Downs meticulously lay out the evidence: that a national system of comprehensive schools delivers the best outcomes.

Molesworth, M., Nixon. E. & Scullion, R. (eds) (2010) *The Marketisation of Higher Education.* London: Routledge

Until recently, government policy in the UK has encouraged an expansion of Higher Education with the express aim of creating a more educated workforce, and in so doing, has sponsored the commodification of Higher Education. This collection explores aspects of this process.

Williams, J. (2013) *Consuming Higher Education: Why Learning Can't Be Bought.* London: Bloomsbury.

This volume explores the status of students within the university and society, and the funding and purpose of Higher Education, drawing on empirical data, UK and USA government policy documents, speeches by policy makers and media representations of students.

References

Adams, R. & Weale, S. (2014) Ofsted chief says struggling schools 'no better off' under academy control. Available at: www.theguardian.com/education/2014/dec/10/ofsted-sir-michael-wilshaw-struggling-schools-academy-neglect

Allen, R. & Burgess, S. (2011) Can school league tables help parents choose schools? *Fiscal Studies*, 32 (2), 245–261.

Bates, R. (2011) Assessment and international schools. In *Schooling Internationally: Globalisation, Internationalisation and the Future for International Schools.* London: Taylor & Francis, pp. 148–164.

Bates, J., Lewis, S. & Pickard, A. (2011) *Education Policy, Practice and the Professional.* London: Continuum.

Bridgehouse, H. (2006) *On Education.* Abingdon: Routledge.

Commission of the European Communities (CEC) (1995) *Teaching and Learning: Towards the Learning Society.* Brussels: Office for Official Publications.

Cresson, E. (1998) *Putting Our Knowledge to Work: A Second Chance for Young People.* Discours prononcé à Harrogate, 5 March 1998, CEC SPEECH/98/45.

Cribb, J., Jesson, D., Sibieta, L., Skipp, A. & Vignoles, A. (2013) *Poor Grammar Entry into Grammar Schools for Disadvantaged Pupils in England.* London: Sutton Trust.

Devine, P., Pearman, A., Prior, M. & Purdy, D. (2009) *Feelbad Britain.* London: Lawrence and Wishart.

DfE (2014) *Schools Causing Concern.* London: DfE.

DfE (2016) Edubase public portal. Available at: www.education.gov.uk/edubase/home.xhtml

Figlio, D. & Loeb, S. (2011) School accountability. In Hanushek, E. A., Machin, S., and Woessmann L. (eds), *Handbook of the Economics of Education.* Amsterdam: Elsevier.

Friedman, M. I. (2003) *Educators' Handbook on Effective Testing.* Columbia, SC: Institute for Evidence-Based Decision-Making in Education.

Glatter, R. (2012) Persistent preoccupations: The rise and rise of school autonomy and accountability in England. *Educational Management Administration & Leadership*, 40 (5), 559–575.

Hatcher, R. (2011) The Conservative-Liberal Democrat Coalition government's 'free schools' in England. *Educational Review*, 63 (4), 485–503.

Keddie, A. (2012) *Matters of Autonomy and Accountability in the English Schooling Policy Context: Constraints and Possibilities.* Brisbane: University of Queensland.

Kishan, N. R. (2008) *Privatization of Education.* New Delhi: A.P.H Pub. Corp.

Lauder, H. (2006) *Education, Globalization, and Social Change*, 1st edn. Oxford: Oxford University Press.

Lauder, H., Hughes, D., Watson, S., Waslander, S., Thrupp, M., Strathdee, R., Simiyu, I., Dupuis, A., McGlinn, J. & Hamlin, J. (1999) *Trading in Futures: Why Markets in Education Don't Work.* Buckingham: Open University Press.

Lawson, N. & Spours, K. (2011) Education for the good society. *FORUM: For Promoting 3–19 Comprehensive Education*, 53 (2), 195–205.

Lawson, H., Boyask, R. & Waite, S. (2013) Construction of difference and diversity within policy and practice in England. *Cambridge Journal of Education*, 43 (1), 107–122.

Lucas, N. and Mace, J. (1999) Funding issues and social exclusion: Reflections on the 'marketization' of further education colleges. In Hayton, A. (ed.) *Tackling Disaffection and Social Exclusion: Education Perspectives and Policies*. London: Kogan Page.

McCaig, C. (2015) The impact of the changing English higher education marketplace on widening participation and fair access: Evidence from a discourse analysis of access agreements. *Widening Participation and Lifelong Learning*, 17 (1).

Nedbalová, E., Greenacre, L. & Schulz, J. (2014) UK higher education viewed through the marketization and marketing lenses. *Journal of Marketing for Higher Education*, 1–18.

Playfair, E. (2015) Market madness: Condition critical. *FORUM*, 57 (2), 213–226.

Prime Minister's Office (2016) PM to set out plans for schools that work for everyone. Available at: www.gov.uk/government/news/pm-to-set-out-plans-for-schools-that-work-for-everyone

Sahlberg, P. (2010) Rethinking accountability in a knowledge society. *Journal of Educational Change*, 11 (1), 45–61.

Slaughter, S. & Rhoades, G. (2009) *Academic Capitalism and the New Economy: Markets, State, and Higher Education*. Baltimore: Johns Hopkins University Press.

Walker P. & Elgot, J. (2016) Justine Greening indicates ban on grammar schools will be lifted. *Guardian*, 8 September. Available at: www.theguardian.com/education/2016/sep/08/justine-greening-confirms-plan-lift-ban-grammar-schools-11-plus

West, A., Mattei, P. & Roberts, J. (2011) Accountability and sanctions in English schools. *British Journal of Educational Studies*, 59 (1), 41–62.

Wilby, P. (2016) Parents out, chief executives in: Our schools will be anything but free. Available at: www.theguardian.com/commentisfree/2016/mar/21/schools-academies-democracy-educational-standards-accountability

5 Creativity in the classroom

Matt Edinger

This chapter explores:

- what creativity is;
- why creativity is important;
- how educators can foster creativity in the classroom.

Introduction

During an educational TED talk in 2006, Sir Ken Robinson suggested that 'creativity is as important as literacy' (Robinson, 2006). He believes that, since educators do not know which types of careers and day-to-day experiences our pupils will have in the future, we must prepare them with skills in creativity. However, creativity, as an act, is a grey area in educational research that has yet to be 'proven' useful with consistently reliable and valid empirical findings. Controversially, researchers of creativity have been pinning their positive findings to it since the 1920s; but the reality is that those involved with the education of children and youth, including pre-service and in-service teachers, may not be aware of creativity, how creativity can be fostered in classrooms, and which pedagogical activities can be used to foster creativity within pupils. This chapter seeks to define creativity, delineate why creativity is important in educational planning, and describe the tools needed to foster creativity in our classrooms.

> **Activity: Defining creativity**
>
> In your opinion, what exactly is creativity? Before reading the following section, write down your definitions of creativity. Then, after reading, compare your responses to those in Table 5.1.

What is creativity?

The Latin root of the word 'creativity' is *creare*, meaning 'to create, to bring forth, produce, bear' (Glosbe, 2016). In 1926, Wallas recorded instances of discovery in science, literary productions and other recognisable output from what he called 'creative geniuses'. His book, titled *Art of*

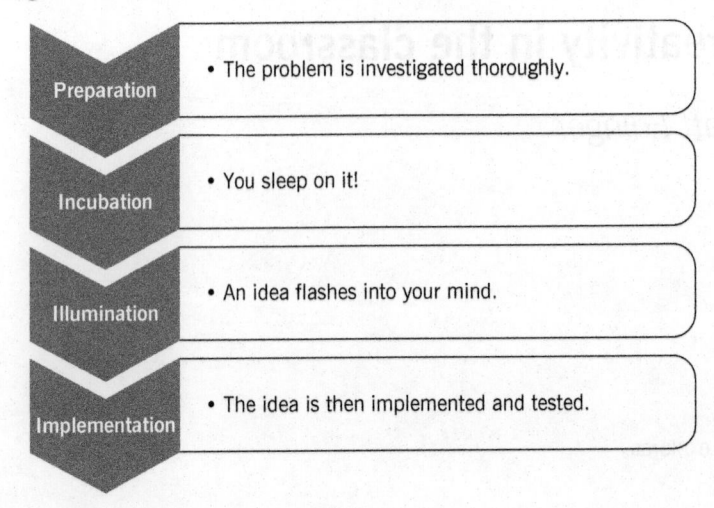

```
Preparation    • The problem is investigated thoroughly.
Incubation     • You sleep on it!
Illumination   • An idea flashes into your mind.
Implementation • The idea is then implemented and tested.
```

Figure 5.1 Steps of creativity (adapted from Wallas, 1926)

Thought (1926), describes creativity as a legacy of the evolutionary process, which allows humans to quickly adapt to rapidly changing environments. Wallas also suggests that the definition of creativity consists of the following steps: preparation, incubation, illumination and elaboration.

On the other hand, Guilford (1950) describes creativity as the ability to manipulate ideas in elaborate and original ways. He suggests that fluency, flexibility, novelty, reorganisation or redefinition of new ideas, degree of complexity, and evaluation could enhance creativity in the classroom. Furthermore, Torrance (1962) states that creativity is the ability to sense gaps in information, formulating solutions that complete the information, testing the potential solutions and communicating the results. Lastly, Perkins (1988) thought that 'a creative result is a result both original and appropriate. A creative person—a person with creativity—is a person who fairly routinely produces creative results' (p. 311).

In the classroom, creativity is the act of making connections between what is known and a specific outcome. For instance, when it comes to connection-making, pupils could create written similarities and differences between the French and American Revolutions, or describe the plant life cycle through a clay, papier-mâché or shoebox diorama creation. On a societal scale, VanTassel-Baska (1998) suggests that creative people are deemed creative if they contribute to society at large. However, for this chapter, Gardner's (1983) understanding that creativity is an aspect of each of the following intelligences: linguistic, logical-mathematical, bodily-kinesthetic, spatial, musical, interpersonal, and intrapersonal is used. Gardner (1997) suggests that each domain has its own parameters for creativity, from Virginia Woolf's linguistic creation of literature to Freud's interpersonal creation of a non-existent domain of psychology. Mohandas Gandhi was also classified by Gardner as an intrapersonal creator who became an influencer of people and a public leader. Gardner's (1997) study of creativity looks beyond a single definition or product of creativity, but applies it to various domains.

Table 5.1 Definitions of creativity

Definitions of creativity	Author(s)
The steps of preparation, incubation, illumination and elaboration	Wallas (1926)
The ability to manipulate ideas in elaborate and original ways, as well as fluency, flexibility, novelty, synthesising ability, analysing ability, reorganisation or redefinition of new ideas, degree of complexity and evaluation	Guilford (1950)
The ability to sense gaps in information, formulate solutions that complete the information, test the solutions and communicate the results	Torrance (1962)
The linguistic, logical-mathematical, bodily-kinaesthetic, spatial, musical, interpersonal and intrapersonal domains have their own parameters for creativity	Gardner (1997)

> **Activity: Creative pupils**
>
> What characteristics will or should creative pupils have? Make a list.

Which characteristics of creativity can teachers find in pupils?

Some characteristics of creativity in pupils can be found within their personality and behaviour traits. VanTassel-Baska *et al.* (2007) suggest that personality traits visible in creative children can include independence in attitude and social behaviour, dominance, introversion, flexibility, intuitiveness, risk-taking, the ability to fantasise and toy with ideas and a moral commitment to work. High energy, stubbornness, inquisitiveness and fast-talking also are behaviour traits of a creative mind in children and youth. Creative indicators, especially in young children, are visible in their kinaesthetic and auditory functioning (VanTassel-Baska et al., 2007). Put another way, pupils can show characteristics of creativity in a most outward way, namely by asking many questions, by asking which variants can pertain to the question or by becoming quickly bored with classroom assignments.

Table 5.2 Characteristics of creative children

Characteristics of creative children	Author(s)
High identification with entire body movements to interpret song and sound	Torrance (1970, as cited in Davis and Rimm, 2004)
Fluency, flexibility of thought, originality, elaboration, visualisation, transformation, concentration, logical/aesthetical thinking, prioritising, planning, making inferences, identifying relevant information and generating different solutions to a problem	(Davis and Rimm, 2004)
Independence in attitude and social behaviour, dominance, introversion, flexibility, intuitiveness, risk-taking, ability to fantasise and toy with ideas, a moral commitment to work, high energy, stubbornness, inquisitiveness and fast-talking	VanTassel-Baska *et al.* (2007)

Similar to Gardner's (1983) bodily-kinaesthetic intelligence, Torrance (1970, as cited in Davis and Rimm, 2004) found that creative children highly identify with entire body movements to interpret song and sound. This link of dramatics to creativity has produced additional characteristic indicators of creativeness such as humour, confidence and having an imaginary playmate (Torrance, 1970 as cited in Davis and Rimm, 2004). The following list of behaviours and abilities, while not exhaustive, can be seen as traits commonly present in a creative child: fluency, flexibility of thought, originality, elaboration, visualisation, transformation, concentration, logical/aesthetical thinking, prioritising, planning, making inferences, and identifying relevant information and generating different solutions to a problem (Davis and Rimm, 2004). For example, children with a penchant for dinosaurs or photography may be happy to tell you all they know about the topic while incorporating it into all subjects or assessments, whether warranted or not.

> **Activity: Fostering creativity**
>
> Do you believe that creativity fosters creativity in individuals? Or is creativity something that is only innate in some individuals? Can teachers facilitate creativity in their pupils? If so, how?

How can teachers foster pupil creativity?

Early in the research, creativity was viewed as a concept that was entirely internal to the creative person. However, Amabile (1983) and Csikszentmihalyi (1996) found that the environment has a strong effect on creative production. Amabile's (1988) model suggests that minor features of the close social environment may influence personal creativity. For example, creativity may be impeded when classroom outcome rewards are previously decided, when undue time pressures are enforced and when intense teacher supervision is applied. Additionally, the evaluation of products, competition, and a lack of method and material choices can also affect creative outcomes (Amabile, 1988).

Piirto (1998, p. 392) states that creativity is born via 'the personality, the process, and the product within a domain in interaction with genetic influences and with optimal environmental influences of home, school, community and culture'. Piirto stresses the importance of social environmental factors in the exercise of fostering creativity. Additionally, given that social relationships are an important feature of any classroom environment, researchers such as Csikszentmihalyi (1988) and Perry-Smith and Shalley (2003) emphasise, along with Piirto (1998), how the act of creativity is a social process, and is therefore important knowledge for all educators. As teachers, we can greatly influence our classroom environment to foster creativity in students.

Sternberg and Lubart (1991) believe that pupils in the classroom should be given confidence to not only find problems, but to define them as well. They also define six elements of creativity as thinking styles, intelligent processes, knowledge, personality, environment and motivation. They believe that pupils should take risks in their work and be taught how to flexibly use knowledge. These elements are important to be aware of since educators must realise the importance of ensuring favourable pupil conditions for creative potential, and we should know what we need to learn and do what we can to foster creativity.

Torrance (1962) delineated seminal findings when studying creative talent in the classroom context. He found a need for educators to guide creative pupils toward creative production since he believed a healthy personality was dependent on the relationship between the classroom and the pupil's own creativity. Torrance suggests that both parents and the school must recognise that all pupils have at least the smallest of seeds of creativity that must be encouraged with experiences and honed with guidance for creative success. Next, Csikszentmihalyi (1991) interpreted the creative process as involving 'flow', or the optimal experience that happens when someone becomes totally involved in something and loses sense of time and surroundings. Additionally, Csikszentmihalyi's (1991) study findings suggest that knowing the creative process as well as how to stimulate creativity via flow in the classroom is important for administrators and teachers. Similarly, Hansen and Feldhusen (1994) studied the effects of trained and untrained gifted and talented teachers on gifted pupils. They found that trained teachers 'placed a greater emphasis on creativity and encouragement of creative thinking and provided a more accepting environment. They encouraged fluency, flexibility, originality, and elaboration; asked more open-ended questions; and encouraged more risk-taking than did untrained teachers in the study' (p. 119).

Table 5.3 What can teachers do to foster creativity?

What can teachers do to foster creativity?	Author(s)
Offer pupil choice and time to complete tasks	Greenberg (1992)
Permit ample room and time for developing a creative reply to problematic circumstances, offer an open 'mental climate' in the classroom that fosters self-esteem and self-worth, and values the viability of products	Shallcross (1981)
Encourage pupils to not only find problems, but define them, take risks in their work and be taught how to flexibly use knowledge	Sternberg and Lubart (1991)
Encourage fluency, flexibility, originality, elaboration, asking open-ended questions, encourage risk-taking, increasing teacher training	Hansen and Feldhusen (1994)
Encourage optimal environmental influences of home, school, community and culture	Piirto (1998)
Encourage divergent and convergent thinking, brainstorming that includes deferring judgment, quantity of ideas and unusual ideas	Treffinger et al. (1997)
Encourage pupil choice, the use of few rules and restrictions, the need for pupil acceptance by teachers, open-ended activities, unstructured time, drawing, flexible directions, more time with technology, more field trips, and more adult guidance in the classroom	de Souza Fleith (2000)
Offer opportunities for pupils to work cooperatively, to learn the skills of creative problem solving, and to have ample, formal reflection activities	Terry (2000)

Factors for nurturing creativity in the classroom

Can creativity be taught? Osborn (1963) believes that it can with appropriate training. He developed training activities within a programme called Creative Problem-Solving (CPS). CPS was further refined by Parnes (1967, 1981), Isaksen and Treffinger (1985) and Treffinger et al. (1997). CPS activities and training use divergent thinking, or solving problems with many possible solutions, and convergent thinking, which is solving problems with a single, correct answer. Also, to conduct appropriate brainstorming, CPS training includes deferring judgement, endeavouring for quantity of ideas as well as unusual ideas, and seeking a combination of these ideas for pupils. Overall, CPS can be seen as a framework for the organisation of a variety of methods that individuals select for specific assignments.

In addition, Terry (2000) reflects that 'students must have opportunities to work cooperatively; to learn the skills of creative problem solving, to have ample, formal reflection activities' (p. 3058A). Finally, researchers of creativity-fostering activities found that specific programmes fostered pupil ability toward fluency and flexibility, diverse skills and novel thinking. To sum up, educators can begin their own understanding of how creativity can be taught in their classrooms by examining collaboration, brainstorming and specific types of thinking.

Renzulli and Callahan (1973) found that, to foster the creation of unique and innovative ideas in the classroom, fluency was aided through the use of teacher training for activities that lacked predetermined answers. The authors emphasised that support includes pupil freedom that allows the development of new ideas.

It makes sense that teachers should be encouraged or directly taught how to think and behave as creative people if they are going to have the skills and experience needed to teach pupils how to be creative and act creatively. Sternberg (2003) suggests that creative instructional strategies lead to creative pupil outcomes, which in turn provide long-term benefits such as improved school performance for pupils.

Teachers and pupils: Academic and personal behaviours needed to foster creativity

Angleoska-Galevska (1996) found that certain specific teacher behaviours foster creativity. These behaviours include a positive attitude toward creativity, creating social relations between educator and pupil and using appropriate materials. Angleoska-Galevska (1996) also found that teacher's level of education benefitted pupil creativity.

Another study suggests that gifted pupils often prefer personal behaviours to their teacher's academic qualities. Lewis (1982) worked with small groups of gifted pupils in third through seventh grade to identify the behaviours of successful teachers of the gifted. The pupils agreed on a list of 22 essential behaviours, the most important of which included creativity, understanding, patience and honesty. The majority of items listed relate to personal traits of the teacher. Sternberg and Lubart (1991) also identify that personality attributes can become essential in the process of teaching creativity. These include tolerance for ambiguity, willingness to overcome complications, perseverance, willingness to grow, risk-taking, having the courage of individual conviction and belief in oneself.

Attitudes and competencies for teachers to foster creativity

In addition to personal and academic behaviours, teachers who are successful at nurturing creativity must also be willing and able to foster all of the personal resources their pupils draw upon in the classroom. Within their investment theory of creativity, Sternberg and Lubart (1991) suggest that building creativity in pupils involves teaching them to use six resources: intelligence, knowledge, intellectual style, personality, motivation and environmental context. Problem definition is another particularly crucial aspect of the intelligence resource. Teachers must avoid non-authentic problems in the classroom and instead develop problems that require insightful solutions to real-world, open-ended questions.

Sternberg and Lubart (1991, 1995) believe that creativity is not just thinking in a definite manner, but is rather an outlook concerning life and what it has to offer. Sternberg (2000) wrote that creative people make a decision to be creative. In a revision of the key resources discussed above, Sternberg (2003) purported that teaching for creativity takes 12 key decisions that motivate creative thinking. These decisions include, to name a few, redefining problems and critiquing and selling your own ideas. He reminds teachers that knowledge is a double-edged sword since it can make individuals think they know everything about a domain, and then suffer from closed-mindedness. Sternberg (2003) believes that creative people must decide to surmount obstacles, take sensible risks and have a willingness to grow. Above all, individuals must decide to believe in themselves and tolerate ambiguity. Truly creative people find what they love to do, and then do it. Teachers must foster these beliefs in the classroom.

Perkins (1999) urges teachers to consider their inventory of pedagogical skills as a 'toolbox' since teaching situations are never truly identical. Once teachers have nurtured and developed the qualities and competencies necessary to effectively teach creativity, they must then turn to methods of creativity introduction into their classrooms. A possible starting point for fostering creativity is utilising informal creative thinking and problem-solving activities such as those outlined in the next section of the chapter.

Activities that foster creativity

Understanding activities that promote creative thinking and problem-solving skills in pupils is another approach teachers can employ to foster creativity skills. The act of teaching and fostering creativity is diverse, and research suggests that there is an intricate artistry required in teaching (Halliwell, 1993; Dadds, 1995; Woods and Jeffrey, 1996; Cropley, 1997). The following strategies allow teachers to implement creativity-fostering activities, but require some advanced planning or preparation. These environmental considerations and thinking process strategies can allow teachers to foster creativity on a daily basis.

Classroom environment and creativity

Raina and Vats (1979) reflect that creative teachers tend to favour a creative classroom environment. Their study found that highly creative teachers facilitate a sense of empathy, a sense of trust, and discovery in the classroom. Teachers with a lower level of creativity tend to reflect the same low level of creativity in their classroom environment. Raina and Vats (1979) found solid connections between teachers' creative personality, teaching style and pupil control beliefs. In their study, creative teachers establish classroom environments with less control and an emphasis on less disciplined control. Similarly, Torrance (1970) describes creative teachers as humanistic, accepting and tolerant in their approach towards the education of their pupils.

Many creative-thinking and problem-solving activities are related to the learning environment of the classroom. Shallcross (1981) recognises an array of strategies she believes to be important in pedagogical advances toward fostering creativity. The first of these strategies includes permitting ample room and time for developing a creative reply to a variety of problematic circumstances. Shallcross (1981) states that many educators often intrude prematurely on their pupils' thinking process. This intrusion may prevent pupils from taking the time to work out ideas. Additionally, she believes that offering an open 'mental climate' in the classroom that fosters self-esteem and self-worth, and values the viability of products, will enhance pupil confidence. Also, the classroom's emotional climate must permit pupil growth in security and personal confidence. She believes that constant scrutiny in the classroom is a creativity killer in any situation. As Shallcross (1981) suggests, 'The ground rules are personal guarantees that allow [pupils] to grow at their own rate, retain the privacy of their work until they are ready to share it, and prize their possible differences' (p. 19).

Another approach to creativity is the Reggio Emilia approach (Katz et al., 1993). The approach suggests environmental classroom modifications that support pupil creativity. This model considers the environment to be an additional educator. The approach believes that teachers should organise different areas for minor and major group projects as well as small intimate spaces for individual pupils. Documentation of pupil work should be displayed in common areas. Shared space is made available for pupils from different classrooms to work together. Similar to Shallcross (1981), the approach suggests that teachers must give pupils adequate time to finish their work while also offering the physical space needed to leave work from one day to the next. In addition, the approach believes that rich resource materials, such as current events or pupil-friendly issues, can be particularly useful when pupils participate in the selection process. The model also suggests that teachers should provide a variety of stimulating encounters that help pupils integrate their outer and inner worlds, or what Gardner (1983) labelled multiple intelligences.

Pupil choice can also be an important environmental consideration in fostering creativity. Greenberg (1992) discovered that pupils who became more creative in the classroom had more choice in identifying which problems they were going to work on and took more time in completing their tasks. She also found that these pupils expressed more positive feelings about their work, which is an important point for teachers, for it could be argued that fostering a positive attitude to one's own creativity is an essential starting point for classroom creativity (Sternberg, 2003).

Amabile (1988) and Isaksen (1995) explored climates that encourage creativity. Their studies suggest that participants in a creative climate should be challenged by their tasks and goals, and should be encouraged to take risks. Consequently, pupils should volunteer new ideas and perspectives freely, and their new ideas should be met with support and encouragement. Furthermore, since ambiguity is most likely tolerated in the creative classroom, pupils should be able to experience debate in an open and status-free environment.

De Souza Fleith (2000) investigates perceptions of classroom environments and their impact on creativity. She sought to determine 'perceptions of characteristics that either stimulated or inhibited the development of creativity in the classroom environment' (p. 148). De Souza Fleith found that creativity-enhancing environments included pupil choice, the use of few rules and restrictions and the need for pupil acceptance by teachers. Teachers in her study also stated that creativity was enhanced by open-ended activities, unstructured time, drawing and flexible directions. The teachers indicated that pupils wanted more time to be spent on the internet, more field trips and more adult guidance in the classroom (de Souza Fleith, 2000).

Tomlinson (1995) suggests that classroom environments should accommodate individual learner interests and abilities in order for the most favourable learning to occur. She emphasises that, when differentiating the curriculum, 'teachers are not dispensers of knowledge, but organizers of learning opportunities' (p. 1). Tomlinson (1995) also believes that when the classroom environment makes allowances for creativity, pupils have a greater chance of becoming creative.

Creative thinking and problem-solving activities involve encouraging pupils to use specific thinking processes, such as de Bono's (1985) 'six hats' method. He believes that creative thinking is fundamentally 'lateral thinking', and his method encourages pupils to consider multiple perspectives of any issue. Pupils 'wear' one of six hats, each with its own fictional colour and permeated with certain qualities. Each hat emphasises a particular approach to thinking. Another thinking process strategy is 'possibility thinking' which encourages pupils to approach learning across the curriculum with a 'what if?' attitude (Craft, 2000). Pupils wonder about possibilities and are prepared to follow, and be supported in, seeing the questions through to an outcome.

Creative dramatics

Using creative dramatics is another activity that can encourage pupils' academic and affective domains since pupils can express themselves in a way that is safe and developmentally appropriate. Creative dramatics, as defined by Johnson (1998), is 'a form of imaginative play that helps pupils learn [and] uses no written dialogue' while simultaneously using 'students' imagination and willingness to act or pretend as a means of reinforcing academic, emotional and interpersonal objectives' (p. 2). Kolczynski and Cepelka (1977) claim that the goal of creative dramatics 'is not performance, but the free expression of the child's creative imagination through the discipline of an art form' (p. 285). The distinction is important: the process of creative dramatics, one in which 'what *is* happening ... is more important than what might or *will* happen' (Kolczynski and Cepelka, 1977, p. 285) is more valuable than the eventual product of those creative dramatics. The next step is recognising which strategies are needed to implement creative dramatics successfully. Johnson explains that 'there are four necessary components of creative dramatics: structure, open-endedness, a safe environment, and feedback' (1998, p. 4). Through these components, we learn that pupils initially 'need structure to guide their actions and dialogues', though 'this structure should be flexible and open ended' (Johnson, 1998, p. 4). Also, a classroom which allows for risk, safety and community is needed, and informal feedback should be employed for effective pupil reflection. When using a simple approach, two types are considered: the first includes an isolated 'warm-up' activity that speaks to the elements of an actor during creative drama, while the second type includes playmaking.

Davis and Rimm suggest that warm-up exercises can help pupils stretch their muscles and require 'little or no thinking' (2004, p. 217). These exercises focus on 'the specific tools an actor uses to create a character ... voice, body, character or imagination and group work' (Johnson, 1998, p. 5). Activities that focus on the actor's voice help pupils learn that speaking loudly, slowly and in varied pitches is key for characterisation (Johnson, 1998, p. 5). To do this, pupils can take on certain qualities (mysterious, angry, scared) to repeat fixed lines (Johnson, 1998, p. 3).

The second element, body, can be addressed through activities that help pupils 'learn how to use their whole body ... to create a character' (Johnson, 1998, p. 6). With these exercises, pupils can walk like different animals, lift heavy/gooey/wiggly objects, use only their faces to show expression (Johnson, 1998, p. 4) or create a 'people machine' (Davis and Rimm, 2004, p. 218).

Third, pupils can participate in exercises that help them make their character believable (Johnson, 1998, p. 6). By acting as a princess who hates dirt but gets mud on her clothes or concurrently playing a wicked wolf and dumb pig, pupils consider unique character traits and how to manage them (Johnson, 1998, p. 5). Davis and Rimm (2004) also offer character exercises, such as animal pantomimes or creating their own environment (p. 219). The final element of group work can be woven into any exercise once pupils are comfortable with creative drama; in fact, 'social or interpersonal skills can be taught in order to make this ... successful' (Johnson, 1998, p. 6).

Playmaking, which is the second type of creative dramatics, 'involves acting out stories and scenes without a script' by giving pupils a simple scene, explaining the characters and allowing pupils to improvise (Davis and Rimm, 2004, p. 219). Through this type of activity, meaningful content can be integrated by having pupils personify a historical figure, embody a scientific concept or contemporise a scene from a novel. Recognising the benefits of creative dramatics is paramount when developing creativity in the classroom. On a basic level, children rely on their emotions to understand the world, thus they use their imagination 'to explore ... their world' (Johnson, 1998, p. 3). Creative dramatics, as an exploratory experience, allows pupils to engage in a process of expressing themselves and seeing their peers express themselves, through which they observe new types of expression and gain comfort with being expressive. Johnson (1998) states that creative dramatics encourages pupils to become 'emotionally involved in lessons' (p. 3), thus creating a meaningful learning experience during which pupils interact with content more deeply. Additionally, this approach leads pupils toward self-direction since, through creative drama, they can become empowered to make and own their decisions (Johnson, 1998, p. 4). Finally, and perhaps most importantly, creative dramatics functions as an equaliser. Through these activities, pupils of different backgrounds can work together, learn from each other and express themselves safely. The entire experience can make pupils aware of the concept of otherness and can allow them to appreciate the pupils and culture that may be different from them. For school teachers, the goal of creativity and awareness are worthy reasons to consider using creative dramatics.

Overcoming barriers to creativity

Even after teachers decide to include and make space for creativity in their classrooms, some pupils may have barriers that preclude them from participating. Evans (1993) delineates three categories of pupil barriers: perceptual, cultural and emotional. One cornerstone of creative thinking is the ability to approach a subject from multiple viewpoints. Therefore, perceptual barriers can include an inability to see an issue from different viewpoints, such as a pupil having 'one right answer' thinking or difficulty identifying problems. Evans (1993) also suggests that cultural barriers can develop from patterns of 'our immediate social and psychological environment' (p. 103). If pupils are in an environment where family or peers devaluate education, a significant difficulty in practising creative thought can arise. Cross (1997) supports this idea in his discussion of gifted pupils and Maslow's (1943) hierarchy of needs, suggesting that pupils will seek a sense of social belonging before they pursue their need for skills related to self-actualisation, such as creativity. Along with perceptual and cultural barriers, pupils can also struggle with creativity due to emotional constraints. Evans (1993) suggests that these emotional barriers can have multiple manifestations, such as a lack of risk-taking, intolerance for ambiguity and a preference for judging ideas rather than creating them. An underlying force behind emotional barriers can be the fear of vulnerability or being wrong. Whether existing together or separately, perceptual, cultural and emotional barriers can threaten pupils' creative ability.

In addition to the barriers pupils bring with them into a classroom, teachers can sometimes add barriers to the use of creativity in classrooms. The classroom environment established by a teacher can have a huge impact on pupils' abilities and motivation to think and act creatively. In her article on creative teaching, Rinkevich (2011) concludes that 'classroom creativity is often actually discouraged' (p. 220). She suggests that teachers can discourage creative behaviours that do not match classroom norms. Rinkevich (2011) argues that one of the main reasons creativity is missing in some classrooms is that some teachers devalue creative behaviours by treating them as non-conforming. Another teacher barrier to a creative classroom is the pressure resulting from standard-based assessments and large class sizes (Rinkevich, 2011). Already stressed by these constraints, one can see how teachers view creativity as a burden and thus, shy away from it. In order to value creativity as a benefit instead of a burden, teachers need proper training. Therefore, another major impediment to teacher creativity, according to Rinkevich, is the lack of training in developing skills and setting up the right environment (2011). It is through professional development that teachers can attempt to dismantle their own barriers to creativity as well as those within their pupils.

We must understand that maximising pupils' creative potential is a long-term effort, spanning from the first days in school until graduation. All pupils, regardless of race, socio-economic status or language can develop as creative thinkers. As pupils move to junior and secondary school, they need a supportive environment to express their creativity freely. By adopting creative dramatics, teachers provide that environment and encourage pupils to think creatively in a format that is engaging to them. Accomplishing that goal requires training, but teachers can start with simple steps such as encouraging different viewpoints or encouraging pupils to take risks. By following these strategies, teachers can begin to foster creativity within their pupils throughout their educational careers.

Table 5.4 Barriers to creativity

Barriers to creativity	Author(s)
Premature intrusion in pupils' thinking processes	Shallcross (1981)
Evaluation of products, competition, a lack of method and material choices, when outcome rewards are previously decided, when undue time pressures are enforced and when intense supervision is applied	Amabile (1988)
Lack of teacher training	Hansen and Feldhusen (1994); Rinkevich (2011)
Pressure resulting from standards-based assessments, large class sizes, and some teachers devaluing creative behaviours by treating them as non-conforming	Rinkevich (2011)

Differentiation

> ✎ **Activity: Differentiation and creativity**
> How might differentiation in the classroom support creativity?

Differentiated instruction supports creativity in the classroom since it consists of providing opportunities for pupils to comprehend information, find logic in ideas and show what they have learned (Tomlinson, 1999). Ward (1961) coined the term 'differential education' for gifted pupils. He created a standard to pilot curriculum planning to challenge pupils of various talents. The terms 'differentiated education' and 'differentiated curriculum' became popular as educators embraced these educational opportunities for accelerated pupils. Differentiation allows educators to fill in educational gaps and enrich students who have mastered the curriculum by creating differentiated plans.

Heacox (2002, p. 5) states that 'differentiating instruction means changing the pace, level, kind of instruction you provide in response to individual learners' needs, styles, or interests'. Differentiation can be described as complex, varied, flexible, relevant and rigorous. To further achievement, teachers should recognise pupil differences and set appropriate learning goals. Differentiation should focus on essential learning and align with pupil choice and demonstration of what was learned. Activities should engage pupils with the depth and breadth of the curriculum (Heacox, 2002).

Teachers who employ differentiation strategies do so with the principle that pupils learn within a variety of diverse approaches. For example, Tomlinson and Allan (2000) wrote that differentiation is a philosophy established on the following set of beliefs:

- Pupils who are the same age differ in their readiness to learn, their interests, their styles of learning, their experiences and their life circumstances.
- The differences in pupils are significant enough to make a major impact on what pupils need to learn, the pace at which they need to learn it and the support they need from teachers and others to learn it well.
- Pupils will learn best when supportive adults push them slightly beyond where they can work without assistance.
- Pupils will learn best when they can make a connection between the curriculum and their interests and life experiences.
- Pupils will learn best when learning opportunities are natural.
- Pupils are more effective learners when classrooms and schools create a sense of community in which pupils feel significant and respected.
- The central job of schools is to maximise the capacity of each pupil.

Tomlinson and Allan (2000) further characterise differentiation 'as a teacher's reacting responsively to a learner's needs' and that the 'goal of [a] differentiated classroom is maximum student growth and individual success' (p. 4). This characterisation infers ownership to differentiation to the field of education since all learners require growth and individual success. Additionally, Tomlinson

(1995) suggests that teachers apply differentiation through consideration of pupil characteristics such as readiness (i.e. level of difficulty), interest and learning profile (i.e. intelligence, talent or learning style). This consideration further reinforces the applicability of differentiation to the broader education environment.

Successful classroom teachers do not differentiate for pupils every moment of every day in the classroom. Non-differentiated, whole-class lessons should still occur. Differentiation gives opportunities for all pupils to perform at their individual level as well as develop their own strengths. In *The Differentiated Classroom*, Tomlinson (1999) uses a metaphor to liken teaching to an equilateral triangle. The pupils and the content are the bottom angles of the triangle while the teacher assumes the effective leadership position at the top. The teacher should learn from pupil experience in order to create effective follow-up lessons. Tomlinson believes 'if any side goes unattended and gets out of balance with the others, the artfulness is lost' (p. 27).

Additionally, Kaplan (1979) developed a framework for designing or developing curricular options. The principles included:

- allow for in-depth learning of a self-selected topic within an area of study;
- develop productive, complex, abstract and/or higher level thinking skills;
- encourage the development of products that challenge existing ideas and produce 'new' ideas.

Later, Kaplan (1986) defines content, process, product and affect as categorical approaches to differentiation. The content section consists of what is actually taught. The process is how it was taught, and the product is the substantial end resulting from pupil appeal and abilities. As a result, Kaplan suggests that these learning experiences are differentiated since they are a match among pupil needs, abilities, interests and educational purposes. However, Kaplan states that the 'differentiation of curriculum and individualization of the curriculum are not similar. Once the curriculum is differentiated, it needs to be individualized for students' (p. 192).

Teachers and differentiation

Renzulli's (1997) five dimensions of differentiation consist of defining individual dimension goals for a truly differentiated approach. His differentiation goals relate to the following five dimensions:

- content – put more depth into the curriculum through organising the curriculum concepts and structure of knowledge;
- process – use many instructional techniques and materials to enhance and motivate learning styles of pupils;
- product – improve cognitive development and the pupils' ability to express themselves;
- classroom – enhance the comfort by changing grouping formats and physical area of environment;
- teacher – use artistic modification to share personal knowledge of topics related to the curriculum as well as personal interests, collections, hobbies and enthusiasm about issues surrounding content area.

Characteristics of differentiation

Differentiated classrooms, according to Tomlinson and Allan (2000), should have all of the following characteristics: flexible grouping, pupil responsibility for their own learning, displayed assignments and scored rubrics, group work and fewer teacher lectures, a variety of responsibilities are encouraged and accepted from pupils, and frequent teacher/pupil conference times. Content-based assignments should vary per pupil readiness and pre-determined goals. Easily accessible records of pupil progress show this goal-setting, achievement of goals and the scoring of a variety of assignments per topic (Tomlinson and Allan, 2000).

The differentiating teacher must understand the subject matter, appreciate pupil differences and have the ability to build upon these differences. Teachers must believe that assessment and instruction are two sides of the differentiating coin, and that they are responsible for the adjustment of content, process and product in response to pupil readiness. Finally, a major goal of the differentiated classroom is maximum growth and measurable individual success (Heacox, 2002; Tomlinson, 1999). Therefore, creativity in the classroom is supported by the many elements and goals of differentiated instruction, and what the researchers in this section believe differentiation could add to our schools.

Conclusion

'Fostering creativity is an integral part of education and should be a guiding principle for teaching all children ... The desire to foster creativity is at the heart of a philosophy or principle that should underlie all teaching and learning in all subject areas and at all times' (Cropley and Cropley, 2001, p. 151). This chapter reviewed the relevance and importance of encouraging creativity. Intentionally employing creative thinking and problem-solving strategies can allow teachers to encourage creativity on a daily, informal basis. Seminal conceptual papers and empirical studies involving the fostering of creativity were examined to shed more light on our understanding of creative concepts. However, truly integrating creativity in the classroom requires more formalised, in-depth approaches such as differentiated instructional strategies.

Teachers who wish to foster creativity in their classrooms must consider several common themes uncovered in this chapter, including characteristics of creative pupils, the classroom environment and barriers to creativity (Amabile, 1983; Csikszentmihalyi, 1996; Edwards and Springate, 1995; Shallcross, 1981). In our current climate of high-stakes standardised testing, teachers must find ways to include creativity as a part of their daily classroom practice.

Additionally, teachers must be cognisant that not all pupils will have the same reaction to creative thinking in the classroom. Creative behaviour contains a degree of risk, and some creative ideas turn out to be product disappointments. Unsuccessful ventures in creativity can affect pupil self-esteem. Those pupils who are averse to taking risks are not likely to see the benefits of teachers fostering creativity and may not be as optimistic towards it (Fernald, 1988; Amabile and Sensabaugh, 1992; Landrum, 1993). In addition to other benefits previously discussed, differentiated instructional strategies could help teachers manage the divergent reactions of their pupil populations to creativity in the classroom.

Case study 5.1: A classroom process for the creative act

For a better understanding of creativity, or to teach the concept of creativity to others, follow the directions below:

What's needed? Space, paper, pencils or pens
Directions (Adjust for special learners as needed):

Gain the attention of a group of pupils or individuals. Indicate two imaginary points on the floor, Point A and Point B, which can be 10 feet (3 metres) apart. Ask the participants to individually list ten ways in which a person can move from Point A and Point B. Some examples include walk, run, skip, hop on one foot, roll and so forth. After four or five minutes have passed, ask some participants to share one idea from their list. If possible, list ten ideas from different pupils on a black or white board, on an overhead projector, or on a computer screen that everyone can see. Next, ask pupils to repeat the activity by individually listing ten additional ways (not already mentioned) in which a person can move from Point A and Point B. After four or five minutes, ask individual pupils to again reveal, one at a time, what they've written. Add these ten ways as 11–20 next to the first list. When finished, ask the pupils to repeat the exercise for a third time. Ask for individuals to state the ways and you can add them as 21–30. Finally, when finished, ask the pupils to repeat the exercise for a fourth and final time. Ask for individuals to state the ways and you should list the fourth set of ten ways as 31–40. In the following discussion, you should ask the question, 'What is the difference between your first ten answers as compared to your fourth list?' Hopefully they might suggest that the obvious, and potentially easiest, answers came first. Then you can ask 'What is the difference in time you spent to find your first ten answers as compared to your fourth list of answers?' Hopefully they might suggest that once the easy solutions were out of the way, they began to spend more time deliberating on what type of 'way' would be appropriate to solve the problem. Also, you could ask a question that indicates how, after the second or third list, they may have begun to ask questions to define the parameters of the 'way' in which a person was allowed to move.

The process they went through represents one process of creativity. This brainstorming process is supported by Wallas's (1926) supposition that creativity consists of similar steps: preparation, incubation, illumination and elaboration.

The end result of the activity can be that participants who may be new to creativity may see that they were able to imagine or 'create' undiscovered or creative ways to move a person from Point A to Point B that they hadn't previously thought of. Hopefully they will understand that creativity can come from understanding the parameters of an activity and using what they know to solve the problem. Additionally, you may find that highly creative pupils may have asked if Points A and B can be placed in different rooms or different schools, with or without gravity, within different atmospheres or maybe even in parallel universes. The point of the activity to me is that creativity occurs once the easy answers have been dismissed and one completely understands the issue or problem. As with all lessons, teachers need to be prepared for anything during this exercise.

Suggested reading

Stanish, B. (1999) *I believe in unicorns: Classroom experiences for activating creative thinking*. Waco, TX: Prufrock Press.

This book offers activities that strengthen skills essential for creative thought—fluency, flexibility, originality and elaboration. It is for teachers interested in encouraging imaginative thinking with activities like getting an elephant down from a tree or removing a porcupine from a lunchbox. The book will challenge students' creativity with activities, most involving writing, designed for primary pupils. Open-ended discussions and brainstorming should be incorporated into these activities.

Wilson, A. (2014) *Creativity in primary education* (Achieving QTS Series). London: Sage.

This book, in its third edition, explores creativity in all areas of the curriculum with case studies and reflective tasks that get the reader thinking about how a teacher could implement different strategies in the classroom. The book retains key material and includes two new chapters – the theme of the creative curriculum and supporting trainees to see how effective curriculum design can enhance creative teaching.

Desailly, J. (2015) *Creativity in the primary classroom*. Los Angeles, CA: Sage.

This second edition offers a practical overview of creative teaching and learning for novice and veteran primary teachers. The book includes content on the National Curriculum in England, such as creativity in multiple subjects as well as creative assessment.

References

Amabile, T.M. (1983) *The social psychology of creativity*. New York: Springer-Verlag.
Amabile, T.M. (1988) A model of creativity and innovation in organizations. In B.M. Staw and L.L. Cummings (Eds), *Research in organizational behavior* (Vol. 10, pp. 123–167). JAI Press: Greenwich, CT.
Amabile, T.M., and Sensabaugh, S.J. (1992) High creativity versus low creativity: What makes the difference? In S.S. Gryskiewicz and D.A. Hills (Eds.), *Readings in innovation*. Greensboro, NC: Center for Creative Leadership.
Angleoska-Galevska, N. (1996) *Children's creativity in the pre-school institutions in Macedonia*. Urbana, IL: ERIC Clearinghouse on Elementary and Early Childhood Education (ED403054).
Craft, A. (2000) *Creativity across the primary curriculum*. London: Routledge.
Cropley, A.J. (1997) Fostering creativity in the classroom: General principles. In M.A. Runco, (Ed.), *The creativity research book. Volume 1*. Cresskill, NJ: Hampton Press.
Cropley, D.H. and Cropley, A.J. (2000) Fostering creativity in engineering students. *High Abilities Studies*, 11(2), 207–218.
Cross, T.L. (1997) Psychological and social aspects of educating gifted students. *Peabody Journal of Education*, 72(3/4), 180–200. Retrieved June 21, 2009, from: www.jstor.org/stable/1493044
Csikszentmihalyi, M. (1988) Society, culture, and person: A systems view of creativity. In R.J. Sternberg (Ed.), *The nature of creativity* (pp. 325–339). New York: Cambridge University Press.
Csikszentmihalyi, M. (1991) *Flow: The psychology of optimal experience*. New York: Harper Collins.
Csikszentmihalyi, M. (1996) *Creativity*. New York: Harper Collins.
Dadds, M. (1995, Autumn/Winter) Continuing professional development: Nurturing the expert within. *Cambridge Institute of Education Newsletter*, 30, 23–27.
Davis, G.A. and Rimm, S.B. (2004) *Education of the gifted and talented* (5th edn, pp. 216–220). Boston: Pearson.
de Bono, E. (1985) *Six thinking hats: An essential approach to business management*. New York: Little, Brown, & Company
de Souza Fleith, D. (2000) Teacher and student perceptions of creativity in the classroom environment. *Roeper Review*, 22(3), 148–153.
Edwards, C.P. and Springate, K.W. (1995) *Encouraging creativity in early childhood classrooms*. Washington, DC: Office of Educational Research and Improvement.
Evans, J. R. (Nov.–Dec. 1993) Creativity in MS/OR: Barriers to creativity. *Interfaces*, 23(6), 101–106. Available at: www.jstor.org/stable/25061826
Fernald, L.W. (1988) The underlying relationship between creativity, innovation and entrepreneurship. *Journal of Creative Behavior*, 22, 196–202.

Gardner, H. (1983) *Frames of mind: The theory of multiple intelligences*. New York: Basic Books.
Gardner, H. (1997) *Extraordinary minds*. New York: Basic Books.
Glosbe – the multilingual online dictionary (2016). Available at: https://glosbe.com/la/en/creare
Greenberg, E. (1992) Creativity, autonomy, and evaluation of creative work: Artistic workers in organizations. *Journal of Creative Behavior*, 26(2), 75–80.
Guilford, J.P. (1950) Creativity. *American Psychologist*, 5, 444–454.
Halliwell, S. (1993) Teacher creativity and teacher education. In D. Bridges and T. Carey (Eds.), *Developing teachers professionally*. London: Routledge.
Hansen, J.B. and Feldhusen, J.F. (1994) Comparison of trained and untrained teachers of gifted students. *Gifted Child Quarterly*, 38(3), 115–123.
Heacox, D. (2002) *Differentiating instruction in the regular classroom: How to reach and teach all learners, grades 3–12*. Minneapolis, MN: Free Spirit.
Isaksen, S.G. (1995) *Some recent developments on assessing the climate for creativity and change*. Paper presented at the International Conference on Climate for Creativity and Change, Buffalo, NY.
Isaksen, S.G. and Treffinger, D.J. (1985) *Creative problem-solving: The basic course*. Buffalo, NY: Bearly.
Johnson, A.P. (1998) How to use creative dramatics in the classroom. *Childhood Education*, 75(1), 2–6.
Kaplan, S.N. (1979) *In-service training manual: Activities for developing curriculum for the gifted and talented*. Los Angeles: National/State Leadership Training Institute on the Gifted and Talented.
Kaplan, S. (1986) The grid: A model to construct differentiated curriculum for the gifted. In J.S. Renzulli (Ed.), *Systems and models for developing programs for the gifted and talented* (pp. 180–193). Mansfield Center, CT: Creative Learning Press.
Katz, L., Edwards, C., Gandini, L. and Forman, G., (Eds.) (1993) *The hundred languages of children: The Reggio Emilia approach to early childhood education*. Norwood, NJ: Ablex Publishing Corporation.
Kolczynski, R.G. and Cepelka, A. (1977) Creative dramatics: Process or product? *Language Arts*, 54(3), 283–286.
Landrum, G.N. (1993) *Profile of genius: Thirteen creative men who changed the world*. New York: Prometheus Books.
Lewis, J.F. (1982 May/June) Bulldozers or chairs? Gifted students describe their ideal teacher. *Gifted Child Today*, 16–19.
Maslow, A. H. (1943) A theory of human motivation. *Psychological Review*, 50(4), 370–396.
Osborn, A.F. (1963) *Applied imagination* (3rd edn). New York: Scribner's.
Parnes, S.J. (1967) *Creative behavior guidebook*. New York: Scribner's.
Parnes, S.J. (1981) *Magic of your mind*. Buffalo, NY: Bearly.
Perkins, D. (1988) The possibility of invention. In R. Sternberg (Ed.), *The nature of creativity*. New York: Cambridge University Press.
Perkins, D. (1999) The many faces of constructivism. *Educational Leadership*, 57(3), 6–11.
Perry-Smith, J.E. and Shalley, C.E. (2003) The social side of creativity: A static and dynamic social network perspective. *Academy of Management Review*, 28, 89–106.
Piirto, J. (1998) *Understanding those who create* (2nd edn). Tempe, AZ: Gifted Psychology Press.
Raina, M.K. and Vats, A. (1979) Creativity, teaching style, and pupil control. *Gifted Child Quarterly*, 23(4) 807–811.
Renzulli, J.S. (1997, July) *Five dimensions of differentiation*. Keynote presentation at the 20th Annual Conference, Storrs, CT.
Renzulli, J. and Callahan, C. (1973) Developing creativity training activities. *Gifted Child Quarterly*, 19(1), 38–45.
Rinkevich, J.L. (2011) Creative teaching: Why it matters and where to begin. *The Clearing House: A Journal for Educational Strategies, Issues and Ideas*, 84(5), 219–223.
Robinson, K. (2006) *Do schools kill creativity?* Available at: www.ted.com/talks/ken_robinson_says_schools_kill_creativity?language=en
Shallcross, D.J. (1981) *Teaching creative behaviour: How to teach creativity in children of all ages*. Englewood Cliffs, NJ: Prentice-Hall.
Sternberg, R.J. (2000) Creativity is a decision. In A.L. Costa (Ed.), *Teaching for intelligence II* (pp. 85–106). Arlington Heights, IL: Skylight Training and Publishing.
Sternberg, R.J. (2003) Creative thinking in the classroom, *Scandinavian Journal of Educational Research*, 47(3), 325–338.
Sternberg, R.J. and Lubart, T. (1991) An investment theory of creativity and its development. *Human Development*, 34, 1–31.

Sternberg, R.J. and Lubart, T. (1995) *Defying the crowd: Cultivating creativity in a culture of conformity.* New York: The Free Press.

Terry, A.W. (2000) *A case study of community action service learning on young, gifted adolescents and their community.* Dissertation Abstracts International, 61(8), 3058A. (UMI No. AAT 9984217)

Tomlinson, C.A. (1995) Deciding to differentiate instruction in middle school: One school's journey. *Gifted Child Quarterly*, 39, 77–87.

Tomlinson, C.A. (1999) *The differentiated classroom: Responding to the needs of all learners.* Alexandria, VA: Association for Supervision and Curriculum Development.

Tomlinson, C.A. and Allan, S.D. (2000) *Leadership for differentiating schools and classrooms.* Alexandria, VA: Association for Supervision and Curriculum Development

Torrance, E.P. (1962) *Guiding creative talent.* Englewood Cliffs, NJ: Prentice-Hall.

Torrance, E.P. (1970) *Encouraging creativity in the classroom.* Dubuque, IA: William C. Brown.

Treffinger, D.J., Isaksen, S.G. and Dorval, K.B. (1997) *Creative problem-solving: An introduction* (3rd edn). Sarasota, FL: Center for Creative Learning.

VanTassel-Baska, J. (1998) *Excellence in educating gifted and talented learners.* Denver: Love Publishing.

VanTassel-Baska, J., Feng A.X. and Evans, B.L. (2007) Patterns of identification and performance among gifted students identified through performance tasks. *Gifted Child Quarterly*, 51(3), 218–231.

Wallas, G. (1926) *The art of thought.* New York, NY: Harcourt Brace.

Ward, V.S. (1961) *Finding the gifted: An axiomatic approach.* Columbus, OH: Merrill.

Woods, P. and Jeffrey, B. (1996) *Teachable moments: The art of teaching in primary schools.* Buckingham, UK: Open University Press.

6 The NEET debate

Jade Murden

This chapter explores:

- when a young person is considered to be NEET;
- the difficulties with labelling a group of people;
- the NEET data and the challenges they present;
- the 'prevention versus re-engagement' debate;
- the 'supply versus demand' initiatives.

Young people have to navigate many social changes including globalisation, an aging population, the economic crisis and the changing educational landscape. Students will be expected to undertake new qualifications using a new 1–9 grading scale. The qualifications have been described as 'more rigorous' and 'challenging' than ever before (Gove 2014; DfE 2015; Morgan 2015). Students will be taught in new educational establishments, such as academies and free schools, and will also be expected to stay in education or training until they are 18 years old. Politician Nick Gibb (2014) stated that the new National Curriculum for England put in place from 2015 will help a generation win the global race, emphasising the responsibility a nation places on its young people.

This is not a recent or solely English phenomenon; EuroFound (2012) declared that the future of Europe is in the hands of 94 million young people aged 15 to 29. When these figures are viewed on a global scale the importance of young people and the choices they make is clear to see. It may not be surprising therefore that a significant amount of research is undertaken on young people regarding their transition from education into employment (Corney 2015; Bajorek *et al.* 2016; Egdell and McQuaid 2016), as this could be considered key to a country's financial stability and industry. One group which is well documented and often labelled as problematic is people aged between 16 and 24 referred to as NEET (Not in Employment, Education or Training) (Simmons *et al.* 2014).

History of NEET

In post-war Britain, the transition from education to employment was fairly straightforward. It was not uncommon for people to leave school at the age of 14 when work was readily available at local mines, mills, shops and factories. A small number of white middle-class males went onto further education, training schemes or university, but for the majority of the young workforce such opportunities were rare (Simmons et al. 2014).

Events during the 1970s radically changed employment opportunities for young people. It is a decade remembered for widespread industrial action resulting in three-day weeks and the closure of many British industries, which are reported to have lost more than six million jobs since the 1960s (Fothergill and Gore 2013). It is also remembered for the collapse of the Labour government and the so-called 'Winter of Discontent' culminating in the election of a Conservative government led by Margaret Thatcher, Britain's first female prime minister (Young and Lambert 2014). This was to signal a new era in politics that moved away from social democracy towards a neoliberal standpoint. Neoliberalism places value on the importance of individualism, entrepreneurialism, competition, consumer choice and accountability.

The shift in the job market is evident in the recent 'Budget Speech' delivered by Osborne (2016) who stated that almost 90 per cent of new jobs are in skilled occupations. Young people who leave school with few or no formal qualifications are finding the transition from education to employment rather different from the young people of the past, who may have previously gone to work in areas which required little or no formal qualifications. This has a significant impact on youth unemployment.

> **Activity: Why do young people become NEET?**
>
> The UK education system can be described as a meritocracy, suggesting that if people work hard and put in the effort then it will yield results. In education this means gaining qualifications and subsequently moving into employment or training. Therefore, some political parties and organisations perpetuate the argument that it is due to a lack of personal aspiration, rather than wider societal influences that young people become NEET.
>
> Which position do you take? Is it this simple or more complex? Who should take responsibility? Can you build a case for either side of this argument?

The concept of NEET is not new. To understand the correlation between youth unemployment and NEET it is helpful to reflect on the origins of the NEET category. The acronym NEET encourages debate as it is considered a deficit model. It implies that there is a problem with the individual due to the category being defined by a set of negative criteria. However, it may be considered slightly less controversial to the previously used phrase 'Status Zero', which was used before the term NEET was coined in the mid-1990s (Rees et al. 1996).

> **Activity: Status Zero**
>
> What images does 'Status Zero' conjure up? Why do you think the category changed to NEET?

Status Zero emerged following changes to unemployment benefits which were implemented in 1988. The changes essentially removed young people under 18 from being eligible for employment benefits.

Consequently people under 18 were no longer recorded as being unemployed and so were not represented in the unemployment statistics (Maguire and Thomson 2007, cited in Maguire 2015).

Unemployed or economically inactive = NEET

Despite the distinction between youth unemployment data and NEET figures, they are often used interchangeably to quantify youth disengagement and inactivity within the youth labour market. The UK government states that someone who is NEET is always either unemployed or economically inactive (Office for National Statistics (ONS) 2016). When considering these two positions of the NEET cohort, there are distinct differences recognised by the state. A young person is identified as unemployed if they have been actively seeking work in the past four weeks and they are able to start work within two weeks (ONS 2016). The key phrase here is 'actively looking for work' which means the young person must be applying for jobs and demonstrating that they are committed to finding work by attending interviews with the intention of starting a position as soon as possible. However it also includes young people who are waiting to take up a position, for example a graduate who has just finished their degree in June and is waiting to start work in a school in September, would be referred to as NEET.

This is in contrast to economically inactive, which means that the young person has been unemployed for more than four weeks and will be unable to start work within the next two weeks (ONS 2016) and therefore they are not contributing to the economy. This category contains young people who are not actively seeking work but also includes young people who are unable to look for work due to being temporarily sick, long-term sick, or young people with caring duties such as looking after a child or parent. The NEET figures are also separated into two further bands of people described as those who 'want a job' and those who 'do not want a job' (ONS 2016). The process of categorising people to a rudimentary level and using polarised grouping systems is not without its problems. As Thomson (2011) argues, the UK NEET policy is a dichotomy between privileged forms of social participation, such as paid work or participation in formal education, and occupations deemed of lesser value such as unpaid domestic labour or students on a gap year (Levitas 2005 cited in Thomson 2011). Consequently the term NEET is complex and multifaceted and applies to a wide range of young people with differing needs and experiences, which is why it is often referred to as a heterogeneous group.

> **Activity: Implications for classifying NEETs**
>
> 1. What are the possible implications for grouping a 16-year-old and a 24-year-old in the same category? Do you think a 16-year-old registered as NEET would have the same experiences as a 24-year-old?
> 2. More females are classed as 'inactive' rather than 'unemployed', and more males are classed as 'unemployed' rather than 'inactive'. What could be the reasons for this?
> 3. Do you agree that unpaid domestic labour should be classed as economically inactive under the NEET system?

NEET figures and Europe

If NEET data is considered from a European perspective then the latest figures state that approximately 4.3 million young people were unemployed (Eurostats 2016a), which equates to just over 20 per cent of young people in Europe in total. To put that into tangible data, youth unemployment within Europe is significant with the youth unemployment rate standing at just over half in Greece (51.1 per cent) and Spain (51.7 per cent); however, in contrast are Norway at 7.8 per cent and Germany at 7.4 per cent. The United Kingdom currently reports 16.1 per cent of young people unemployed. There could be a tendency to equate high levels of youth unemployment to recent political unrest in both Greece and Spain; however, when reviewing the data for youth unemployment, the figures have not significantly changed in the last decade nor are any significant changes predicted in the near future (Eurostats 2016b), demonstrating that there are multiple and complex reasons for this trend.

> **Activity: NEET figures in Europe**
>
> 1. Why do you think there are significant differences in the number of people registered as NEET across Europe?
> 2. Do you think comparing the number of people registered as NEET countries in league tables is useful?

NEET figures and the UK

According to the latest government figures, the number of young people who are NEET in the UK has declined over the past year by just over 78,000 (Mirza-Davies 2016). This leaves the new reported figure in the second quarter of 2016 to be 843,000 young people on the NEET register (Mirza-Davies 2016). This is an apparent positive trend, as according to Hancock (2014) the previous year's figures were even more successful. Hancock (2014) claims that in 2014 the number of young people on the NEET register was at the lowest it had been since 2008 and that the number of 16–18-year-olds on the NEET register was at the lowest since records began. However, when considering this from a global perspective, despite the recent decline, the UK NEET figures for 15–19 year olds is 8.7 per cent, which is still above the OECD average of 6.3 per cent (Mirza-Davies 2016).

As with many statistics which claim to put a number on a group of people, there are questions regarding the accuracy of the data and the methods used for collecting it. The ONS acknowledges that the NEET figures are estimated, but stress that they have calculated for a level of uncertainty which makes their data viable (ONS 2016). ONS uses data gained from household surveys; consequently, this data cannot include young people who are not in households, for example those who are homeless, in traveller families or who live in an institution such as a prison or residential care. As young people who are registered as NEET are at risk of some of these factors (Miller *et al.* 2015; Buchanan and Tuckerman 2016; YMCA 2015) then not including these young people in the figures could distort the data.

Characteristics of NEETs

Research into the characteristics of people on the NEET register found that people already on, or at risk of being on, the NEET register can be classed as some of the most vulnerable people in society and are at high risk of social exclusion (Miller *et al.* 2015; Buchanan and Tuckerman 2016; YMCA 2015). Mirza-Davies (2016) outlines specific characteristics of people who are most likely to be added to the NEET register as:

- those eligible for free school meals (FSM);
- those who have been excluded or suspended from school;
- those with their own child before they are 19;
- those who do not achieve the educational threshold, which is set at five A*–C GCSE grades;
- those who have a disability.

A gender imbalance is also notable with more females being on the NEET register.

When reviewing the NEET data regarding these characteristics, certain trends emerge. People who are eligible for free school meals (FSM) are also less likely than their peers to achieve the educational threshold. Only 33.1 per cent of those eligible for FSM achieved the educational threshold compared to 60.9 per cent not on FSM (DfE 2016). In England FSM is often used as an indicator of low socioeconomic status. The socioeconomic attainment gap was greatest for white boys on FSM with just 28.3 per cent (EHRC 2015) achieving the educational threshold. Using this data, if the characteristic indicators are correct, around 70 per cent of white boys on FSM are at risk of joining the NEET register.

In the case of young people who have a disability or learning difficulty (SEND), an attainment gap is also visible with just 20 per cent achieving the educational threshold; though this is an improvement on previous years (DfE 2016). However, when this achievement figure is coupled with the fact that a young person with SEND continues to be much more likely to be excluded from school (EHRC 2015) their chances of becoming NEET also rise. In addition, teen mothers are less likely to finish their education than their peers, more likely to experience poor mental health and more likely to bring up their children in poverty (Hobcraft and Kiernan 1999 and Tinsley 2014, both cited in Russell 2016).

These trends suggest that the specific characteristics put forward by Mirza-Davies (2016) for people on the NEET register cannot be so easily defined as most people fall into more than one category. The disadvantages of facing multiple barriers to learning, and consequently opportunity, are well documented; Ball (2013) claims that the relationship between opportunity, achievement and social class remains stubbornly entrenched in the UK, which is mirrored in these latest figures.

> **Activity: Characteristics of NEETs**
>
> A key strand running through these characteristics is low socioeconomic status. Does this move the debate to be an education and social class issue?

NEET – a 'negative umbrella' term?

The NEET concept has been described as a 'negative umbrella' under which to place young people (Reiter and Schlimbach 2015) and one which is neither a helpful concept nor correct. Yates and Payne (2006, cited in Reiter and Schlimbach 2015) pursue the idea that the status of NEET is grossly over-simplified, which perpetuates the NEET stereotype through the representation of NEET as a group of young people on the cusp of social exclusion and with 'hard to reach/teach' labels. Research suggests that this does not accurately represent young people on the NEET register as almost two-thirds of this group do not face complex barriers to engaging in education, training or employment (Hutchinson and Kettlewell 2015). Like most stereotyping, this has a negative impact not only for those on the NEET register but also for people who work on NEET schemes and the politicians who serve them. This is evident in the images projected by the former prime minister. During a speech on NEET reforms he stated, 'That well-worn path – from the school gate, down to the jobcentre, and on to a life on benefits – has got to be rubbed away' (Cameron 2015, cited in BBC 2015). This view gives no consideration to the reasons why young people are on the NEET register and has undertones of young people and unemployment being a 'life-choice'. This underpins the concept of NEET as a deficit model, thereby suggesting that it is a problem created by the young people themselves (Macdonald, 2011 cited in Hutchinson and Kettlewell 2015) rather than acknowledging wider societal influences. Hutchinson and Kettlewell (2015) argue that it is because of these negative stereotypes that research has focused on re-engaging young people with complex barriers and effectively ignored two-thirds of the NEET cohort.

The NEET initiatives debate

Being on, or at risk of being on, the NEET register can have a lasting effect on young people. It can impact on the young person's mental and physical health and their ability to relate to peers, which can have a direct impact on their work opportunities (Veldman et al. 2015; Scarpetta et al. 2010 cited in De Luca et al. 2015). Young people who are registered as NEET are at a higher risk of a process referred to as 'churning'. This happens when a young person gets caught in a cycle of short-term employment and being on the NEET register. In addition to the health costs for the young person there is also the estimated 'lifetime' economic cost to the state. This is estimated at between £11.7 and £32.5 billion (Morse 2014) due to benefits which are claimed, services which are often used and lost revenue in taxes. Possibly due to these high costs and high stakes for young people, there are key debates surrounding the effectiveness of strategies and initiatives regarding people who are registered as NEET.

> **Activity: Responsibility for NEETs**
> 1. With whom should a NEET model place responsibility – with the individual or with the state?
> 2. Should NEET policy be decided by government or independent thinktanks?
> 3. What are the pros and cons of each?

Prevention versus re-engagement

Prevention implies that it is possible to predict who is likely to be registered as NEET and intervene before it happens using 'at-risk' categories, such as the ones proposed by the NEET characteristics, and putting strategies in place in schools. Re-engagement refers to the ability to manage or reduce the number of people on the NEET register through a range of re-engagement and transition initiatives, such as specific courses to increase the employability of a person or creating apprenticeships (Hutchinson et al. 2015).

The financial cost to the state, the emotional cost for young people registered as NEET and the involvement of the media (Monogan 2016; Harris 2015) encourages all political parties to state in their manifestos how they will address youth unemployment (Miliband 2015; Clegg 2015; Cameron 2015; Young Greens 2015). Historically, the election of a new government often involves dismantling previous services and the introduction of new services which reflect the current government's ideological stance on young people and unemployment in general. Consequently young people are exposed to a pendulum effect, swinging between political ideologies with no long-term stability.

> **Activity: Prevention or re-engagement**
>
> 1. Which approach would be the most effective: prevention or re-engagement?
> 2. Is it possible to predict someone's future?

Supply versus demand

In addition to prevention versus re-engagement there is a distinction between NEET policies; this is the 'supply versus demand' debate. Supply policies focus on the individual, increasing their qualifications, employability skills and attitude, but they have been criticised for projecting that being on the NEET register is due to an individual failing which could add to the pressure (Beck 2015). 'Demand' policies focus on trying to shape employer demand through changing their perceptions of young people or by offering financial incentives such as apprenticeships (Hutchinson et al. 2015). Successive governments have engaged with the supply and demand debate in different ways.

Government and NEET policy

Labour

Under the Labour government, education was perceived as a key mechanism to address social exclusion with NEET initiatives reflecting this (McDonald and Shildrick 2010, cited in Hutchinson et al. 2015). Labour commissioned the Wolf Report (2011) which recommended that the curriculum should value skills and work experience and should be relevant for the learner and linked to job opportunities. This suggests that a reduction of NEET figures can be achieved by engaging young people with a relevant curriculum, giving them choice and acknowledging that not everyone values an academic route, thereby giving status to vocational choices. The Wolf Report's (2011) recommendations address both prevention and re-engagement as they aim to prevent NEET through a relevant school curriculum but also re-engage with a strong vocational education for people over 16.

A course specifically designed and commissioned to meet the needs of young people at risk of becoming NEET was the Entry to Employment programme (E2E). E2E was an innovative programme funded by the Learning and Skills Council (LSC) for post-16 students not yet ready for mainstream college, employment or apprenticeships. E2E comprised three independent core strands: basic and key skills, vocational skills and personal and social development. It also advocated personalised learning to engage young people (Spielhofer et al. 2003). However, France (2016) argues that these types of courses do not really offer the skills that are required in high-paid workplaces and that they are in fact 'warehouses' due to there being limited alternatives for young people.

Labour also introduced a holistic approach to NEET with the introduction of learner-centred services. A flagship policy was the creation of Connexions, which was phased in from 2001. Connexions was aimed at teenagers and proposed to offer a range of services from high-quality careers advice to sexual health advice, in which the Labour government invested £450 million (Hutchinson et al. 2015). Connexions was considered to be successful by the Department for Education and Skills, which reported that it was on target to reduce the number of NEET in a short amount of time (Bourn 2004). However, it could be perceived to be quite ambitious to state the effectiveness of a programme during the relatively early stages and with a decline of just 8 per cent in NEET figures (Bourn 2004).

The service also tracked people registered as NEET (Beck 2015) using personal advisers. Their role was to support young people to engage in further education or employment. However, Connexions received criticism due to the tension between informality (as they were trying to appeal to young people) and accountability (as a public service). Some practitioners believed being accountable to central government and recording information and tracking young people created difficulties and erected barriers which hindered, rather than supported, their clients (Hoggarth and Smith 2004; Ofsted 2002).

Despite this concern, centralised tracking was a key strength of the service. Now tracking young people who are registered as NEET is the responsibility of more than one organisation, such as schools and Local Authorities. If the young person's whereabouts are not known then the organisations have the option of recording the status as 'unknown'. This has a direct impact on the final published NEET data as a calculation is made using the 'unknown' status which makes the assumption that only one in every eight 'unknown' status are actually NEET and the other seven are in work or further learning (Brooks 2014). This has a significant impact on the NEET figures (Maguire 2015). The method of assuming that almost all 'unknowns' are actually not NEET has resulted in criticism of current NEET data with claims that the UK 'has lost track of over 150,000 young people aged 16–18 as their working or education status is now reported as "unknown"' (Brooks 2014, p. 16).

The Labour government also tried offering financial incentives to students in post-16 education in the form of an Educational Maintenance Allowance (EMA). This was a means-tested grant of up to £30 a week for children from low-income households, resulting in approximately 650,000 young people in England claiming EMA (DfE 2011). According to the Institute for Fiscal Studies, Save the Children and Centre for British Teachers, EMA significantly raised the stay-on rates for post-16 learners, particularly low-attaining students, students from single parent households and certain ethnic minority groups (Fletcher 2009 cited in Smith 2012). A notable difference to this initiative was that the payment was made to the student's bank account rather than to the primary carer, as is the case for Child Benefit (Holford 2015). EMA was the student's responsibility to spend how they saw fit, rather than the government funding an institution or giving money to the student's family. However, this controversial decision opened the debate regarding students spending their EMA on 'non-learning' activities and therefore questioning if they actually 'needed' it for education.

Activity: Supply and demand policies

1. Do you think that the 'earn and learn' approach to study can be effective?
2. Do you think there are any drawbacks in paying students to study?
3. What do these strategies tell us about the government's view of young people who are NEET?
4. Are these supply or demand policies?

The Coalition government

The election of the Coalition government in 2010 saw changes to NEET services. With a change of government came new priorities, with the mantra of austerity and cuts directly impacting NEET policy. In 2011 the Coalition government announced plans to abolish EMA in England, claiming that the initiative cost £560 million a year with alleged administration costs of £36 million a year (DfE 2011). These costs, they argued, could not be justified due to the 'deeply worrying state of finances' and proposed that the money would be better spent targeting the 'most in need' through bursaries (DfE 2011). Despite opposition from some Labour MPs, the Coalition government won by a majority of 59 votes, with Michael Gove insisting that EMA was poorly targeted and that the government could not spend money that it did not have (BBC 2011). Interestingly, EMA was only stopped in England and continues in Northern Ireland and Wales. Scotland not only continues to have the EMA initiative but its government plans to expand its remit to include part-time students in 2016 (SOED 2015). Jeremy Corbyn (2015) also stated that if Labour are elected in 2020 then he will bring back EMA for young people in England, thus presenting a cyclic approach to NEET initiatives and reinforcing the debate that societal influences are intrinsically linked with opportunity for young people.

Connexions, Sure Start and Youth Service funding were also cut in line with government austerity policy. However, this received criticism from education unions with NASUWT referring to it as 'scandalous' (Keates 2014) and ATL accusing the government of dismantling valuable careers services for young people. Deputy Prime Minister Nick Clegg and Chris Grayling from DWP (2012) launched a new government scheme which focused on organisations working with young people to support them moving into work or training. Clegg pledged money to third-sector services and private services, offering them £126 million, which equates to approximately £2,200 for every young person 'helped' into learning or employment. The underlying philosophy for these changes was that 'payment by results is the best way to deliver the best possible support for young people' (Clegg and Grayling 2012). Similarly to the Labour Party, large amounts of money were invested but in a different way, offering incentives to organisations rather than the individual. Consequently the methods could be perceived as a more neoliberal approach to NEET programmes by encouraging competition in the education sector.

Raising of the participation age (RPA)

One policy which continued despite the change in government was the proposal to raise the participation age (RPA), as outlined in the 2008 Education and Skills Act under the Labour government. This proposed that by 2015 young people should be expected to stay in education or training until 18. Clearly this has the potential to significantly reduce the recorded 16–17-year-olds in the NEET figures through the power of legislation.

RPA is voluntary, however for parents in receipt of child benefit it is tied to their child staying in education after their 16th birthday and will stop if the child leaves education (HM Revenue and Customs 2015). Despite full implementation of RPA the latest figures from January to March 2016 state that there were still 58,000 young people aged 16 and 17 who were considered NEET, which is up 7,000 from the previous year (ONS 2016). However, this initiative is still in the early stages so a fuller understanding of the effectiveness of this approach is not yet achievable.

Activity: The power of legislation

1. If learning is tied to the receipt of benefits, is it voluntary? Does this NEET strategy have the potential to target some groups more than others?
2. What do these strategies tell us about the government view of young people who are labelled NEET?

Conservative

In 2015 a majority Conservative government was elected that had previously declared that it had plans to change NEET policy. Prior to the election, Cameron (2014) ambitiously vowed to abolish youth unemployment, starting with the removal of key benefits for young people under 21. He declared this would help prevent a life on welfare and offer the chance for young people 'to make something of themselves' (Cameron 2014). The tagline of the new initiative, 'earn or learn', has a focus on getting young people to find work, arguably to ensure that they do not create a financial burden on the state (France 2016). The government's Skills Minister stated, 'a life on benefits is simply not an option' (Hancock 2015), reinforcing the initiative's aim to target benefit claimants. The concept of removing benefits for young people was also mentioned in the pre-election Labour manifesto (Miliband 2015) which highlights how the NEET debate and proposed policy had progressed within this party since the 'incentive-style' approach of the previous Labour administration.

The policy also identifies a distinct age group within the NEET cohort of people aged 18 to 21 rather than extend the initiative to the maximum age of someone who is NEET, which is 24. The segregation of the group does not appear to be supported by 'the greatest need' as the highest number of young people registered as NEET fall into the 18 to 24 age bracket and the highest number of people in full-time education are aged 18 to 21, therefore the reason for targeting this specific age group may need further exploration (Corney 2015).

The 'earn or learn' policy has essentially two aspects: the first is to drive social mobility through increasing educational opportunities for young people. This is through wider access to Higher Education (BIS 2016) and the assurance of three million apprenticeships or traineeships for young people (Cameron 2014). The second strand to this policy is a stronger obligation on young people aged 18 to 21 who are in receipt of benefits to enter full-time employment or education (Corney 2015).

Young people in receipt of benefits will have to complete a mandatory 'employability boot camp'. This is an intensive six-month 'work-ready' programme which includes activities such as job searching, interview techniques and support in completing job applications. After the completion of the 'boot camp' the young person must take employment, or if they are unable to find employment they must participate in unpaid work or enrol on a traineeship (Corney 2015). This policy apparently fosters a 'no excuses culture' and results in benefit sanctions or benefits being stopped altogether if the young person is not 'earning or learning' (Hancock 2015). However, the proposal to remove benefits has been criticised by the YMCA (2015) who state that for most young people under 21 claiming Universal Credit and /or housing benefit it is not a 'choice' but a clear need.

The YMCA (2015) argue that under 21s in receipt of these benefits have often recently left care, have been homeless, are estranged from their family or bringing up children and that it is only a very small proportion who 'abuse the system' (YMCA 2015). Leishman and Young (2015) declare that as a financial exercise removal of benefits would realistically only save £3.3 million, which is a small sum in public finance, because potentially other public service costs could increase significantly, for example social services, emergency shelters and criminal justice.

Activity: The use of language

1. At times the Conservative government adopt military language when describing NEET initiatives, which is echoed in their support for a 'military ethos' approach to behaviour management in schools. What are the implications of this?
2. What do these strategies tell us about the government view of young people who are labelled NEET?

Conclusion

As with most aspects of education, it is difficult to offer a solution. The figures representing young people can be perceived as inaccurate but also unrelenting. The heterogeneous nature of the young people who are registered as NEET also challenges the effectiveness of a blanket approach. However, despite the differences in this group, there are similarities, such as low educational achievement and poor mental and physical health. Another common thread appears to be low economic status, which perpetuates the cycle of social inequalities bound with educational inequalities (Reay 2012), pushing the NEET debate into the education and inequalities arena.

Due to the financial burden of young people who do not contribute to the economy and the personal and social implications for a young person who is on the NEET register, it is clear that strategies are needed. However, it is arguably the government's dominant view and ideological standpoint regarding young people which is reflected in the current deficit model and NEET policy. This is observed through the different approaches to the young people, offering them financial incentives to learn, proposing benefit sanctions to people who are not learning or in employment, or by using the power of legislation to enforce students to stay in education or training regardless of their will. Historically, political parties offer different approaches to social issues. However, despite changes in the elected government the NEET policies appear to share similar approaches. This is evident in the Labour and Coalition support for the RPA or the 'pre-Corbyn' Labour support for the Conservative approach of benefit sanctions for unemployed young people. Consequently, if there is a solution it may lie with research conducted by Simmons and Smyth (2016) who argue that understanding the reasons why young people disengage with education is critically important in reducing the numbers of NEET in the UK. Therefore, until the voices of people on the NEET register are listened to and acted upon, then regardless of whether it is a 'carrot' or 'stick' initiative engagement in employment or education may be difficult to enforce.

Case study 6.1: Billy

Billy is a 'looked after child' who lives in a residential children's home. He has no specific learning difficulties or disabilities; however, his basic levels of maths and English are lower than average. Billy struggles with school and does not feel inspired by the academic curriculum; he is frequently disruptive and challenges authority. He would like to take a vocational option in Year 10 but due to him being excluded from school several times he is told that he must attend an alternative curriculum at the local college or be permanently excluded. Billy does not get to choose his curriculum which is focused on English, maths and personal development. Billy does not have to complete any GCSEs and instead completes Functional Skills in maths and English. Billy completes his final two years at the college and achieves Entry Level 3 Functional Skills and a Personal Development qualification. When he applies to do a construction course he is told that due to a lack of relevant experience and qualifications, he must enrol on a Level 1 Construction Course and complete his Level 1 Functional Skills in maths and English. Billy is excellent at construction and completes his practical course with ease. His tutors say that he has a real flare for the trade. Unfortunately Billy still struggles with his maths and his English and fails both. The following year he is told that despite his outstanding skills in construction, he is unable to move to the Level 2 Construction Course as he has not achieved his maths and English at Level 1. Billy goes to another training provider to do his Functional Skills but he also has to complete a 'core qualification', they do not do construction so he chooses hospitality. Billy becomes bored and disruptive as he is not really interested in his course so he is asked to leave. He is disillusioned with education and tries to find work, but with minimal qualifications and no work experience he is unsuccessful. Billy joins the NEET register.

Key questions:

1. Are there key points during Billy's educational experience where becoming NEET could have been avoided?
2. Should lack of maths and English qualifications disbar young people from vocational courses? How about other academic courses, such as teacher training?

Case study 6.2: Chelsie

Chelsie is a good attender at school and has no specific learning difficulties or disabilities identified. She leaves school with 5 GCSE D–G grades and applies to her local college to do a child care course as she has always enjoyed looking after her younger brothers and sister. As Chelsie has not achieved a GCSE C or above in maths or English, she must take a skills test. Upon completion of the skills test Chelsie is told that she is working at Functional Skills Level 1 (the equivalent of D–G) and so is advised to apply for a Level 1 Child Care Course and study maths and English Functional Skills at Level 1. Chelsie completes the child care course and English and maths at Level 1. The following academic years Chelsie completes her Level 2 and Level 3 child care courses and her Level 2 English and maths. However Chelsie decides that she no longer wants to work with children and that she would like to do a beauty therapy course. As she has not studied beauty therapy before she is advised that a Level 2 course would be the most appropriate; however, she no longer needs to study for her English and maths as it is only a government requirement up to Level 2. Chelsie applies for and completes the Level 2 Beauty Therapy Course. She would like to enrol onto a Level 3 Beauty Therapy Course but is informed that as she already has a Level 3 qualification (in child care) she would now have to pay for this qualification, which she feels she would be unable to do. Chelsie decides that she needs to find employment. When she leaves college and tries to find a job in the beauty therapy industry she is told that she needs at least a Level 3 beauty qualification for any position. Chelsie takes up a low-skilled job in her local supermarket and two years later becomes pregnant. She leaves work and joins the NEET register.

Key questions:

1. Are there key points in Chelsie's educational experience where becoming NEET could have been avoided?
2. Why do you think Chelsie feels unable to fund her Level 3 beauty qualification?
3. Is it the government's responsibility or the individual's responsibility to fund post-18 learning? Why or why not?

Suggested reading

France, A. (2016) *Understanding Youth in the Global Economic Crisis*. Bristol: Policy Press.

This book offers a global perspective on the apparent 'NEET crisis', making direct reference to the 2008 financial crash and the implications this has had for young people. Case studies are used from eight countries to demonstrate that the neoliberal agenda affecting the young is happening on a global scale.

Simmons, R. and Smyth, J. (2016) Crisis of youth or youth in crisis? Education, employment and legitimation crisis. *International Journal of Lifelong Education*, 35 (2), 136–152.

Simmons is a key writer regarding young people who are at risk of becoming NEET. In this paper Simmons and Smyth present their longitudinal ethnographic study of the lives of young people on the NEET register. They propose that the neoliberal government initiatives to re-engage young people may actually reinforce their marginalisation.

References

Bajorek, Z., Donnaloja, V. and McEnhill, L. (2016) *Don't Stop Me Now: Supporting young people with chronic conditions from education to employment*. London: The Work Foundation.

Ball, S. (2013) *Education, Justice and Democracy: The struggle over ignorance and opportunity*. London: Centre for Labour and Social Studies.

BBC News (2011) Labour loses vote to stop scrapping of EMA. Available from: www.bbc.co.uk/news/education-12228466

BBC News (2015) David Cameron: Unemployed young 'should do community work'. Available at: www.bbc.co.uk/news/uk-politics-31500763

Beck, V. (2015) Learning providers' work with NEET young people. *Journal of Vocational Education & Training*, 67 (4), 482–496.

BIS (2016) *The Teaching Excellence Framework: Accessing quality in Higher Education*. London: House of Commons.

Bourn, J. (2004) *Connexions Service Advice and Guidance for all Young People*. National Audit Office, DfES: The Stationery Office.

Brooks, R. (2014) *Out of Sight: How we lost track of thousands of NEETS, and how we can transform their prospects*. London: Fabian Society.

Buchanan, S. and Tuckerman, L. (2016) The information behaviours of disadvantaged and disengaged adolescents. *Journal of Documentation*, 72 (3), 527–548.

Cameron, D. (2014) Leader's speech, Conservative Conference, Birmingham. Available at: www.britishpoliticalspeech.org/speech-archive.htm?speech=356

Cameron, D. (2015) *The Conservative Party Manifesto. Strong leadership, a clear economic plan a brighter, more secure future*. Conservative Party. Available at: https://s3-eu-west-1.amazonaws.com/manifesto2015/ConservativeManifesto2015.pdf

Clegg, N. (2015) *Young People Manifesto. Policies to create opportunities for all young people*. Liberal Democrat Party. Available at: hError! Hyperlink reference not valid.ttps://d3n8a8pro7vhmx.cloudfront.net/libdems/pages/9284/attachments/original/1430600098/Final_Youth_MiniManifesto_2015_27_04_15v3.pdf?1430600098

Clegg, N. and Grayling, C. (2012) Radical scheme to rescue NEETs. London: DfE, DWP. Available at: www.gov.uk/government/news/radical-scheme-to-rescue-neets

Corbyn, J (2015) *A Better Future for Young People*. Available at: https://d3n8a8pro7vhmx.cloudfront.net/jeremyforlabour/pages/123/attachments/original/1439232082/Youth.pdf?1439232082

Corney, M. (2015) *'Earn or Learn' for 18 to 21 Year Olds: New age group, new policies*. London: NCFE.

DeLuca, C., Godden, L., Hutchinson, N. and Versnel, J. (2015) Preparing at-risk youth for a changing world: Revisiting a person-in-context model for transition to employment. *Educational Research*, 57 (2), 182–200.

DfE (2011) *Plans to End the Maintenance Allowance (EMA) Programme*. Available at www.gov.uk/government/news/plans-to-end-the-education-maintenance-allowance-ema-programme

DfE (2015) *2010–2015 Government Policy: School and college qualifications and curriculum*. Available at: www.gov.uk/government/publications/2010-to-2015-government-policy-school-and-college-qualifications-and-curriculum/2010-to-2015-government-policy-school-and-college-qualifications-and-curriculum

DfE (2016) *21st January 2016. Revised GCSE and equivalent results in England, 2014 to 2015*. Available at: www.gov.uk/government/uploads/system/uploads/attachment_data/file/494073/SFR01_2016.pdf

Egdell, V. and McQuaid, R. (2016) Supporting disadvantaged young people into work: Insights from the capability approach. *Social Policy and Administration*, 50 (1), 1–18.

Equality and Human Rights Commission (2015) *Is Britain Fairer? The state of equality and human rights 2015*. London: EHRC.

Eurofound (2012) *NEETs – Young people not in employment, education or training: Characteristics, costs and policy responses in Europe*. Luxembourg: Publications Office of the European Union.

Eurostats (2016a) *Statistics Explained: Youth Unemployment*. Available at: http://ec.europa.eu/eurostat/statistics-explained/index.php/File:Table_1_Youth_unemployment,_2014Q4_(%25).png

Eurostats (2016b) *Labour Market Statistics at Regional Level*. Available at: http://ec.europa.eu/eurostat/statistics-explained/index.php/Labour_market_statistics_at_regional_level

Fothergill, S. and Gore, T. (2013) *The Implications for Employment of the Shift to High-Value Manufacturing*. London: Foresight.

France, A. (2016) *Understanding Youth in the Global Economic Crisis*. Bristol: Policy Press.

Gibb, N. (2014) New curriculum will make education system 'envy of the world'. Available at: www.gov.uk/government/news/new-curriculum-will-make-education-system-envy-of-the-world

Gove, M. (2014) Michael Gove speaks about the future of education reform. Available at: www.gov.uk/government/speeches/michael-gove-speaks-about-the-future-of-education-reform

Harris, S. (2015) Shame of 500,000 'Neets' who don't even want to work: Alert over the young not in jobs, training or education. Available at: www.dailymail.co.uk/news/article-3098467/British-Neets-numbering-500k-don-t-want-work.html

Hancock, N. (2014) Number of NEETS in England drops for all age groups between 16 to 24, Available at: www.gov.uk/government/news/number-of-neets-in-england-drops-for-all-age-groups-between-16-to-24

Hancock, N. (2015) Every young person should be either earning or learning from April 2017. Available at: ww.gov.uk/government/news/hancock-every-young-person-should-be-earning-or-learning-from-april-2017

HM Revenue and Customs (2015) Child benefit when your child turns 16. Available at: www.gov.uk/child-benefit-16-19

Hoggarth, L. and Smith, D. (2004) *Understanding the Impact of Connexions on Young People at Risk*. Nottingham: DfES.

Holford, A. (2015) The labour supply effect of Education Maintenance Allowance and its implications for parental altruism. *Review of Economics in the Household*, 13 (3), 531–538.

Hutchinson, J. and Kettlewell, K. (2015) Education to employment: Complicated transitions in a changing world. *Educational Research*, 57 (2), 113–120.

Hutchinson, J., Beck, V. and Hooley, T. (2015) Delivering NEET policy packages? A decade of NEET policy in England. *Journal of Education and Work*, 29 (6), 707–727.

Keates, C. (2015) NASUWT comments on rise in NEETs. Available at: www.nasuwt.org.uk/Whatsnew/NASUWTNews/PressReleases/NASUWTCommentsOnRiseInNEETs

Leishman, C. and Young, G. (2015) *Lifeline not Lifestyle: An economic analysis for the impacts of cutting housing benefit for young people. Full report*. Heriot-Watt University: End Youth Homelessness.

Maguire, S. (2015) NEET – unemployed, inactive or unknown- why does it matter? *Education Research*, 57 (2), 121–132.

Miliband, E. (2015) *A manifesto for Britain. Young People*. Available at: www.labour.org.uk/manifesto/young-people

Miller, J., McAuliffe, L., Riaz, N. and Deucher, R. (2015) Exploring youths' perceptions of hidden practice of youth work in increasing social capital with young people considered NEET, in Scotland. *Journal of Youth Studies*, 18 (4), 468–484.

Mirza-Davies, J (2016) *NEET: Young People Not in Employment, Education or Training*. Briefing Paper Number 06705. London: House of Commons Library.

Monogan, A. (2016) Number of UK 'Neets' increases for second consecutive quarter. *Guardian*. Available at: www.theguardian.com/business/2016/may/26/number-of-uk-neets-increases-for-second-consecutive-quarter

Morgan, N. (2015) New reforms to raise standards and behaviour. Available at: www.gov.uk/government/news/new-reforms-to-raise-standards-and-improve-behaviour

Morse, A. (2014) *16–18-Year-Old Participation in Education and Training*. London: DfE/National Audit Office.

Office for National Statistics (2016) *Young People Not in Education Employment or Training (NEET): May 2016*. Available at: www.ons.gov.uk/employmentandlabourmarket/peoplenotinwork/unemployment/bulletins/youngpeoplenotineducationemploymentortrainingneet/latest

Ofsted (2002) *Connexions Partnerships: The first year 2001–2002*. London: Ofsted.
Osborne, G. (2016) Budget 2016: George Osborne's speech. Available at: www.gov.uk/government/speeches/budget-2016-george-osbornes-speech
Reay, D. (2012) *What Would a Socially Just Education System Look Like?* London: Centre for Labour and Social Studies.
Rees, G., Williamson, H. and Istance, D. (1996) 'Status Zero': A study of jobless school leavers in South Wales. *Research Papers in Education*, 11 (2), 219–235.
Reiter, H. and Schlimbach, T. (2015) NEET in disguise? Rival narratives in troubled youth transitions. *Educational Research*, 57 (2), 133–150.
Russell, L. (2016) Complex pathways for young mothers outside employment, education and training. *Ethnography and Education*, 11 (1), 91–106.
Scottish Office Education Department (SOED) (2015) 22,000 more young people eligible for EMA. Available at: https://news.gov.scot/news/22000-more-young-people-eligible-for-emas
Simmons, R. and Smyth, J. (2016) Crisis of youth or youth in crisis? Education, employment and the legitimation crisis. *International Journal of Lifelong Education*, 35 (3), 136–152.
Simmons, R., Thomson, R., Tabrizi, G. and Nartey, A. (2014) *Engaging Young People in Education, Employment or Training. The case for a Youth Resolution*. London: University and College Union.
Smith, E. (2012) *Key Issues in Education and Social Justice*. London: Sage.
Spielhofer, T., Mann, P. and Sims, D. (2003) *Entry to Employment (E2E) Participation Study: Final report*. London: Learning and Skills Development Agency.
Thomson, R. (2011) Individualisation and social exclusion: The case of young people not in employment, education or training. *Oxford Review of Education*, 37 (6), 785–802.
Veldman, K., Reijneveld, S., Ortiz, J., Verhulst, F. and Bultmann, U. (2015) Mental health trajectories from childhood to young adulthood affect the educational and employment status of young adults: Results from the TRAILS study. *Journal of Epidemiology & Community Health*, 69 (6), 588–593.
Wolf, A. (2011) *Review of Vocational Education – The Wolf Report*. Available at: www.gov.uk/government/uploads/system/uploads/attachment_data/file/180504/DFE-00031-2011.pdf
YMCA (2015) *Uncertain Futures: A report examining the impact of removing automatic entitlement to Housing Benefit for 18 to 21 year olds*. London: YMCA.
Young, M. and Lambert, D. (2014) *Knowledge and the Future School*. London: Bloomsbury.
Young Greens (2015) *Generation Vote Green: The youth manifesto*. Green Party. Available at: http://younggreens.org.uk/assets/images/younggreen%20images/documents/Youth_manifesto1.pdf

7 Sexuality and education

Trevor Cotterill

This chapter explores:

- the dilemmas faced by LGBT students and teachers surrounding their sexuality within education;
- the effects disclosure about their sexuality might have on their identity and the subsequent consequences of such disclosure;
- the portrayal of an LGBT student as a 'victim' or a 'hero';
- the nature of intersecting identities and stigma in the classroom in relation to LGBT teachers.

If statistics are to be believed, Lesbian, Gay, Bisexual, Transgendered and Questioning (LGBTQ) individuals make up a significant part of both the student population and the workforce in education. Often, however, there is an internal debate to be had about issues such as disclosure of their sexuality, the perceived impact of their sexuality on others and the role that education can have in ameliorating some of the issues which these individuals may face.

LBGT students

> ✏️ **Activity: What are young people saying?**
>
> The Youth Chances Report (2014) which surveyed over 7,000 young people aged 16–25 found that the experience of LGBT ideation and activity starts early for many, particularly when compared with the age at which targeted provision for LGBTQ people generally starts. Over half of LGBTQ respondents (53 per cent) knew they were LGBTQ by the age of 13. Over half of trans respondents (58 per cent) knew they were trans by the same age.
>
> Most young LGBTQ people feel that their time at school is affected by hostility or fear, with consequences such as feeling left out, lower grades and having to move schools. Most report that their school supported its pupils badly in respect of sexuality or gender identity. Schools also neglect areas that are known to be public health concerns. Sex and relationships education is not inclusive of LGBTQ relationships and does not provide young people with the emotional and sexual health information they need. This is a particular concern for young gay and bisexual men who are at higher risk of STIs and HIV. However, LGBTQ

young people experience less discrimination at university and work, which are also rated as environments that are much more tolerant and supportive than school.

LGBTQ young people report significantly higher levels of mental health problems including depression and anxiety, self-harm and suicidal thoughts. High rates of poor mental health were found in the whole sample, presenting a concerning picture in the youth population at large.

Youth Chances, 2014. Survey of 16–25 year olds: First reference report.
London: METRO. www.youthchances.org/

If you were talking to the government about the findings of the report, what recommendations would you suggest and why?

✏ Activity: What are the statistics?

The Integrated Household Survey (ONS, 2015) identified the following: In 2014 the IHS found 1.6 per cent of adults identified themselves as lesbian, gay or bisexual (LGB). This comprised of: 1.1 per cent who identified as gay or lesbian and 0.5 per cent who identified as bisexual.

The size of the LGB population has remained the same since 2013 (1.6 per cent) and has experienced a small increase since 2010 (from 1.5 per cent), although this increase was not statistically significant. The likelihood of an adult identifying as LGB decreased with age. In 2014, 2.6 per cent of adults aged 16–24 identified as LGB. This decreased to 0.6 per cent of adults aged 65 and over. In 2014, twice as many men identified themselves as gay (1.5 per cent) when compared with women who identified themselves as gay or lesbian (0.7 per cent). By contrast, women were more than twice as likely to identify themselves as bisexual (0.7 per cent) compared to men (0.3 per cent). In 2014, London had the highest proportion of adults identifying themselves as LGB (2.6 per cent). Differences between other regions of the UK were relatively small and mostly not statistically significant, with LGB identification ranging from 1.0 per cent (East Midlands) to 1.8 per cent (South-East). Adults in managerial and professional occupations were more likely to identify themselves as LGB (2.1 per cent) than those in either intermediate occupations (1.3 per cent) or routine and manual occupations (1.4 per cent).

You can access the findings at: www.ons.gov.uk/peoplepopulationandcommunity/culturalidentity/sexuality/bulletins/integratedhouseholdsurvey/2015-10-01

- What could account for these differences?
- Do you think that these statistics are accurate, or are over- or under-estimations, and why?

The school culture and LGBT students

LGBT students are part of a wider school culture involving various groups and subgroups with differing identities, but in general LGBT students tend to have more negative attitudes toward school (Espelage et al., 2008; Russell et al., 2001) with many being invisible within school settings. It has been suggested that LGBT students are part of a heteronormative culture and institutionalised heterosexism may be experienced by many LGBT students in their daily interactions (Herek, 2002). This experience can often be stressful and a survey conducted by GLSEN (Gay, Lesbian, Straight Education Network) in the USA found that the majority of LGBT students surveyed had experienced negative incidents at school, from overt homophobia and violence to more subtle manifestations of institutionalised heterosexism (Kosciw et al., 2010). They also found that over 60 per cent of sexual and gender minority respondents felt unsafe in their school environment because of their sexual orientation, and 40 per cent reported being physically harassed in schools because of their sexual orientation, creating atmospheres that often fail to be conducive to the learning, personal growth and other educational needs of LGBT students.

As far back as the 1980s, McAnarney (1985) noted the goal of adolescence should be the development of a secure identity, a positive sense of self and the capability to form intimate relationships. However, for youth who are LGBT 'achieving these tasks can be difficult because of the stigmatisation of homosexuality' (Espelage et al., 2008, p. 203). Often, LGBT youth are attempting to develop their identities without the support of various social systems that include families, schools and peers (Morrison and L'Heureux, 2001). Consequences of such homophobic school environments on LGBT students include ostracism, physical violence, verbal harassment, a decline in academic performance, school failure, truancy and a decrease in involvement in school and extracurricular activities (Kosciw et al., 2009). Furthermore, Kosciw et al. (2010) found that nearly 34 per cent of LGBT youth who reported a homophobic incident to school staff indicated that nothing was done in response to the report. Perhaps parents, teachers and others are often reluctant to ask such individuals direct questions about their sexual orientation and they themselves may be often hesitant about identifying themselves as lesbian, gay or bisexual.

You might think that moving from secondary to higher education might be a positive experience for many LGBT students. For many students, higher education provides a setting in which they can freely experiment with alternate roles and identities while gaining a sense of themselves as individuals (Adams et al., 2006). But as individuals struggle to accept their non-normative sexual identity, they often feel isolated and find the journey into higher education difficult. Waldo (1998) points to the promise that higher education holds for many of these individuals with this being the first time that many LGBT students are exposed to the LGBT community. Post-secondary education and the autonomy associated with it offers hope for many young people in their struggle to accept their sexuality. Unfortunately, research also shows that some colleges and universities do not provide a safe and nurturing environment for non-heterosexual students (Dilley, 2005).

Victimisation, homophobic bullying and possible consequences

Research suggests that a large majority of LGBT youth experience peer victimisation at school, which can include verbal, physical and relational forms of victimisation (Coker et al., 2010; Espelage et al., 2008; Poteat et al., 2012a; Robinson and Espelage, 2011). Consequences of such victimisation include anxiety, depression, suicidal ideation and traumatic stress (Robinson, and Espelage, 2011), isolation and stigmatisation from peers, and externalising behaviours such as substance use (Poteat et al. 2012b). Homophobic teasing and peer victimisation, in combination with heterosexist school policies and passive acceptance of students' homophobic behaviour by schools, are identified as contributing to the perpetuation of mental health and educational concerns such as absenteeism, lowered educational aspirations and lowered academic achievement. (Aragon et al., 2014). Secondary schools, in particular, are frequently heterosexist and homophobic institutions creating atmospheres that often fail to be conducive to the learning, personal growth and other educational needs of LGBT students. Indeed, the goal of adolescence should be the development of a secure identity, a positive sense of self and the capability to form intimate relationships. However, for youth who are LGBT or questioning their sexual orientation, 'achieving these tasks can be difficult because of the stigmatisation of homosexuality' (Espelage et al., 2008, p. 203). Munoz-Plaza et al. (2002) described the classroom as 'the most homophobic of all social institutions' (p. 53).

Research suggests that LGBT students differ statistically on three educational outcomes in comparison to their non-LGBT peers. Students have higher rates of truancy, earn lower grades and have lower educational intentions. Robinson and Espelage (2011) suggested that victimisation partially accounted for these differences. They found secondary-aged LGBT students to be at a much-elevated level of truancy risk compared to their non-LGBT peers. This level of unexcused absences remained consistent throughout secondary school.

Research has suggested that many LGBT students experience compromised opportunities for academic success. They may be more prone to school-related problems, including feeling less socially integrated, having difficulty paying attention in class and skipping classes more often, which can lead to lower academic achievement. One such study on students in New Zealand who came out as LGBT reported lower levels of educational attainment. This low performance at school was associated with increased bullying and verbal assault (Henrickson, 2008).

> **✎ Activity: Reflection**
>
> What does the research outlined above tell you about the consequences of such bullying and stigmatisation for the individual and the school?

Heroes or victims?

How are LGBT students portrayed within the school? Allen (2015) makes an important point by identifying that often representations of the experience at school necessitate understanding LGBT within a binary of either victims or heroes, and this constitution obscures these young peoples' lived schooling realities. Harwood and Rasmussen (2004) argue that 'there is a tendency to conflate LGBT adolescence with "woundedness" in educational discourses' (p. 306) and argue that along with their depiction as wounded victims of homophobia and other discriminatory practices, LGBT youth have also been heralded as resilient heroes. Such dualistic representations can be seen to flatten their lived experiences and produce a binary that reduces LGBT youth to either wounded or hero. There are often cases of resiliency whereby LGBT youth transform from wounded to hero (Talburt, 2004).

This notion of the 'woundedness' discourse depicts schools as unwelcoming, unsafe and subsequently unhealthy spaces for LGBT students (McCarty-Caplan, 2013). Homophobia is rendered a particular problem and commonly evidenced in physical and/or verbal harassment of LGBT students (Msibi, 2012; Taylor et al., 2011). For example, in the USA results from the Gay, Lesbian, and Straight Education Network's (GLSEN's) 2011 National School Climate survey of the experiences of lesbian, gay, bisexual and transgender youth in U.S. schools, 'indicated that in the past year 81.9% were verbally harassed (e.g., called names or threatened), 38.3% were physically harassed (e.g., pushed or shoved) and three fifths (63.5%) felt unsafe at school because of their sexual orientation' (Kosciw et al., 2012, p. 5). In other international studies homophobia is also reported to occur via rumours, graffiti, schoolyard intimidation and cyberbullying (Jones and Hillier, 2012; Kjaran and Jóhannesson, 2013; Hunt and Jenson, 2007; Sexton, 2012). The cumulative effect of these statistics is to depict a schooling environment of gloom and negativity in which LGBT are constituted as vulnerable and in need of protection.

However, there are also studies which report on LGBT students 'fighting back'. One example is Kjaran and Jóhannesson's (2013) examination of the way LGBT youth respond to heterosexism in upper secondary schools in Iceland. These researchers recount the story of one participant, Hrafn, whose peers pestered him about whether he was sure he was gay. Finding these questions offensive, Hrafn would answer his male heterosexual classmates by countering with questions about 'whether they were "sure" about their sexuality' and 'how could they be certain if they had never been with a boy?' The authors write, 'His reactions demonstrate that LGBT students can create their own discursive space and do not have to be positioned as victims, as has sometimes been the case among scholars on LGBT youth' (Kjaran and Jóhannesson, 2013, p. 361). Through this analysis, Hrafn is constituted as the hero who fights back against oppressive heterosexism and who offers hope for a brighter future against the bleak backdrop of LGBT victimisation. However, such depictions once again establish a binary in which LGBT youth can only be victims or heroes.

Activity: Is it all bad news?

Gay teenagers who come out at school emerge with higher self-esteem and lower levels of depression than if they had not – and are no more likely to be bullied. New research, said to be the first to document the benefits of coming out during adolescence, suggests that teenagers should not be advised to keep their sexuality quiet in the hope of minimising the risk of classroom abuse.

Stephen Russell, the director of the University of Arizona's Frances McClelland Institute for Children, Youth and Families, and the lead author of the study, said: 'Being out is good for you. Being able to be who we are is crucial to mental health.' After examining data on 245 gay and lesbian people in their early 20s, the researchers found that teenagers experienced victimisation and bullying in school over their gender identity or sexuality regardless of whether they came out or not. Those who had come out in school, however, reported higher self-esteem and life satisfaction as young adults than those who had tried to hide their sexuality or gender identity. Coming out in school also led to lower levels of depression in early adulthood. 'Our study points to the positive role of coming out for youth and young adult well-being' (Lusher, 2015).

What factors may influence a young person's decision to come out at school?

'I am what I am': Disclosing and coming out

For LGBT youth, coming out (i.e. disclosure of their identity to others) can be a key developmental milestone, one that is associated with better psychological well-being. However, this greater visibility may come with increased risk of peer victimisation. Being out, therefore, may reflect resilience and may unfold differently depending on ecological context as some spaces may be more or less supportive of LGBT youth than others. Kosciw et al. (2015) explored a model of risk and resilience for 'outness' amongst 7,816 LGBT secondary school students. They found that 'outness' was related to higher victimisation but also to higher self-esteem and lower depression. Greater victimisation was related to negative academic outcomes directly and indirectly via diminished well-being. The increases in victimisation associated with 'outness' were larger for rural youth, and benefits to well-being partly compensated for their lower well-being overall. They suggest that being out reflects resilience in the face of a higher risk of victimisation, in addition to promoting well-being in other ways.

Activity: Read the following account

Actually for me there were two closets. Coming out of the first closet was more difficult, it meant coming out towards yourself, accepting your feelings and get rid of any prejudices towards yourself. When I had gone through that, I needed to come out of the second closet, telling people around me about my feelings and sexuality. I was, however, very scared as to how others would react. I was especially afraid of how my family would react, whether they would disown me or not. I was also afraid of being somehow different from others, being a freak or something, not being able to be like everybody else. What made me often feel worse was that my mother was often asking me whether I had a girlfriend at school or not. Actually I find it a bit sad that one needs to go through this difficult process, spending so much time feeling badly only to become oneself, to be happy. It would be the perfect world if people did not need to go through this ordeal in order to become happy.

(Kjaran and Jóhannesson, 2015)

What are your thoughts on what this individual experienced?

LGBT youth are forced to be continuously aware of who they are out to and mindful of how to manage their disclosure across contexts. It is assumed that LGBT youth, after disclosing their sexual orientation, may receive positive and/or negative feedback that will in turn impact academic and school experiences. LGBT youth are faced with complex decisions regarding sexual identity disclosure across multiple contexts.

It is clear from the existing literature that the coming-out process and in particular the task of self-disclosure is a highly salient issue for LGBT youth and is associated with various psychosocial outcomes. It is less clear how the individual or group to whom one comes out relates to experiences at school (i.e. academic achievement and harassment). Being out at school has been shown to be associated with more harassment yet, at the same time, feeling less socially isolated (Kosciw et al., 2010). Therefore, LGBT youth appear to experience a range of consequences resulting from coming out, which is related to the contexts (people and places) in which they are out.

In one study, Morris et al. (2014) found that coming out to different groups of people (i.e. at school and/or at home) was associated with academic achievement and harassment depending on the patterns of 'outness'. Youth who were not out at all or out to everyone reported the highest grades and lowest rates of harassment; these youth had to manage their 'outness' the least. They found that being out to more friends solely or in combination with other groups of individuals (i.e. family members) was generally associated with higher grades and less school harassment. In addition, youth who reported being out at home but not at school reported the worst grades and more harassment. Students who feel the need or are required to constantly manage to who they are out may perform worse at school, while students who are out to the majority of others in their social environment perform better in school.

Although out LGBT students may indeed be targets of harassment at school, those who remain in the closet may experience maladaptive developmental outcomes as well. The results of this study suggest different experiences for youth based on the context and social relations that define their being out. This leads to two important questions: Are LGBT youth so involved and concerned about how to negotiate coming out to others that they may ignore their studies and thus perform lower than their heterosexual counterparts? Or, can problems with coming out be attributed to the school context, in that schools that engage youth academically are more helpful in encouraging LGBT youth to express themselves, therefore allowing them to come out to more individuals? Findings seem to suggest that if students cannot disclose their sexual identity to multiple groups at the same time, their achievement may be undermined. With the exception of those youth who did not disclose their sexual identity to anyone, youth that were out to only one or two targets of disclosure reported lower academic achievement and higher rates of harassment. It is compelling that youth who were only out to family fared the worst. Because LGBT individuals must oftentimes rely on surrogate support systems such as friends (in comparison with families that may lack the tools to socialise their non-heterosexual child in a heteronormative society), it may be particularly difficult for young people to disclose their sexual identity to family members only. In summary, their findings implicate that it is not as simple as youth being better or worse off based on their decision to disclose or not disclose their sexual identity. There are both advantages and costs of remaining in the closet or disclosing sexual identity to multiple groups of individuals; youth that disclose their sexual orientation during school may be doing so when conforming and fitting in is most important.

Studies have found that young people grow up surrounded by homophobic language and attitudes, living within a social and legal system biased towards heterosexuals (Flowers and Buston 2001). These narratives of oppression are shown to be particularly deleterious in educational settings, with homophobic bullying rife and lesbian, gay, bisexual and transgender (LGBT) students maintaining elevated levels of absenteeism compared to their heterosexual peers (Ryan and Rivers, 2003). Research has documented that coming out as a sexual minority can be a difficult and stressful process (Flowers and Buston (2001), one that occurs over an extended period of time and, as Evans and Broido (1999) comment, is not an 'either/or' concept. It also describes how these issues are exacerbated for bisexuals, who face discrimination from both heterosexuals and other sexual minorities (Ochs, 1996).

Bisexual students

Given the unique discrimination faced by bisexuals (Burleson, 2005), often described as 'biphobia' (Eliason, 1997), it is necessary to examine the influence of decreasing homophobia on bisexual youth and whether decreasing homophobia influences biphobia in the broader culture. Research carried out in the UK on the changing experiences of bisexual male adolescents by Morris et al. (2014) drew upon in-depth interviews with 15 openly bisexual males aged 16–18 from sixth-form colleges. They found that these participants' experiences were significantly improved on those described in the academic literature, with the majority having positive coming out experiences. Furthermore, the dominant narrative is one of acceptance and inclusion, both among friends and within their local cultures. Despite this, some students continue to experience biphobic and heteronormative assumptions about their identities. Nonetheless, these instances are greatly decreased and the majority of participants reported positive experiences of being openly bisexual.

It is evident that bisexual youth are aware of the social implications of coming out, and they are often strategic in determining who to come out to and in what context (Gorman-Murray, 2008). They most frequently opt to tell their friends about their same-sex desires before their parents, and tend to tell their mothers before their fathers (Savin-Williams and Ream, 2003). Furthermore, bisexual youth examine how other sexual minorities are treated, and consider the prevalence of homophobic language when determining whether to come out (Anderson, 2011). Even so, there is limited research on the experiences of bisexual youth specifically – despite bisexuals facing unique forms of discrimination (Klein, 1993). Morris et al. (2014) identified only two boys having difficulty in coming-out experiences. Indeed, 13 of the 15 participants were accepted by their friends, with the majority commenting that the process had improved their relationships with peers and even increased their popularity at school. The majority of participants had very positive experiences of coming out as bisexual with participants also highlighting the strategies they employed in planning their coming out. Nine of the bisexual boys interviewed decided to tell their 'best' or 'closest' friends first. Aaron said he came out to his closest friends because 'I knew they would truly accept me' (p. 404). Expressing his view that younger people are more accepting of bisexuality, Edward said, 'I figured my friends would be cooler about it. It's a generational thing' (p. 405).

However, contrast this with the stories of Daniel and Will (see Case studies 7.1 and 7.2), who are also bisexual (Rivers, 2001).

Case study 7.1: Daniel

Rivers (2001) found that while the majority of bisexual boys reported entirely positive coming-out experiences, there were some negative narratives as well. Two participants faced bullying similar to that experienced by openly gay and bisexual students in the 1980s and 1990s.

For example, Daniel spoke of the negative treatment he received from other students while at secondary school: 'It was absolutely horrible. I had bullies take the piss out of me, call me loads of names like "fag" and "queer". I got beaten up, and I lost most of my friends.' He went on to describe the physical violence and verbal harassment directed at him, adding, 'They punched me in my stomach and privates, kicked me, and pushed me over lots of times into the dirt. They used to say that I was a piece of dirt, so I deserved to be on the floor.' Daniel further reported that when he came out, a few of his friends stopped speaking to him. He commented, 'They didn't want to know me anymore. They thought I was like some sort of freak.'

When interviewed, Daniel no longer attended the same school, having moved to a different sixth-form college. Asked if he still faces problems, he replied, 'Not anymore. Since I've been at college people accept me for who I am and support me. It's much better now.' He added, 'People accept me. Treat me as a normal person and not as some sideshow freak. They support me.' When asked why he thinks things have improved, he said, 'The fact that everyone on your course chose to be there, so you can focus easier. Tutors support you if you have any problems you need to talk about, and people are generally more mature.'

Case study 7.2: Will

The other participant who experienced significant discrimination because of his sexuality was Will, who attended a private religious secondary school. Like Daniel, he also experienced verbal and physical abuse for being openly bisexual. Talking about the physical violence, he said, 'I was pushed over a wall, punched in the head repeatedly, and someone threw me into a tree.' Will also reported homophobic slurs directed at him, and reported other significant incidents of homophobia: 'One person graffitied my whole desk so there was "gay" written everywhere. I came in the next day and all my books, all my notes, had "gay" written across them.' Asked what he thought the bullies' motivation was, Will said, 'Being different. Because I've always been over-caring of people.'

Will also has dyspraxia, and suggested that some of the bullying might be attributable to his physical and behavioural differences. Will later added, 'I think the bullying, for them, was about seeing whether they could get me to snap. And I think that's what it became about. When they got thinking about me being bisexual, I think that suddenly started adding fuel to the fire.'

What do these case studies tell you about attitudes in general towards bisexual individuals?

Case study 7.3: Adam, 25

Read the case study of Adam at the link below:
 Source: LGBT Foundation (2016) at: http://lgbt.foundation/information-advice/coming-out-support/coming-out-your-stories/

How does this compare to the experiences of Daniel and Will?

> **Case study 7.4: School for LGBT pupils planned for Manchester (Hill, 2015)**
>
> The proposed school will teach 40 lesbian, gay, bisexual and transgender students who are struggling in mainstream education.
>
> Ellie (not her real name) turned to the LGBT Youth North West charity after she was outed by a school friend. 'School was awful,' she said. 'The PE teacher made me change clothes with the lads because she said I wasn't attracted to them. It annoyed me so much that I stopped going to PE, which meant I got in trouble for missing the lessons,' she added. Ellie eventually changed schools at 16. 'There were comments all the time, in most of the classes and in the corridors, and none of the teachers did anything to help me.'
>
> Rob (also not his real name) said homophobic bullying made his education in a mainstream school horrendous. Teachers need to teach about how homophobia is bad and how it affects the lives of LGBT people, he said. 'They need to help us feel safe in our own environment of school. And they should teach the other students how LGBT people just want to be like anyone else. But none of this happens and, as a result, LGBT pupils routinely experience bullying that, if it was racist or sexist, wouldn't be accepted by the school for a second.'
>
> **What do you consider are the advantages and disadvantages of such a proposal?**

LGBT teachers

Not only does the debate pertain to LGBT students and their experiences in education, but also to the teachers themselves. A key issue for many of these staff is to balance their personal and professional identity, while assessing the impact declaring their sexual orientation may have on themselves, their students and the institution.

> **Activity: First impressions**
>
> Read the following statements:
> Kate, a PE teacher, says she almost wishes her students would ask about her sexuality, because it might push her into being open. But she also fears the reaction of pupils and staff, and wonders if she would be ready for the extra responsibility. 'There's part of me that feels I could be a positive role model, but it could completely change the dynamic of my lessons – you've got a lot to handle as a teacher, regardless of talking about issues that are outside your classroom.'
>
> Jonathan decided not to be open with pupils about his sexuality at the school he now works at. In fact, he suspects that coming out there would be trouble-free, but his previous experience plays on his mind. 'I love everything about teaching, but what happened made me not want to go to work,' he says. 'It's a scandal that there are still teachers who aren't able to be open about their sexuality' (Williams, 2012).
>
> - What are you first impressions of these teachers?
> - Why might they have differing points of view?

Section 28 and its legacy

Section 28 of the Local Government Act 1988 was a controversial amendment to the UK's Local Government Act 1986, enacted on 24 May 1988 and repealed on 21 June 2000 in Scotland, and on 18 November 2003 in the rest of the UK by Section 122 of the Local Government Act 2003. The amendment stated that a local authority shall not intentionally promote homosexuality or publish material with the intention of promoting homosexuality or promote the teaching in any maintained school of the acceptability of homosexuality as a pretended family relationship. Many believed that Section 28 prohibited local councils from distributing any material, whether plays, leaflets, books, etc. that portrayed gay relationships as anything other than abnormal. Teachers and educational staff in some cases were afraid of discussing gay issues with students for fear of losing state funding (legislation.gov.uk, 2016).

In the UK the removal of Section 28 from the statute book in 2003, despite the considerable political and media opposition, was a significant milestone for non-heterosexual teachers (Nixon and Givens, 2007) and despite being legally ineffectual, academics agree that the legislation had a powerful and lasting cultural effect (Epstein, 2000).

One of the most plausible reasons for the sociocultural impact of Section 28 was that it functioned as a panoptic schema of surveillance (Foucault, 1992). Not only did the amendment refer to the promotion of homosexuality, it also encouraged teachers to self-censor their own behaviours in case they were 'seen' to be in some way promoting homosexuality in schools. Thus a panoptic schema is a coerced form of what Bourdieu (2001) refers to as 'invisibilisation' and although teachers may not necessarily change their sexualities in order to conform to the prevailing heteronormative orthodoxy, it could be argued that even today, many teachers are reluctant to identify as LGBT.

> **Activity: The impact of Section 28**
>
> - Why do you think Section 28 was introduced in 1988? What influences in society might have led to this amendment?
> - What changes in cultural norms and attitudes might have led to the removal of this in 2003?

Have things changed?

Evidence seems to suggest that the visibility of LGBT people within education seems to be lacking, and heteronormative attitudes seem to prevail. International research on this matter (Buston and Hart, 2001; Epstein, 1994; Herek, 2004) has revealed schools to be rather heteronormative and heterosexist, generally assuming that everyone within their settings is heterosexual. Kjaran and Kristinsdóttir (2015) similarly indicated that institutionalised heterosexism prevails in the structure and culture of the schools in Iceland and is part of the teachers' setting that they need to address. However, Lundin (2016) suggests that LGBT teachers are also a part of these norms, and therefore it is important to understand their perspectives. A LGBT teacher is likely not only to experience prevailing sexuality norms but also contribute to their development.

It is also taken for granted that the adults in school, both by their diversity and by their work to counteract traditional gender patterns, contribute to fulfilling the mission expressed as diversity. However, it can be questioned if the school is yet the arena for this mission or if schools are slightly behind. Eribon (2004) describes how a homosexual teacher constantly fears being insulted by the students and he suggests that the teaching profession could be one of the more difficult sectors of the workforce. In educational settings certain behaviours and interests are assumed, whereas others are perceived as odd. King (2004) illustrates this as he describes school as a setting where sexuality does not seem to exist – students are regarded as sexually inexperienced, and teachers as sexually inactive.

Personal or professional identity?

International studies have consistently highlighted the difficulties experienced by lesbian, gay and bisexual teachers from around the world as they attempt to negotiate their personal and professional identities within the context of an often hostile work environment (Connell, 2015; Endo et al., 2010; Irwin, 2002; Piper and Sikes, 2010; Rudoe, 2010). Both Nixon and Givens (2004) and Connell (2015) highlight the continuing threat and fear of harassment, which obliges LGBT teachers to cover or 'mask' their sexuality. Indeed, deliberate self-censorship is an identity management technique employed by LGBT teachers as they endeavour to protect themselves from instances of verbal/physical abuse/harassment from pupils or from instances of subtle ostracisation/exclusion on the part of some colleagues (Wardle, 2009). Paradoxically, an unexpected outcome of these feelings of insecurity is that some LGBT teachers report that they work harder and more effectively in order to safeguard their professional reputation and, in so doing, make themselves less likely to be targeted for harassment or dismissal (Jackson, 2007).

Gray (2013) states that coming out as a lesbian, gay or bisexual teacher necessitates the negotiating of both private and professional worlds. Coming out in disclosing one's sexuality is a phenomenon unique to LGBT people, and coming out is part of a lifelong process of what Grace and Benson (2000) identify as a risky business of choosing visibility. Rasmussen (2004) argues that the coming out process may be complicated by a range of (private) factors (age, race and familial background), which, for educators, can be further complicated by (professional) factors such as the wider community, ethos and management team of the school within which the LGBT teacher is located. Therefore, it is useful to think about the coming-out strategies of LGBT teachers as encompassing a negotiation between private and professional worlds.

Negotiating private and professional worlds is a key issue for a LGBT teacher. Although the intersections between private and professional selves are a factor in the lives of most people, for example the separation of our 'work selves' and 'home selves', for LGBT teachers the negotiation between the private and the professional is of particular concern. Thus there may be a view that teaching is a moral profession where the private world of a teacher exists separately from the world of teaching, learning and pedagogy. If disclosure relating to a teacher's sexual identity occurs, LGBT teachers could be particularly vulnerable to accusations of deviancy and, indeed, sex abuse (Piper and Sikes, 2010). On the other hand, there is agreement as to the key role for teachers in educating young people about LGBT issues (Craig et al., 2011).

Thus there is a metaphorical tightrope to be walked. Hardie (2012) points out the dilemmas and issues that have to be handled as a risk management by the homosexual teacher and says,

'School contexts provide challenges that needed to be weighed in terms of personal risk' (Hardie, 2012, p. 275). These risks include the possibility of being insulted, harassed or worse. Eribon (2004) points out that the risk is then that the homosexual person can experience sarcasm and cruelty and be unable to perceive the reason. For example, in a biology lesson words such as phagocytosis or homozygote can provide amusement and innuendo. LGBT teachers may need to be more vigilant or take precautions to comply with the heterosexual norm in an acceptable way. This notion suggests that there is still work to be done to avoid schools remaining a closet while society around changes, and one suggestion is to gain the explicit support and trust of colleagues.

The idea that a gay teacher's identity might be 'bayoneted' from two sides powerfully illustrates a double bind for LGBT teachers. On the one hand, coming out as an LGBT teacher fractures the boundary between private and professional worlds, and, as such coming out is a potentially dangerous speech act that can mark one as 'other' within the heteronormative space of school (Ferfolja, 1998). On the other hand, coming out as an LGBT teacher can be a political act of defiance or psychological necessity in order to live private and professional lives that are tolerable. In addition, as Khyatt (1997) argues, the sexual identity of an educator may not be spoken by LGBT educators themselves, but be read by students through the dress, speech or content of syllabus a teacher chooses to deploy.

The LGBT teacher as a role model

> **Activity: Role models?**
>
> What would be the advantages for both LGBT and heterosexual students, of having a LGBT individual within the teaching staff?

There are a number of advantages of students being exposed to a role model from the LGBT community. Other LGBT students could identify with someone in authority, discuss issues relating to their own identity, as well as increasing the diversity of organisations in mirroring society. However, there is also a dilemma which could mean producing a dissociated personality (Eribon, 2004). A relevant question is to ask what professional impact the considerations, exemplified by King (2004), could have? To break the norm by coming out might be perceived as expressing something very personal and maybe inappropriate. This is one of homo- and bisexual teachers' dilemmas: A heterosexual teacher can talk about a partner without being accounted for talking about sexuality, whereas the homo- or bisexual teacher is at risk of being understood as talking inappropriately about sexuality. King (2004) identifies a key issue in that as teachers and prospective teachers gay men have made a very bad bargain. They have tacitly agreed that they would not promote homosexuality and do so by keeping themselves in the closet. By not 'acting gay' they would not be visible as practising homosexuals, but this bargain has set up countless occasions for paranoia, monitoring one's teaching behaviour and policing oneself for evidence of homosexuality, lest a colleague, parent, or head teacher deduces the sexual persona.

A disruptive alternative to others' perception, a gay teacher may model a possible life for young children who will later be gay and lesbian adults. As part of teaching practice, a gay teacher may provide narratives (and/or counter narratives) in response to media portrayals of 'morally dangerous' homosexual lives and individuals who should not be around children. There are also dangers of social media revealing rather more information to students than a teacher would like. Staff should be extremely careful to adopt the highest security settings, not to befriend students on Facebook and to be cautious about which photos they upload.

Disclosure

This notion of disclosure is an important one and one in which there are many positive outcomes. The classroom is a place where learning is co-constructed through interactions between teachers and their students, with class discussions often being facilitated by self-disclosures between students. Whereas teachers spend the majority of their time in class covering relevant course content; highly effective teachers often disclose personal stories in order to foster a better student–teacher relationship (Schrodt, 2013). Research has also suggested that through self-disclosure, teachers are able to enhance student participation (Cayanus et al., 2009), student motivation, effective learning, classroom climate (Mazer et al., 2007) and teacher credibility. However, important though it may be, the use of self-disclosure is made more complicated for teachers with potentially stigmatising private information to share, as disclosing such information might undermine the benefits traditionally associated with self-disclosure in the classroom. Due to the sensitive nature of some private information – such as one's sexual identity – the use of self-disclosure by teachers of sexual minority status often is a challenging endeavour.

Self-disclosure becomes a more complicated issue and potential risk for teachers who identify as LGBT as they navigate coming out, a self-disclosure that may be perceived as negative by students, colleagues or parents. Despite vehemently urging LGBT teachers to continue to come out in the classroom, Russ et al. (2002) demonstrated that students view a teacher's sexual orientation as a salient – and often stigmatised – issue when it comes up in class. When a teacher was perceived as gay by his or her student audience, students rated that teacher as significantly less credible, were more likely to offer critical comments on feedback forms and were significantly less likely to suggest hiring the teacher in question (Russ et al., 2002).

Although not disclosing one's sexual orientation may seem like the obvious 'choice', withholding such a personal characteristic potentially hurts a LGBT teacher's immediacy and/or credibility and privileges heterosexual teachers who are free to disclose such information. LGBT teachers may feel like they are being dishonest to their own identities by not disclosing their sexual orientation and view coming out in the classroom as an effective teaching strategy.

Intersecting identities and stigma in the classroom

In labelling theory (Riddick, 2012) recognises the tendency of the majority to negatively label minorities as deviant from the physical, psychological, social or cultural norms. Labels become descriptors or categorisations that can carry a 'stigma'. A stigma is a label that has a powerfully negative character that influences a person's self-concept and social identity. Stigmas may be seen as personal attributes that are deeply discrediting, to the effect that they mark an individual as different from socially acceptable identity categories. Meisenbach (2010) suggests that any stigma necessitates a sense of 'not-us' in order to designate stigmatised persons as different from socially accepted identities. To a large extent, sexual orientations that transgress the societal assumption and positive valence of heteronormativity or heterosexuality remain stigmatised in many cultures, prompting many LGBT teachers to avoid declaring their sexual orientations in an attempt to evade the potentially negative ramifications of doing so (Barker and Reavey, 2009). In other words, the stigma against homosexuality faced by LGBT teachers and perceived by their students depends on how teachers view the stigma themselves and how they manage the stigma in the context of the classroom.

Activity: Labelling

- What labels might someone attach to a teacher who declares their sexual orientation?
- How might these labels then be used to stigmatise an individual?
- Would it make a difference if the teacher was heterosexual?

Of course, an individual rarely experiences stigma in relation to a single marginalised identity category, which makes it necessary to acknowledge the intersectionality of so-called 'identity markers'. Intersectionality refers to 'the multidimensionality and complexity of human experience and describes the site where multiple identities come together or intersect' (Marsiglia and Kulis, 2009, p. 42). For example, ethnic minority LGBT individuals often face complicated layers of racism and heterosexism in different contexts (Allen, 2011). Ultimately, intersectionality avoids seeing sexual orientation on the basis of a single socially constructed identity and examines the complexity of marginalised individuals' identities. Hendrix et al. (2003) explain that 'when the multiple identities we bring to the classroom are not acknowledged and appreciated, [a] sense of invisibility is felt' (p. 178).

In contrast, intersectionality calls for recognition of the varying and competing identities that individuals who identify as LGBT navigate in the classroom. LGBT teachers are uniquely challenged with the decision to disclose their sexual orientation, a disclosure that might enhance student familiarity and motivation, or polarise students and result in demotivation. Because persons of sexual minority status sometimes lack visible markers of their stigmatised identities, many LGBT individuals feel pressured to 'pass' or conceal information about oneself to 'preserve, sustain, and encourage others' predisposed assumptions about one's identity' (Spradlin, 1998, p. 598). Additionally, many LGBT teachers have lamented that disclosing sexual orientation is often seen as 'flaunting' their sexuality, while not speaking of it can be seen as lying to one's self – essentially placing LGBT teachers in a 'double-bind' position. Thus it may well be that the individual identifies the costs and benefits of disclosing their sexual identity before making a decision.

Activity: To disclose or not to disclose? That is the question

- What dilemmas might a teacher thinking about disclosing be faced with?
- Fill in the table below, with some suggestions.

	Me as a person	My organisation
Why I should disclose my identity		
Why I should not disclose my identity		

In their research, McKenna-Buchanan et al. (2015) suggest that there are a number of strategies used when teachers disclose sexual identity. These are given in Table 7.1 below.

Table 7.1 Strategies for disclosing sexual identity

Strategy	Example
Intentional and direct verbal or non-verbal disclosure of sexual orientation	'I basically told them the first day, I'm gay, and sometimes I'll talk about gay topics, like things on television, gay characters, things like that. I'm going to talk about those things.'
Reciprocity: intentional disclosure of private information in response to others' disclosure of or request for personal information	'When they come out to me, I always come out to them.'
Ambiguity: intentional use of ambiguous or indirect messages to subtly indicate one's sexual orientation	'When a student asks me "what are you doing this weekend?" instead of sharing I have a date with my "girlfriend", I intentionally shift the pronoun to 'partner' to remain neutral.'
Intentional disregard of someone's inquiry, or redirection of someone's attention to another topic of discussion	'I would deflect the intrusiveness of such a question. I would say something like, "that's funny, and I never ask you about your relationships."'
Avoidance: intentional avoidance of any possible reference to sexual orientation so as to maintain full concealment of one's own sexual orientation	'I don't come out because I feel like it will jeopardize my credibility even more.'

> **Activity: Consequences of adopting a strategy**
>
> - What could be the positive consequences for the teacher in resorting to these strategies?
> - Are there any potential risks?

Conclusion

The area of sexuality within education is fundamentally a key contemporary issue which affects many lives now and in the future. Not only is there a debate surrounding challenging the heteronormative assumptions inherent in the discourses currently played out within compulsory and non-compulsory education, there are a growing number of individuals who identify as GSM, a term that covers sexuality (bisexual, asexual, lesbian, gay, queer or questioning) and sex/gender (intersex, transgender, transsexual, queer or questioning). Debates are inherent throughout education, but nowhere are these more profound as in the area of sexuality. 'Do I disclose? What might happen if I do?' 'How can we make schools a safe environment for these individuals?' 'What about an inclusive curriculum which challenges stereotypes?' 'Should educational policy and practice reflect society?' ... the list of questions internally or externally verbalised are fundamental if we are to engage in meaningful discussion in an aspect which affects so many lives.

Case study 7.5: Peter

When it came to 'coming out', I dithered for quite some time as I had no idea how to approach the subject. Eventually in a Year 11 physics lesson a student noticed me absent-mindedly playing with my engagement ring (I had recently proposed to my boyfriend) and said, 'Ooh watch out sir, if you drop that your girlfriend will be really angry.'

I quietly replied, 'It's a he actually; I'm getting married to a man.' A wave of silence swept the classroom, followed by a barrage of curious questions. 'How come you're gay sir, you don't sound camp?' and 'But you don't sound at all like [an openly gay student in the year]' or 'Is it legal to marry a man then?' We spent a few minutes calmly discussing it and then carried on with the lesson without any problems – I even managed a proper plenary! I was truly relieved, and somewhat surprised that there had been not even the slightest hint of a critical or negative reaction. In fact, one student, a very imposing Asian boy, said to me at the end of the lesson 'Seriously Sir, that was big – pretty [sic] ... respect for being honest.'

Since then I've done short, age-appropriate assemblies to every year at school on the meaning of words such as 'gay', 'lesbian', 'transvestite', 'transgender', and about the effect of using 'gay' as a derogatory word. I've done other assemblies on the structure and growth of the teenage brain and why it makes coming out particularly hard.

(Weston, 2012)

- What does this example tell you about the positive consequences for both the individual and the school, of identifying as a gay teacher?
- Is answering questions in a matter-of-fact way a suitable response?

Case study 7.6: John

I'm not ashamed of being gay, and it's a completely natural thing for me to be, erm ... I guess there's kind of two sides to the argument. One is whether I'm just kind of a good role model, I do what I do and people find out and, 'Oh, he's gay'. ... I think sometimes by going out of your way to force an issue, there's then more opportunities for people to pick up on and criticise, 'Because he's gay, it's because he's gay' ... Part of me would love to be in a job where I could just be me. I do feel that on occasion, I'm in school, and I'm not allowed to ... 'Not allowed' perhaps is the wrong phrase but I feel that I shouldn't share the fact that I live with a man, share my life with a man, that I like having sex with men.

(Gray, 2013)

- How does this teacher view the notion of being a role model?
- How does John view the relationship between professional and private life?

Case study 7.7: Anon

Scared about the kids, scared about the parents, scared about the impression it makes of yourself, scared about their judgement, their comments, their opinions and their sweeping statements they will make, what rumours will go around school, speculation that starts. I'm assuming here, I'm probably wrong in saying this; they [parents] probably would have a negative image of me if they knew that I was gay and they would be afraid to let their kids come into my lessons … I'd hate to have all those complaints in school and me being told that some kids can't be in my lessons because their parents don't want them to.

(Edwards et al., 2014)

As a closeted, gay primary teacher, I constantly monitored my behaviours around children. I was anxious about how other teachers, parents, and principals would interpret my interactions and relationships with my students.

(Magnusa and Lundin, 2016)

If you were interviewing these teachers, what questions would you ask them about how it felt not be open about their sexual identity within their schools?

Suggested reading

Bowl, M. (ed.) (2012) *Gender, Masculinities and Lifelong Learning*. London: Routledge.

This book reflects on current debates and discourses around gender and education in which some academics, practitioners and policy-makers have referred to a crisis of masculinity.

Dijk, L. van and Driel, B. van (eds) (2007) *Challenging Homophobia: Teaching About Sexual Diversity*. Stoke-on-Trent: Trentham.

This book tells how educators in various national and cultural contexts deal with prejudice, discrimination, stereotyping and sometimes overt violence against sexual minorities, particularly lesbians and gays. This book focuses on the importance of changing the attitudes of people who believe that their homophobic views on sexuality are morally superior.

McCormack, M. (2012) *The Declining Significance of Homophobia: How Teenage Boys Are Redefining Masculinity and Heterosexuality*. New York and Oxford: Oxford University Press.

Research has traditionally shown high schools to be hostile environments for LGBT youth. Boys have used homophobia to prove their masculinity and distance themselves from homosexuality. Despite these findings over the last three decades, The Declining Significance of Homophobia tells a different story. Drawing on fieldwork and interviews of young men in three British high schools, the author shows how heterosexual male students are inclusive of their gay peers and proud of their pro-gay attitudes. He finds that being gay does not negatively affect a boy's popularity, but being homophobic does.

Taylor, Y., Hines, S. and Casey, M. E. (eds) (2011) *Theorizing Intersectionality and Sexuality*. Basingstoke: Palgrave Macmillan.

This book re-examines political, conceptual and methodological concerns of 'intersectionality', bringing these into conversation with sexuality studies. As a whole, the collection seeks to weave a more complex, shifting and contested map of sexual identifications, politics and inequalities as these (dis)connect across time and place, re-constituted in relation to class, disability, ethnicity, gender and age. Empirical, methodological and theoretical concerns are brought together, serving to demonstrate contemporary intersections as imagined by researchers in desiring and questioning.

References

Adams, G. R., Berzonsky, M. D. and Keating, L. (2006) Psychosocial resources in first-year university students: The role of identity processes and social relationships. *Journal of Youth and Adolescence* 35:1, 679–680.

Allen, K. D. (2011) *Self Object Needs, Homophobia, Heterosexism Among Gay Men During Emerging Adulthood*. Available at: http://pqdtopen.proquest.com/pubnum/3434973.html?FMT=AI

Allen, L. (2015) Picturing queer at school. *Journal of LGBT Youth*, 12:4, 367–384.

Anderson, E. (2011) Updating the outcome: Gay athletes, straight teams, and coming out in educationally based sport teams. *Gender & Society* 25:2, 250–268.

Aragon, S. R., Poteat, V. P., Espelage, D. L. and Koenig, B. W. (2014) The influence of peer victimization on educational outcomes for LGBTQ and non-LGBTQ high school students. *Journal of LGBT Youth*, 11:1, 1–19.

Barker, M. and Reavey, P. (2009) Self-disclosure in sexualities teaching. *Feminism & Psychology*, 19:2, 194–198.

Bourdieu, P. (2001) *Masculine Domination*, (trans. R. Nice), Cambridge: Polity Press.

Burleson, W. E. (2005) *Bi America*. New York: Harrington Park Press.

Buston, K. and Hart, G. (2001) Heterosexism and homophobia in Scottish school sex education: Exploring the nature of the problem. *Journal of Adolescence*, 24:1, 95–109.

Cayanus, J. L., Martin, M. M. and Goodboy, A. K. (2009) The relation between teacher self-disclosure and student motives to communicate. *Communication Research Reports*, 26:22, 105–113.

Coker, T. R., Austin, S. B. and Schuster, M. A. (2010) The health and health care of lesbian, gay, and bisexual adolescents. *Annual Review of Public Health*, 31, 457–477.

Connell, C. (2015) *School's Out: Gay and Lesbian Teachers in the Classroom*. Oakland, CA: University of California Press.

Craig K., Bell, D. and Leschied, A. (2011) Pre-service teachers' knowledge and attitudes regarding school-based bullying. *Canadian Journal of Education*, 34:2, 21–33.

Dilley, P. (2005) Which way out? A typology of non-heterosexual male collegiate identities. *Journal of Higher Education*, 76, 56–88.

Edwards, L. L., Brown, D. H. K. and Smith, L. (2014) 'We are getting there slowly': Lesbian teacher experiences in the post-Section 28 environment. *Sport, Education and Society*, 21:3, 299–318.

Eliason, M. J. (1997) The prevalence and nature of biphobia in heterosexual undergraduate students. *Archives of Sexual Behavior* 26:3, 317–326.

Endo, H., Reece-Miller, P. C. and Santavicca, N. (2010) Surviving in the trenches: A narrative inquiry into queer teachers' experiences and identity. *Teaching and Teacher Education*, 26:4, 1023–1030.

Epstein, D. (1994) Introduction: Lesbian and gay equality in education – problems and possibilities. In Epstein, D. (ed.) *Challenging Lesbian and Gay Inequalities in Education*. Buckingham: Open University Press.

Epstein, D. (2000) Sexualities and education: Catch 28. *Sexualities* 3:4, 387–394.

Eribon, D. (2004) *Insult and the Making of the Gay Self*. Durham, NC: Duke University Press.

Espelage, D. L., Aragon, S. R., Birkett, M. and Koenig, B. W. (2008) Homophobic teasing, psychological outcomes, and sexual orientation among high school students: What influence do parents and schools have? *School Psychology Review* [Special issue], 37:2, 202–216.

Evans, N. J. and Broido, E. M. (1999) Coming out in college residence halls. *Journal of College Student Development* 40:6, 658–668.

Ferfolja, T. (1998) Australian lesbian teachers – a reflection of homophobic harassment of high school teachers in New South Wales government schools. *Gender & Education*, 10:4, 401–415.

Flowers, P. and Buston, K. (2001) 'I was terrified of being different': Exploring gay men's accounts of growing-up in a heterosexist society. *Journal of Adolescence*, 24:1, 51–65.

Foucault, M. (1992) *The Use of Pleasure. The History of Sexuality: Volume 2* (trans. R. Hurley). London: Penguin Books.

Gorman-Murray, A. (2008) Queering the family home. *Gender, Place and Culture*, 15:1, 31–44.

Grace, A. B. and Benson, F. J. (2000) Using autobiographical queer life narratives of teachers to connect personal, political and pedagogical spaces. *International Journal of Inclusive Education*, 4:2, 89–109.

Gray, E. M. (2013) Coming out as a lesbian, gay or bisexual teacher: Negotiating private and professional worlds. *Sex Education*, 13:6, 702–714.

Hardie, A. (2012) Lesbian teachers and students: Issues and dilemmas of being 'out' in primary school. *Sex Education*, 12, 273–282.

Harwood, V. and Rasmussen, M. L. (2004) Studying schools with an ethic of discomfort. In Baker, B. and Heyning, K. (eds) *Dangerous Coagulations? The Uses of Foucault in the Study of Education*. New York: Peter Lang.

Hendrix, K. G., Jackson, II, R. L. and Warren, J. R. (2003) Shifting academic landscapes: Exploring co-identities, identity negotiation, and critical progressive pedagogy. *Communication Education*, 52:3–4, 177–190.

Henrickson, M. (2008) 'You have to be strong to be gay': Bullying and educational attainment in LGB New Zealanders. *Journal of Gay & Lesbian Social Services*, 19:3–4, 67–85.

Herek, G. M. (2002) Heterosexuals' attitudes toward bisexual men and women in the United States. *The Journal of Sex Research*, 39:4, 264–274.

Herek, G. M. (2004) Beyond "homophobia": Thinking about sexual stigma and prejudice in the twenty-first century. *Sexuality Research and Social Policy*, 1:2, 6–24.

Hill, A. (2015) School for LGBT pupils planned for Manchester. Available at: www.theguardian.com/education/2015/jan/16/school-for-lesbian-gay-bisexual-transgender-pupils-manchester

Hunt, R. and Jenson, J. (2007) *The School Report: Young People's Experiences of Young Gay People in Britain's Schools*. London, UK: Stonewall.

Irwin, J. (2002) Discrimination against gay men, lesbians, and transgender people working in education. *Journal of Gay and Lesbian Social Services*, 14:2, 65–77.

Jackson, J. M. (2007) *Unmasking Identities: An Exploration of the Lives of Gay and Lesbian Teachers*. Lanham, MD: Lexington Books.

Jones, T. and Hillier, L. (2012) Sexuality education school policy for Australian GLBTIQ students. *Sex Education*, 12:4, 437–454.

Khyatt, D. (1997) Sex and the teacher: Should we come out in class? *Harvard Educational Review*, 67:1, 126–143.

King, J. (2004) The (im)possibility of gay teachers for young children. *Theory into Practice*, 43:2, 122–127.

Kjaran, J. I. and Jóhannesson, I. Á. (2013) Manifestations of heterosexism in Icelandic upper secondary schools and the responses of LGBT students. *Journal of LGBT Youth*, 10:4, 351–372.

Kjaran, J. I. and Jóhannesson, I. Á. (2015) Inclusion, exclusion and the queering of spaces in two Icelandic upper secondary schools. *Ethnography and Education*, 10:1, 42–59.

Kjaran, J. I. and Kristinsdóttir, G. (2015) Schooling sexualities and gendered bodies: Experiences of LGBT students in Icelandic upper secondary schools. *International Journal of Inclusive Education*, 19:9, 978–993.

Klein, F. (1993) *The Bisexual Option*, 2nd edn. Binghamton, NY: The Haworth Press.

Kosciw, J. G., Greytak, E. A., Diaz, E. M. and Bartkiewicz, M. J. (2009) Who, what, where, when, and why: Demographic and ecological factors contributing to hostile school climate for lesbian, gay, bisexual, and transgender youth. *Journal of Youth and Adolescence* 38:7, 976–988.

Kosciw, J. G., Greytak, E. A., Diaz, E. M. and Bartkiewicz, M. J. (2010) *The 2009 National School Climate Survey: The Experiences of Lesbian, Gay, Bisexual, and Transgender Youth in Our Nation's School*. New York, NY: GLSEN.

Kosciw, J. G., Greytak, E. A., Bartkiewicz, M. J., Boesen, M. J. and Palmer, N. A. (2012) *The 2011 National School Climate Survey: The Experiences of Lesbian, Gay, Bisexual and Transgender Youth in Our Nation's Schools*. New York: GLSEN.

Kosciw, J. G., Palmer, N. A. and Kull, R.M. (2015) Reflecting resiliency: Openness about sexual orientation and/or gender identity and its relationship to well-being and educational outcomes for LGBT students. *American Journal of Community Psychology*, 55:1, 167–178.

Legislation.gov.uk (2016) Available at: www.legislation.gov.uk/ukpga/1988/9/section/28

LGBT Foundation (2016) *Coming Out: Your Stories*. Available at: http://lgbt.foundation/information-advice/coming-out-support/coming-out-your-stories/

Lundin, M. (2016) Homo- and bisexual teachers' ways of relating to the heteronorm. *International Journal of Educational Research*, 75, 67–75.

Lusher, A. (2015) Gay pupils end up happier if they come out at school, new research suggests. *Independent*, 11 February. Available at: www.independent.co.uk/life-style/health-and-families/health-news/gay-pupils-end-up-happier-if-they-come-out-at-school-10039801.html

Magnusa, C. D. and Lundin, M. (2016) Challenging norms: University students' views on heteronormativity as a matter of diversity and inclusion in initial teacher education. *International Journal of Educational Research*, 79, 76–85.

Marsiglia, F. F. and Kulis, S. (2009) *Culturally Grounded Social Work: Diversity Oppression and Change*. Chicago, IL: Lyceum.

Mazer, J. P., Murphy, R. E. and Simonds, C. J. (2007) 'I'll see you on Facebook': The effects of computer-mediated teacher self-disclosure on student motivation, affective learning, and classroom climate. *Communication Education*, 56:1, 1–17.

McAnarney, E. (1985) Social maturation: A challenge for handicapped and chronically ill adolescents. *Journal of Adolescent Health Care*, 6, 90–101.

McCarty-Caplan, D. (2013) Schools, sex education, and support for sexual minorities: Exploring historic marginalization and future potential. *American Journal of Sexuality Education*, 8, 246–273.

McKenna-Buchanan, T., Munz, S. and Rudnick, J. (2015) To be or not to be out in the classroom: Exploring communication privacy management strategies of lesbian, gay, and queer college teachers. *Communication Education*, 64:3, 280–300.

Meisenbach, R. J. (2010) Stigma management communication: A theory and agenda for applied research on how individuals manage moments of stigmatized identity. *Journal of Applied Communication Research*, 38:3, 268–292.

Morris, M., McCormack, M. and Anderson, E. (2014) The changing experiences of bisexual male adolescents. *Gender and Education*, 26:4, 397–413.

Morrison, L. L. and L'Heureux, J. (2001) Suicide and gay/lesbian/bisexual youth: Implications for clinicians. *Journal of Adolescence*, 24:1, 39–49.

Msibi, T. (2012) 'I'm used to it now': Experiences of homophobia among queer youth in South African township schools. *Gender and Education*, 24:5, 515–533.

Munoz-Plaza, C., Crouse Quinn, S. and Rounds, K. A. (2002) *High School Journal*, 85:4, 52–63.

Nixon, D. and Givens, N. (2004) 'Miss, you're so gay.' Queer stories from trainee teachers. *Sex Education: Sexuality, Society and Learning*, 4:3, 217–237.

Nixon, D. and Givens, N. (2007) An epitaph to Section 28? Telling tales out of school about changes and challenges to discourses of sexuality. *International Journal of Qualitative Studies in Education*, 20, 449–471.

Ochs, R. (1996) Biphobia: It goes more than two ways. In Firestein, B. A. (ed.), *Bisexuality: The Psychology and Politics of an Invisible Minority*. Thousand Oaks, CA: Sage.

Piper, H. and Sikes. P. (2010) All teachers are vulnerable but especially gay teachers: Using composite fictions to protect research participants in pupil–teacher sex-related research. *Qualitative Inquiry*, 16:7, 566–574.

Poteat, V. P., O'Dwyer, L. M. and Mereish, E. H. (2012a) Changes in how students use and are called homophobic epithets over time: Patterns predicted by gender, bullying, and victimization status. *Journal of Educational Psychology*, 104, 393–406.

Poteat, V. P., Sinclair, K. O., DiGiovanni, C. D., Koenig, B. W. and Russell, S. T. (2012b) Gay–straight alliances are associated with student health: A multischool comparison of LGBTQ and heterosexual youth. *Journal of Research on Adolescence*, 23:2, 319–330.

Rasmussen, M. L. (2004) 'That's so gay!': A study of the deployment of signifiers of sexual and gender identity in secondary school settings in Australia and the United States. *Social Semiotics*, 14:3, 289–308.

Riddick, B. (2012) Labelling learnings with 'SEND': The good, the bad and the ugly. In D. Armstrong and G. Squires (Eds.), *Contemporary Issues in Special Educational Needs* (pp. 25–34). Glasgow: McGraw Hill.

Rivers, I. (2001) The bullying of sexual minorities at school. *Educational and Child Psychology*, 18:1, 32–46.

Robinson, J. P. and Espelage, D. L. (2011) Inequities in educational and psychological outcomes between LGBTQ and straight students in middle and high school. *Educational Researcher*, 40:7, 315–330.

Rudoe, N. (2010) Lesbian teachers' identity, power and the public/private boundary. *Sex Education*, 10:1, 23–36.

Russ, T. L., Simonds, C. J. and Hunt, S. K. (2002) Coming out in the classroom ... an occupational hazard?: The influence of sexual orientation on teacher credibility and perceived student learning. *Communication Education*, 51:33, 311–324.

Russell, S. T., Seif, H. and Truong, N. L. (2001) School outcomes of sexual minority youth in the United States: Evidence from a national study. *Journal of Adolescence*, 24, 111–127.

Ryan, C. and Rivers, I. (2003) Lesbian, gay, bisexual and transgender youth: Victimization and its correlates in the USA and UK. *Culture, Health & Sexuality*, 5:2, 103–119.

Savin-Williams, R. C. and Ream, G. L. (2003) Sex variations in the disclosure to parents of same-sex attractions. *Journal of Family Psychology*, 19:3, 429–438.

Schrodt, P. (2013) Content relevance and students' comfort with disclosure as moderators of instructor disclosures and credibility in the college classroom. *Communication Education*, 1:24, 116–121.

Sexton, S. (2012) Queer Otago secondary students' views of their schooling environment. *New Zealand Journal of Educational Studies*, 47:1, 93–105.

Spradlin, A. L. (1998) 'The price of passing': A lesbian perspective on authenticity in organizations. *Management Communication Quarterly*, 11:4, 598–605.

Talburt, S. (2004) Constructions of LGBT youth: Opening up subject positions. *Theory into Practice*, 43:2, 116–121.

Taylor, C., Peter, T., McMinn, T., Elliott, T., Beldom, S. and Ferry, A. (2011) *Every Class in Every School: The First National Climate Survey on Homophobia, Biphobia, and Transphobiailn Canadian Schools. Final Report.* Toronto, ON: Eagle Canada Human Rights Trust.

Waldo, C. R. (1998) Out on campus: Sexual orientation and academic climate in a university context. *American Journal of Community Psychology*, 26:5, 745–774.

Wardle, M. (2009) *Prejudice, Acceptance, Triumph: The Experience of Gay and Lesbian Teachers in Secondary Education.* London: Athena Press.

Weston, D. (2012) 'Coming out' at school. Available at: www.theguardian.com/teacher-network/2012/jan/30/coming-out-gay-teacher-sexuality

Williams, R. (2012) Being gay at school remains difficult for teachers. Available at: www.theguardian.com/education/2012/nov/26/gay-teachers-homophobia-stonewall-research

8 Special educational needs and disability

Categorisation and naming

Deborah Robinson

This chapter will explore:

- England's policy for Special Educational Needs and Disability (SEND);
- the relationship between categorisation, naming and power within social and educational systems;
- the theory of inclusion phobia;
- the dilemma of difference;
- conceptual and practical solutions.

Introduction

This chapter outlines current systems of *categorisation* and *naming* in England with a particular focus on SEND. In doing so it invites consideration of some of the difficulties that arise when social systems identify individuals who are in need of additional educational support. Though such systems may secure equal opportunities for those who need more from an education system than it might ordinarily provide, they can also incite the labelling and categorisation of human beings in ways that stigmatise and marginalise. For this reason, vociferous debate surrounds the practice of labelling within the field of SEND, with much of this focusing on how power is gained or lost in the fracas. This chapter explores the nature and scope of this debate with particular reference to the concepts of *inequality and biopower*, the *dilemma of difference* (Norwich, 2008) and the *inclusion phobia* (Robinson and Goodey, 2018; Goodey, 2015). Finally, potential solutions are explored while a case study illustrates the manner in which educational practitioners may mediate labels and categories in ways that foreground the uniqueness and capacities of individual children (Trussler and Robinson, 2015).

The policy context in England

This section will describe the current context for SEND in England. This context will serve to illustrate how naming and categorisation become weaponry in the battle for equality and, paradoxically, inequality within the same system.

In England, the 2014 Children and Families Act uses the term *special educational needs* (SEN) to identify children and young people who have significantly greater difficulty learning than their peers and/or who have a disability which makes access to mainstream education of the type generally available more difficult (DfE and DoH, 2015, p. 15). Those signified by SEN receive *special provision* defined as *additional to or different* from that which is usually provided. Fundamentally, this means that it costs more since such provision may include transport, placement in a special school, educational therapies or additional staffing. In England, children and young people who have SEN may also be identified as disabled. Disability under the law is 'a physical or mental impairment which has a long-term and substantial adverse effect on their ability to carry out normal day-to-day activities' (Equality Act, 2010, Section 6, 1). The SEN Code of Practice (DfE and DoH, 2015) notes that this definition includes sensory impairments such as those affecting sight or hearing, and long-term health conditions including asthma and epilepsy. Where a disability may affect access and opportunity in educational contexts such as schools and colleges, those so named 'disabled' will also qualify for special educational provision and occupy the category SEN. For this reason and for the purposes of professional shorthand, this cohort of children and young people are often identified by the group signifier *Special Educational Needs and Disabilities* (SEND).

In England, 1.3 million (15.4 per cent) children and young people are identified as having SEND. Just over 235,000 (2.8 per cent) have more exceptional and complex needs and will have a Statement or an Education, Health and Care Plan (EHCP)[1] along with a more significant level of different or additional provision (such as a place in a special school, transport costs, social care). This cohort is signified by the term *SEN with an EHCP*. Children and young people whose level of disability or learning difficulty do not warrant an EHCP are supported through funds that are delegated to schools and/or available from Local Authorities through an application process. This cohort is signified by the term *SEN Support*. Individuals who have an EHCP have more guarantees about additional resource allocation. Their right to appeal is also more firmly protected in law (DfE and DoH, 2015).

The levels of additional resource allocated to individuals are, at least in principle, proportional to the degree to which their learning difficulties and/or disabilities are exceptional or complex. The system can be likened to the system of *triage* commonly adopted in medical settings where those with the most urgent wounds or illnesses are treated first in situations where resources are stretched (Slee, 2010). Given that education systems have finite resources, the system is charged with identifying those worthy of additional expenditure in ways that are as fair and equitable as possible. Such a situation may demand a cold, hard and pragmatic approach to finding the most deserving among an educational population that contains more deserving individuals than the system can actually afford. In such a context, systems of naming and categorisation emerge as a necessary means to an end. In the same context, some names and categories gain worthiness (and hence expenditure) over others. Perhaps inevitably, practitioners, parents and learners find themselves engaged in a battle over scarce resources. Labels become weapons with which to call the state to order.

However, this can become a war game, one in which there are winners and losers and, potentially, one which results in collateral damage to those with less social and economic capital. For example, evident in England is the strong association between SEND and social deprivation. With little furore, the DfE (2015, p. 3) have reported, that 'across all age groups and levels of support, children who are eligible for free school meals are twice as likely to be identified as having SENDs than those who are not eligible.' However, Peer and Reid (2016) note that the association between

SEND and social deprivation is significantly more marked for some types of difficulty than others, specifically, social, emotional and mental health (SEMH) and moderate learning difficulties (MLD). Such categories are less likely to garner the additional protection and resource provided by an EHCP (DfE, 2015). Peer and Reid (2016) also argue that EHCPs are allocated to children living in more socially advantaged areas of the country and in this naming game autistic spectrum disorder is a front runner in garnering a more secure and significant contract of support (DfE, 2015). It is possible to surmise that those with the social and economic capital are more likely to *take* the powerful, resource-garnering labels while those with less are more likely to be *given* labels that garner little benefit but gain more stigma (Perry and Frances, 2010).

With such power play in mind, Dyson (2012) argues that the identifier SEND is not only a response to children and young people who happen to experience difficulties in school because of their impairments or individual idiosyncrasies. Rather it is a response to the educational impact of wider social inequalities, including those related to poverty, race and gender. Individuated identification and intervention habituated through policy means that the system can absolve itself from responsibility for radical change as 'much less attention is paid to contextual factors in children's social backgrounds' (Dyson, 2012, p. 52). For this reason, those who are more powerful, the *status quo*, can retain the traditional practices that gained them their privileged position in the first place. However, that contextual factors have a role to play in naming and categorisation is evident in contemporary data since, as noted, there are significant imbalances in the number of children identified as having SENDs among boys and children who are socially disadvantaged. Further, children and young people who speak English as an additional language are less likely to be identified with the marker SEND than those who speak English as a first language (DfE, 2015). Although complex factors are likely to be influencing these outcomes, statistics on who is being named, categorised and resourced may both mirror and perpetuate wider inequalities.

An important question surrounds whether the identification and interventions associated with the signifier SEND actually deliver more equitable outcomes for individuals within an education system. On this point there is some account of the positive impact of carefully designed and delivered interventions where children achieve more than they might do without them (Kavale, 2007; Mitchell, 2008) though other studies in the USA (Bielinski and Ysseldyke, 2000) imply that such interventions do not transform outcomes but ameliorate inequalities in ways that make them less visible. Blatchford *et al.* (2009) identify that where children and young people in schools are allocated support in the form of a teaching assistant, their progress in academic subjects is less than those with SENDs who do not have such support. Blatchford *et al.* (2009) suggest that this is, in part, a consequence of less time spent with teachers. In this way, SEND becomes a separator – one which puts distance between those so labelled and those who are not. What was originally conceived as a means of supporting equality (the allocation of teaching assistants to students with SENDs in mainstream schools) becomes an agent of segregation and poorer outcomes. If the system of naming and categorisation in England is not delivering emphatically on equality, what is it delivering? Tremain (2011) offers some explanation with reference to the concept of *biopower*.

Naming, categorising and biopower

Disability theorists have demonstrated sustained interest in the oppressive dynamic of naming and categorising. Tremain (2011) draws on the work of Foucault (1978) to explain how those who are powerful in a society construct the ideal (or normal) human body and mind. Where an individual is not of an ideal (or normal) body and mind, they become a focus for measurement, appraisal, categorisation and qualification. They also become a focus for intervention and correction as the state is licensed to intrude upon their physiological and psychological space. Foucault (1978, p. 144) argued that this was the expression of a 'normalising society' which operated 'power centred on life' which could be named *biopower*. The eventual consequence is the subjugation of disabled people. Those labelled as 'disabled' might come to believe that their 'defects' or 'abnormalities' make them governable and in need of governance. Hence, being categorised as an individual with learning difficulties or disabilities incites the surrendering of power and control. Returning to the question posited earlier about what the SEND system is delivering, Tremain (2011) would argue that what is delivered is in the service of the status quo.

Of course, such theories seem grand and prophetic. However, Gray and Ridden (2005) present a series of life-maps that recount the real experiences of some disabled people growing up in the 1960s, 1970s and 1980s in England and these represent a more complex picture of how identification and naming can both help and hinder the achievement of equality. For example, Matthew (who has autistic spectrum disorder) found more happiness and stability after his diagnosis than before it. He recounts negative memories of his mainstream school where 'they didn't understand, did they, my problem' and his experience of special schools where 'they were fair'. However, Matthew's story, as he tells it, implies that he had little choice or influence over what placements or supports were provided for him. He also experienced placements in specialist further education that were 'a nightmare. They treated me like a thirteen-year old' (Gray and Ridden, 2005, p. 102), and communicates some yearning for independence. Similarly, Sue yearned for and valued her independence. She had experienced brain damage after being knocked down by a car when she was nine years old and following her recovery she was placed in special schools, something she resented. She also resented being told that she had communication difficulties and that she had to go to a residential college because, as her parents said, 'she would have to grin and bear it as there was nowhere else to go' (Gray and Ridden, 2005, p. 83) and all of this added to her feelings of helplessness and frustration about the lack of control she had over her own life. Such stories are common among disabled people (Barnes and Mercer, 2010), though Norwich (2008) explains that the act of identification creates dilemmas that bring positive and negative consequences in ways that are, to some extent, unresolvable.

The dilemma of difference

Norwich (2008) offers the concept the *dilemma of difference* to explain why naming and categorisation are both helpful and unhelpful, and in doing so offers a more moderate and less weaponised account of the system and what it is challenged by. Drawing on Minow (1990), Norwich explains how education systems struggle to manage children who are 'different' without stigmatising them or denying them relevant opportunities. The problem arises when delivery of special benefits can be used to reinforce stereotypes in implicit or explicit ways. For example, where children and young people have an allocated support assistant, the received message is that this is because they cannot manage, they are not capable and they are to some extent helpless and separate. The system demands some departure from an identity of 'normality' in order for needs to be taken into account and, in doing so, may marginalise those so provided for. With this in mind,

Norwich (2008, p. 3) argues that the *dilemma of difference* is best explained through understanding the term 'dilemma' to mean a situation where 'there is a choice between alternatives, all of which are unfavourable and risk negative consequences'. Hence, the identification dilemma takes the following form:

- If children and young people experiencing difficulties in learning are identified, categorised and labelled they are more likely to be treated as different and even stigmatised, devalued and marginalised.
- If children and young people experiencing difficulties in learning are not identified, then it is less likely that they will garner the recognition and additional resources that can support their equal opportunity.

In this way, the process of naming is inevitably and paradoxically both helpful and harmful in its pursuit of equitable outcomes. Relatedly, Dyson *et al.* (2012) have considered equitability in education systems across the world, noting that liberal democracies adopt policies that reflect a basic contradiction in the following form:

- There is an intention to treat all learners as essentially the same so that they might be entitled to occupy a universal education system.
- There is an equal and opposite intention to treat them as different.

Dyson *et al.* (2012) argue that policy and practice is, in fact, an attempt at resolving these dilemmas. Further, these resolutions are unstable in character since they change as cohorts, social contexts, economic contexts and cultures do. For this reason, policy for SEND will always be imperfect and subject to tumult, though the core tension, the *dilemma of difference*, will remain as a more constant presence. Though the *dilemma of difference* is widely debated under the question of naming or not naming, Riddick (2012) offers a more practical analysis of the positive and negative consequences of identification while also offering some solutions which are discussed later in the chapter.

Riddick (2012) argues that labelling is wrongly vilified and that it is more helpful to consider labelling as process that can be managed to secure positive outcomes. Riddick (2012) explores the advantages of labelling and notes that the naming or categorising of an individual's difficulties under the banner of, for example 'dyslexia' or 'autistic spectrum disorder' may support acknowledgement and understanding of a learner's difficulties in ways that enable appropriate provision. Such naming also offers constructs that can be researched. Practitioners can turn to this body of research for guidance on the most effective forms of intervention and support.

Being named or categorised might also enable those with similar types of difference to develop their own culture and advocacy forums in ways that are empowering and, in so doing, support greater self-understanding. Labels (such as 'autistic spectrum disorder') may also perpetuate more acceptance from the wider public about behaviour that may seem odd or culturally distasteful. Hence, labels may support the construction of 'greater tolerance and understanding' (Riddick, 2012, p. 28). However, also acknowledged is the fact that labels can do all of these things in reverse and that they can be a method of control, pathologisation and an arbiter of inappropriate support. In support of Dyson (2012), Riddick (2012) suggests that the process of naming places blame for learning difficulty within the learner in faulty social systems. Riddick (2012, p. 28) argues that stigmatisation is not always the consequence of labelling but may simply be an encapsulation of wider negative attitudes – withholding a label in the hope that this will avoid stigmatisation can, in some cases, be 'like burying your head in the sand, thus denying the reality of everyday experiences'. MacDonald (2010) notes that where people have 'hidden' disabilities such as autism and dyslexia, they are somewhat positive about being so named since this supports greater self-understanding, tolerance and acceptance. An important question centres on whether it is just for society to demand a label or a category before it gives permission for difference, and other points of critique can be drawn from Asprey and Nash (2006, p. 23) who provide a rich illustration of the ambivalence that children and young people feel about their labels. For example, in recounting the comments of a 14-year-old boy with a degenerative muscle condition:

> I suppose I do get treated differently now and again, I think that's a good thing and sometimes I feel it's a bad thing. I mean obviously I want to be treated the same, but then sometimes I'd like to be treated differently ... I like to be asked.
> (Asprey and Nash, 2006, p. 23)

Riddick (2012) suggests that the process of identification could be mediated by the application of wise labelling (discussed more fully later). In the call for voice in the quotation above ('I like to be asked'), it is important to ask why Riddick (2012) does not account for the way in which individuals so labelled may also be charged with mediating the impact of their labels or in deciding whether or not one is to be applied.

Learning disability and the inclusion phobia

Goodey (2015) argues that the label *learning disability* (and related diagnoses such as autistic spectrum disorder) is conventionally regarded as a permanent and natural state, identified by an objective system of measurement based on 'reliable' scientific accounts of classifiable human difference. However, the permanence of such labels and categories is questionable since Goodey's systematic analysis of the history of intellectual disability reveals that, as a construct, learning disability has not always existed (Goodey, 2011). Rather, it is an artefact of a more contemporary obsession with intelligence, so measured by psychologists. It is also the consequence of a society dominated by the need to produce and prosper.

Goodey (2015) draws on Timimi (2011, p. 5) to explain how constructs such as 'autism' emerge to serve needs and obsessions of neo-liberal societies whose economies demand particular personalities and competencies – autism becomes a 'catch-all metaphor' for a set of unrelated behaviours that represent 'a lack of the type of social and emotional competences ... necessary for societies dominated by neo-liberal political foundations'. In more straightforward terms, what this means is that individuals who do not behave in ways that serve conventional forms of productivity and 'money making' are labelled as defective so that they may either be corrected and made more productive or taken out of the way so they do not impede the productivity of wider society.

Goodey (2015) argues that systems of labelling and categorisation represent the innate propensity of social systems to manifest phobic responses to human difference. In the past (for example in the Middle Ages) inclusion phobia was not targeted at those with learning disabilities (which as a concept did not exist) but towards other groups such as heretics. A heretic was an individual who lived by a religion not practised or permitted by rulers and sovereigns. Heretics were considered a danger and a threat to the powerful and systems of violent punishment were permitted and mandated. Heretics, then, were an extreme outgroup for whom segregation, punishment and exile were considered appropriate (and even sacred) forms of intervention.

In the case of the inclusion phobia, dominant secondary institutions (such as those allied to education and medicine) perpetuate categorisation and labelling and identify an extreme outgroup for whom segregation (in special schools for example) is sanctioned in law. However, Robinson and Goodey (2018) argue that the basis of this practice, as it stands on labelling and categorisation, is shaky to say the least. For example, the word 'autism' was coined only a century ago; moreover, since then, having denoted for the first half of its existence a retreat into the imagination, it has been transformed into something like an absence of imagination. Criteria for identification have also been continually re-assembled and re-defined to absorb an increasingly varied spectrum of individuals who may defy categorisation. Robinson and Goodey (2018) argue that this reveals an essential contradiction which lies in the urge to preserve a system that runs on *fixed* diagnoses from contamination by a reality that is *fluid*. To the extent that psychological categories risk being exposed as temporary and tied to current, passing forms of social organisation, the more firmly they must be tied down by a research vocabulary that links to seemingly stable and permanent medical certainties ('diagnosis', 'genes', etc.). In summary, the system strives to validate itself and continues to label and categorise in ways that may be both inaccurate and stigmatising.

Conclusion

This chapter has exposed some of the dilemmas and contradictions inherent in a system that seeks to identify those in need of additional educational support. It has explored the debate that surrounds the positive and negative consequences of naming and categorisation through analysis of the theories of *biopower*, the *dilemma of difference* and the *inclusion phobia*. What emerged was that labels and categories are not always the scientifically stable, pure, reliable or simple entities that it may be assumed they are. Educational debate portrays them as powerful weapons through which the state, education systems and individuals may give and take power and resources. The question remains, what can educators and education systems do to resolve the tensions created by a system of naming?

Riddick (2012) offers the practice of *wise labelling* as a potential solution. Wise labelling is conceptualised as a collaborative process that should start through the positing of key questions including:

- Is there a need for a label or with better teaching will needs be met?
- Will the label enable more positive self-evaluations and self-awareness or not?
- Will the label help educators to decide on appropriate and effective interventions?

Riddick (2012) argues that the negative effects of naming and categorisation can be mediated by well-informed practitioners who operate reflectively in this way. The case study presented below offers support for Riddick's argument since it demonstrates (in the face of what has been the pessimistic tone of this chapter), that those working in the field of education do have a sophisticated awareness of the dangerous power of labels and categories. In case study 8.1, Tom (a teaching assistant) is actively diminishing the power of a label in pursuit of equality and recognition for the unique qualities of an individual child. The case study (presented at the end of this chapter) is an interesting example of the manner in which practitioners (who are wise enough) can mediate the negative power of labels and categories. Trussler and Robinson (2015) argue that where teachers can use informed professional judgement to construct practices that include children with SENDs through the use of systematic enquiry, they will be more likely to mediate the negative impact of labelling on their learners and on themselves. However, Robinson (2017) argues that this is less likely to happen in contexts where teachers are over-directed by a centralised curriculum, state interference and teacher training programmes that emphasise 'learning on the job' over intellectual engagement with the challenges of meeting diverse needs in education systems that have finite and increasingly limited resources.

Similarly, Norwich (2008) and Lewis and Norwich (2005) purport that it is wise to expose and explain the dilemma of difference to new and experienced teachers so that they might better understand (and manage) the contradictions they are faced with in the classroom context. They should also be exposed to the vociferous debates about current categories and their accuracy and usefulness. All of these solutions emphasise the importance of not being blind to the power of naming and categorisation to do good and evil, nor to the contradictions that arise in trying to provide additional educational support for those who might need it. In the end, wise and politically aware teachers are those most able to resolve this dilemma in ways that enable social justice for diverse learners in education systems. They are potential peacemakers in the war of naming.

Case study 8.1: Wise labelling

Key questions
While you are reading this case study consider the following:
- How and why does Tom keep Christopher's label at a distance?
- In what ways does Tom's management of a label reflect wise labelling?
- To what extent does this reflect the dilemma of difference playing out in the real world?
- What approach to 'training' could help practitioners to develop wise labelling?

Tom has been appointed by a primary school to support a child called Christopher with the label of SEND and Williams Syndrome. Tom explained that his previous experience was as an assistant at a pre-school and that on acquiring an NVQ qualification he had applied to be a Teaching Assistant at the school, specifically in relation to supporting Christopher. He didn't feel experienced as a TA and didn't want anyone to think he was an expert.

When reflecting on how important it was to know about Christopher's 'condition', Tom said that for him, the most important thing was getting to know Christopher. He explained that he had done some reading and research on Williams Syndrome but that 'no child is a textbook child'. He also commented that meeting with Christopher's mother was the most important thing since it put things into context since 'she told me exactly how it was for them'. Tom explained that the 'theory' of the condition had not yet applied much to Christopher. For example, he didn't have as much difficulty with mathematics and number skills as was usually said to be the case and the list of characteristics for the condition on the one hand didn't relate to him, but on the other could have related to lots of other children in the class. Tom said, 'For me, it was getting to know Christopher and getting to know his mum, meeting his family that was the most useful thing.' He also said that he thought that knowledge of the 'theory' might be relevant though because behaviours like maths difficulties might emerge as he got older and he would know how to interpret that and what to do if it emerged.

Suggested reading

Blatchford, P., Bassett, P., Brown, P., Martin, C., Russell, A. and Webster, R. (2009) *Deployment and Impact of Support Staff Project*. Research Report RB148. London: DCSF.
Goodey, C. (2015) *Learning Disability and the Inclusion Phobia: Past, Present, Future*. London: Routledge.

Note

1 An EHC plan replaces a statement of SEN. It is a legally binding summary of the provision that is to be made for an individual in response to their needs and aspirations. It focusses on positive outcomes in the areas of health, education, and independent living.

References

Asprey, A. and Nash, T. (2006) The Importance of Awareness and Communication for the Inclusion of Young People with Life-Limiting and Life-Threatening Conditions in Mainstream Schools and Colleges. *British Journal of Special Education*, 33: 10–18.
Barnes, C. and Mercer, G. (2010) *Exploring Disability*. London: Polity.
Bielinski, J. and Ysseldyke, J. E. (2000) *Interpreting Trends in the Performance of Special Education Students. NCEO Technical Report No. 27*. Minneapolis, MN: University of Minnesota, National Centre on Educational Outcomes.
Blatchford, P., Bassett, P., Brown, P., Martin, C., Russell, A. and Webster, R. (2009) *Deployment and Impact of Support Staff Project*. Research Report RB148. London: DCSF.
Department for Education (2015) *Statistical First Release: Special Educational Needs in England, January: 2015*. London: DfE.
Department for Education and Department of Health (DoE and DoH) (2015) *Special Educational Needs and Disability Code of Practice: 0 to 25 years*. London: DfE.
Dyson, A. (2012) Special Educational Needs and the 'World Out There'. In *Contemporary Issues in Special Educational Needs: Considering the Whole Child*. London: Open University Press/McGraw Hill Education.
Dyson, A., Ainscow, M., Goldrick, S. and West, M. (2012) *Developing Equitable Education Systems*. London: Routledge.
Equality Act (2010) Chapter 5. London: The Stationery Office.
Foucault, M. (1978) *The History of Sexuality Volume 1: An Introduction*. London: Allen Lane.
Goodey, C. E. (2011) *A History of Intelligence and 'Intellectual Disability': The Shaping of Psychology in Early Modern Europe*. Oxon: Ashgate.
Goodey, C. (2015) *Learning Disability and the Inclusion Phobia: Past, Present, Future*. London: Routledge.
Gray, B. and Ridden, G. (2005) *Lifemaps of People with Learning Disabilities*. London: Jessica Kingsley.
Kavale, K. A. (2007) Quantitative Research Synthesis: Meta-Analysis of Research on Meeting Special Educational Needs. In Florian, L. (ed.), *Handbook of Special Education*. London: Sage, pp. 207–221.
Lewis, A. and Norwich, B. (2005) *Special Teaching for Special Children?* London: David Fulton.
MacDonald, S. J. (2010) Towards a Social Reality of Dyslexia. *British Journal of Learning Disabilities*, 38, 271–279.

Minow, M. (1990) *Making All the Difference: Inclusion and Exclusion and American Law*. Ithaca, NY: Cornell University Press.
Mitchell, D. (2008) *What Really Works in Special and Inclusive Education? Using Evidence-based Teaching Strategies*. Abingdon: Routledge.
Norwich, B. (2008) *Dilemmas of Difference, Inclusion and Disability: International Perspectives and Future Directions*. London: Routledge.
Peer, L. and Reid, G. (2016) *Special Educational Needs: A Guide for Inclusive Practice*. London: Sage.
Perry, E. and Frances, B. (2010) *The Social Class Gap for Educational Achievement: A Review of the Literature*. London: RSA.
Riddick, B. (2012) Labelling Learners with SEND, the Good, the Bad and the 'Ugly'. In Armstrong, D. and Squires G. (eds), *Contemporary Issues in Special Educational Needs: Considering the Whole Child*. Maidenhead: Open University Press/McGraw Hill Education.
Robinson, D. (2017) The Problem of Inclusive Pedagogy in Initial Teacher Education: Some More Thoughts on the Way Forward. *Teaching and Teacher Education* (forthcoming).
Robinson, D. and Goodey, C. (2018) The Inclusion Phobia and its Measurement: Repositioning the Pathology. *British Journal of Special Education* (forthcoming).
Slee, R. (2010) Political Economy, Inclusive Education and Teacher Education, In C. Forlin (ed.), *Changing Paradigms and Innovative Approaches to Teacher Education for Inclusion*. London: Routledge, pp. 13–22.
Timimi, S. (2011) *The Myth of Autism*. London: Macmillan.
Tremain, L. (2005) *Foucault and the Government of Disability*. Michigan: University of Michigan Press.
Trussler, S. and Robinson, D. (2015) *Inclusive Practice in the Primary School*. London: Sage.

9 Self-harm

Dispelling the myths

Ang Davey and Anna Davey

This chapter explores:

- the evolution of the meaning of self-harm;
- what is self-harm;
- who self-harms – characteristics of people who self-harm and incidence rates;
- why people self-harm – antecedents and consequences;
- strategies to prevent and manage self-harm.

> **Activity: Defining terms**
>
> Before beginning this chapter, write down what you think self-harm is. What sort of behaviours do people who self-harm exhibit? At the end of the chapter, revisit your thoughts here to see if your views have changed.

Evolution of the meaning of self-harm

Before 1945, self-harm was often regarded as attempted suicide. This was because self-harm was a secretive and hidden activity and only came to light if someone 'overdid' it and had to take themselves to the Accident and Emergency department at their local hospital or summon an ambulance to transport them there. The development of the Welfare State after World War II (1945) provided opportunities to support people who self-harmed to an extent where emergency treatment was not needed. From this time, self-harm was seen as a 'cry for help' and the National Health Service offered support for underlying causes through a range of treatments including counselling and/or antidepressants. In the latter part of the 20th century, self-harm started to be seen not as communicative (i.e. a cry for help) but instead as a behaviour designed to self-manage internal emotional pain. From the 1970s, self-harm was considered generally to mean self-cutting rather than other more serious acts of attempted suicide such as taking an overdose, and the intention is seen to be different – self-harm is to manage pain while attempted suicide is to end the pain (Millard 2015).

A major report by the Camelot Foundation (2006) in collaboration with the Mental Health Foundation, following a two-year inquiry into the voice of young people aged 11 and 25 who self-harmed, concluded that self-harm is a significant public health issue in Britain but that support is poor because of the lack of understanding of self-harm. This therefore poses a major challenge to young people who self-harm, their families, their schools and hospitals including Accident and Emergency departments.

Self-harm is not just a British issue. Walsh (2006) shows that there is a growth in the number of self-harmers in many countries including Canada, the USA, Europe, Japan and Taiwan. The World Health Organisation (2014) provides data that globally, self-harm is the fifth top cause of illness or disability for young people, but the Royal College of Psychiatrists (2010) and the Camelot Foundation (2006) both claim that the UK has one of the highest rates in Europe, with self-harm being one of the top five causes of acute hospital admissions. Two-thirds of these admissions are people under the age of 35.

What is self-harm?

The Camelot Foundation (2006) highlights that self-harm is a symptom and not a cause – the underlying cause is the core problem and self-harm is the strategy used to manage that underlying cause. It can be ritualistic, compulsive, either episodic or repeated on a regular basis (Whitlock 2010), and is non-fatal (Moran *et al.* 2012). Self-harm typically involves cutting, burning, scratching, hair-pulling, head banging, interfering with wound healing and taking toxic substances (Camelot Foundation 2006; Royal College of Psychiatrists 2010). While cutting is seen as the most common form of self-harm and the most repetitive of self-harming behaviours (Royal College of Psychiatrists 2010), there is little research on the forms of, and extent of, cutting. Where cutting is the form of self-harm, the most common areas to cut are the arms or back of the legs with a blade (Young Minds and Cello 2012). After cutting, overdoses are the most common form of self-harm (Hawton and Rodham 2006). Self-harm then covers a wide range of behaviours but it is clear that the self-harm is deliberate (Bell 2003) and usually hidden, being carried out in secret, and designed to cope with the underlying cause.

Young people often use more than one method to self-harm based on their preferences and the circumstances they are in at the time. A young person might choose cutting as a means of coping with anxiety but then choose burning as a means of coping with anger. Similarly, a young person's choice of the means of self-harming might be limited by where they are – so, if they are in hospital or a young offenders' institution, they might not have access to the tools required to cut or burn and so use biting as the tool of self-harm. As a hidden and secret activity, self-harm is not normally carried out with others and is called the silent scream (Bell 2003; Walsh 2006), although Walsh (2006) found that two people might act together to harm themselves or each other and therefore it can be an interpersonal act.

Self-harming is a series of activities and reducing the number of and severity of incidents is seen by self-harmers as a road to recovery, although this may not be a view shared by professionals who consider that recovery is only achieved when self-harming ceases. In agreement with Bell (2003), the Camelot Foundation (2006) considers that self-harm is rarely an attempt at suicide and can actually prevent a suicide attempt. A young person's voice from the Mental Health Foundation (2006) says,

> People often link self-harm to suicide but for me it was something different; it was an alternative to suicide, my way of coping even though I sometimes wished my world would end.

Self-harm: Dispelling the myths 131

> ✎ **Activity: Self-harm and suicide**
>
> This young person's voice tells us that she has self-harmed and wishes her world would end. How could this be reconciled with a claim that she does not want to commit suicide?

The seriousness of self-harm is shown by Hawton and Rodham (2006), as deliberate (as opposed to accidental) self-harm represents one of the most common reasons for young people attending hospitals. They add that this certainly does not represent the total number of young people self-harming. However, while the incidence rate is high, Hawton and Rodham (2006) also explain that most cutting or other self-harm is not designed to cause serious harm – most cuts are minor and can be made at home, again often in secret. However, even though most self-harm is minor, the Mental Health Foundation (2006) advocate that all self-harm should be taken seriously as it is an indicator of underlying emotional harm.

Who self-harms?

Figure 9.1 Ball and chain by Sophie Harward

> **✏ Activity: Self-harm myths**
>
> The Mental Health Foundation (2006) claim that the predominant myths about self-harm are:
>
> - They are attention seeking.
> - It's a Goth thing.
> - Only girls self-harm.
> - People who self-harm do it because they enjoy it.
> - People who self-harm are suicidal.
> - They have a personality disorder.
>
> Think about your own perceptions of people who self-harm and list what you think are the characteristics of people who self-harm. You might agree with some of the above and you might be able to add other characteristics. Think also about why identifying characteristics of people who self-harm might be helpful or unhelpful.

According to the Association for Young People's Health (2013), there is a shortage of reliable data about who self-harms because not all people who self-harm access support services. This view is echoed by the Camelot Foundation (2006) who recognise that self-harm is kept secret and people who self-harm treat themselves at home unless they have taken toxic substances, in which case they are more likely to go to hospital. A further difficulty in assessing the number of young people who self-harm is that there is no clear definition of what self-harm is. The Mental Health Foundation (2006) consider that 10 per cent of young people self-harm and this would mean that at least two young people in every secondary classroom have self-harmed at some point. Guilt, secrecy and shame surround self-harm with one young person's voice declaring that she felt ashamed about having emotional problems in the first place and ashamed again about self-harming (Camelot Foundation 2006). The size of the problem is highlighted by data from the Priory (2005) that one in five girls aged 15–17 self-harm, which would mean 800,000 young people had self-harmed in the UK in that year. Walsh (2006) highlights that before the late 1990s, people who self-harmed tended to fall into particular groups – young people with mental health issues, young people in detention centres, people with special education needs and prison inmates. In the late 1990s, Walsh (2006) observes that the profile has changed – the previously mentioned groups are still at a higher risk of self-harming, but in addition are young people in secondary schools, colleges and universities, and adults generally.

The Royal College of Psychiatrists (2010) claim that children as young as eight years old self-harm but the most common age group is age 15–24 (Moran et al. 2012; Walsh 2006). The Camelot Foundation (2006) suggest that the average age for starting to self-harm is 12 years and this can extend into adulthood, middle age and beyond.

Self-harm is more prevalent in female young people, but in later teens and adulthood the difference is reduced between males and females. The Association for Young People's Health (2013) suggests that self-harm is higher in adolescent females because they are more likely to suffer from depression and anxiety, and there is an established link between these mental health issues and self-harm. The prevalence of self-harm in females is supported by Fox and Hawton (2004) who found that 80 per cent of young people who self-harmed were female. The Mental Health Foundation (2006), however, considers that there is no such thing as a typical young person who self-harms – any young person can self-harm if they find it is a coping strategy for their emotional problems. They do agree, however, that having a mental health disorder, being a child in care, a care leaver, LGBT (lesbian, gay, bisexual or transgender) or having lost a relative through suicide are factors making it self-harm more likely, but this is not an inclusive group and agreement for this claim is made by Young Minds and Cello (2012) that anyone can self-harm. The Royal College of Psychiatrists (2010) agrees that those confused over sexual orientation and sexuality are more likely to self-harm although, again, anyone can. It is important to remember that not everyone in these categories does self-harm and young people outside these categories might self-harm.

There are groups of marginalised young people who are more likely to self-harm – young people in custody (with a higher rate of males), victims of abuse and victims of sexual exploitation as they are more at risk of emotional poor health and less likely to have the support of family and friends. They are also more likely to know other young people who use self-harm as a coping strategy and can copy this behaviour. A major study by Child and Adolescent Self-Harm in Europe (CASE) (2004) of 30,000 young people surveyed over two years in seven European countries found factors associated with self-harm. In males, there was a higher risk if they have a family member who had committed suicide or self-harmed, while for females there was a higher risk if they suffered from anxiety. While bullying and family problems were cited, these were low-risk factors according to CASE (2004), but bullying was cited by the Camelot Foundation (2006) as a significant factor.

Data on black, minority and ethnic young people who self-harm is lacking in the literature but Soni-Raleigh (1996) considers that Asian females are three times more likely to self-harm. However, this is contradicted by a more recent study of over 20,000 individuals aged 16–64 years who self-harmed that shows that self-harm rates were the highest in young Black females, but that there was no difference between self-harm rates in White females and Asian females (Cooper et al. 2010). Young people with learning difficulties are more likely to self-harm (Duperouzel 2004) generally because they are more likely to suffer from depression or anxiety.

> **Activity: Gender and self-harm**
>
> Why are self-harmers more likely to be female? How reliable do you think statistics are on who self-harms?

Why people self-harm

Consideration of the antecedents of self-harm and the desired consequences or benefits of self-harm are important. There are perhaps no surprises about the causes leading to young people self-harming. Young people who self-harm talk generally about the distress and profound emotional pain that they are suffering and behind these are a raft of reasons. Both the Camelot Foundation (2006) and Fox and Hawton (2004) recognise that there are often multiple triggers rather than one single cause. Bullying is high on the list of causes of self-harm, together with poor body image and poor relationships (Mental Health Foundation 2006). Problems at home and at school can equally lead to feelings of isolation that ultimately cause deep distress and emotional pain. As well as relationship issues at school, young people face the stress of current school performance with worries about future poor job prospects and keeping up with commercial trends (Young Minds and Cello 2012). Sex abuse can also be a historical reason for self-harming emerging in teenage years (Turrell and Armsworth 2000). Poor relationships can often be made worse by social media, which can make young people feel isolated and alone. The Mental Health Foundation (2006) also recognised the stresses of transitional changes such as changing schools or moving home. Co-existent conditions often present with self-harm are anxiety and depression that can be the cause of, or consequence of, self-harm; and can indeed be a vicious circle.

With these underlying causes, it is no surprise that young people need a solution, but an understanding is needed of why young people choose self-harm as their solution. It is sad to hear that young people often articulate that they do not know of any other ways to cope with their emotional pain. Self-harm is a tangible way of coping as opposed to talking about or reflecting upon their actions. It is also available at any time of the day or night and does not need help or permission from anyone else. For some young people, even if there was someone else to talk to, this would not help them communicate their emotions in a way that self-harming can – even though this means they are communicating to themselves. Self-harm gives a release to built-up tensions and helps to manage strong emotions by providing an outlet (Association for Young People's Health 2013), similar to screaming when facing a threat. As a means of coping with and expressing deep pain, a young person's voice said that self-harm went further and was an 'escape from a terrible state of mind' (Royal College of Psychiatrists 2010, p. 24) and young people indicate that self-harm makes them feel better and makes them feel alive. A young person's voice from the Camelot Foundation's study (2006, p. 22) declared, 'Pain works. Pain heals. If I had never cut myself, I probably wouldn't still be around today.'

A reason for self-harming then can be to allow a young person to live – to self-harm but live, rather than commit suicide. Self-harming can be the one means of allowing a young person to continue living a normal life – self-harming might enable them to attend school whereas without self-harming they would not be able to face the stress and pain of doing so and would stay at home and therefore not engage in education at all. Many young people have remarked that self-harming is easier pain to manage than emotional pain and is also less painful in itself. Smith et al. (1998) explain that there is a chemical release in the brain when people self-harm that gives them a positive feeling of calm and wellbeing, so physical pain can lead to a reduction or elimination of emotional pain. Acts of self-harm can still be a cry for help with an intention that others know what they are doing as such behaviour might lead to extra attention being given or even of being loved by another. Secretive self-harm can also be an act of seeking love from oneself – after self-harming, young people generally care for themselves, cleaning wounds and applying dressings and this is an opportunity for them to feel that they are loved by themselves.

However, self-harming does not address the antecedents or underlying problems but merely masks them. To this end, it is a temporary solution that gives temporary relief and therefore self-harm often becomes a repetitive, even addictive, behaviour. Another reason sometimes given for self-harm is that it is a self-punishment for being a failure – the issue of failure being the inability to manage underlying psychological problems. As a self-punishment, self-harm benefits the young person by providing deserved attention which can act as a form of comfort or closure. Young people who self-harm are sometimes comforted by the effects of self-harm, even though they are certain to upset their families and friends. Examples are by frightening others by their behaviour or by using self-harm as a form of revenge against another by seeking to impose guilt on them (Royal College of Psychiatrists 2010).

Strategies to manage and prevent self-harm

Trying to prevent and manage self-harm is a complex area because prevention and management are generally only possible once it is known that a young person has self-harmed and it has already been established that this is often a secretive and private activity. Therefore, strategies are needed that address all young people – this will include those who self-harm, those who might self-harm in the future and those who might be in a position to support a self-harmer.

As a secretive activity, once a young person has self-harmed, they will need to know how to care for the physical damage that they have done to themselves to avoid further complications such as septicaemia or blood loss. On the basis that most self-harmers do so by cutting themselves, education on keeping clean any tools used for cutting is needed in order to reduce the risk of infection. After self-harming, young people should be aware of the decisions they might need to take about managing the physical damage they have caused themselves or seeking help from another source. Most self-cutting consists of multiple surface and superfluous cuts that can be managed by cleaning and a dressing. Young people who self-harm then should have access at all times to an appropriate first-aid kit. Young people also need to be aware of the potential dangers of taking poisonous substances, the impact of which they will not be able to assess because there may be no tangible visual signs. For the ingestion of poisonous substances (including overdoses of medication) and for substantial wounds caused by cutting, young people need to know how to get further help including calling for an ambulance and to feel confident that it is the right thing to do in the circumstances (Bell 2003). Basic first-aid training would be a valuable enrichment activity in schools for a variety of reasons and would certainly help with self-harm, either as the self-harmer or someone supporting.

Strategies also need to be in place to raise awareness of self-harm. As most people who self-harm are of school age, a good place to start would be in schools. The Camelot Foundation (2006) and Young Minds and Cello (2012) found that 97 per cent of young people in schools consider that self-harm should be addressed in schools, with 66 per cent saying that it should be addressed in lessons.

> **Activity: Support in schools**
>
> What support for self-harm was available at your school? What support do you think is needed?

Education about what self-harm is and the alternatives available such as counselling can be included in Personal, Social and Health Education (PSHE) classes, together with how to support others who disclose self-harm. PSHE education also gives young people the opportunity to discuss issues affecting them that might lead to self-harm and is supported by a raft of resources that promote mental health in the curriculum by understanding one's own emotions and those of others, thus reducing the stigma of coping mechanisms such as self-harming. PSHE can help children and young people to understand what self-harm is, and develop their confidence in being able to ask for help or disclose self-harming activities to others. Awareness-raising of alternatives to self-harm can help to reduce the incidence of self-harming in schools or reduce its seriousness.

Raising awareness of self-harm and producing guides for young people, their parents, schools, the health service and the public in general is recommended by the Camelot Foundation (2006) who suggest that this should sit with health departments as self-harm is a public health issue that has an impact on young people and their education. Edward Timpson, the Minister of State for Children and Families (2013), recognised that any mental health issue (including self-harm) can have a huge impact on a young person's life chances because they are more likely to struggle at school (Gov.UK 2013). Self-harm awareness raising should, to meet the recommendations of the Camelot Foundation (2006), cover what is self-harm, why people self-harm, how to respond sensitively to disclosure, what support is available, and being able to signpost self-harmers to appropriate services. As one of the difficulties of self-harming is disclosure, a guide for young people on what to expect upon disclosure would be useful, either at school or national level. The Association for Young People's Health (2013) welcomes the opportunity to challenge the myths surrounding self-harm and believes that improved awareness would help to reduce the stigma of self-harm. This, in turn, could lead to a reduction in self-harm or an increase in the number of disclosures, whilst at the same time raising awareness to young people and the general public of the dangers of self-harm and possible alternative strategies for coping with emotional distress.

Peer support has been recommended as a positive and effective strategy for self-harming with young people declaring that they are three times more likely to talk to a friend than a teacher about self-harm or underlying reasons for self-harming. The Camelot Foundation (2006) found that while young people do indeed prefer to talk to peers, it is not necessarily about self-harming but more the reasons why they self-harm. As well as peer support, some schools have introduced adult support workers to offer a counselling service to young people as an alternative to peer support; young people have expressed a preference for this rather than teacher support.

One of the underlying causes of self-harm is bullying and, by law, all state schools must have a behaviour policy in place that includes measures to prevent all forms of bullying among pupils, including cyber-bullying (Gov.UK 2015).

As well as understanding what self-harm is and what support can be put in place in schools, there is also a range of multi-disciplinary support available through the health service and voluntary sector. Childline is a long-established voluntary organisation that most young people have heard of, but there is also Parentline that can offer support to parents and other carers who are similarly experiencing emotional distress because of their child's self-harming. Through the health service, a range of support mechanisms can be put in place through the young person's GP, including psychological therapy services, family therapy, psychiatric treatment and in-patient care.

Activity: Differences between mental health issues and illness

What is the difference between 'mental health issue' and 'mental illness'? Using online sources, explore these two concepts to ensure that you understand them and could explain them to others.

Distraction techniques can be helpful to young people who self-harm because it puts them or leaves them in control by having strategies that do not involve other people, thus not risking others taking over. These range from gentler techniques such as talking to friends, keeping a diary, drawing and painting, and researching self-harm on the internet (Camelot Foundation 2006) to more active techniques suggested by both the Camelot Foundation (2006) and Bell (2003). Making a loud noise, shouting, screaming over loud music and smashing pots can release tension. Instead of biting oneself, a young person can bite an object; instead of cutting oneself, a young person can cut an object. To replicate cutting, young people can use marker pens to draw cuts and blood so that they have a visual representation of their usual self-harm. Fake blood can also be purchased and used for this purpose. To replicate the physical pain of self-harm, suggestions are to break an egg on one's hand, place one's arms in a bucket of ice and flick one's legs with rubber bands or keep a rubber band on one's wrist to flick when the need for a physical sensation is needed. Walsh (2006) also recommends applying a temporary tattoo to the area that a young person wants to harm and then scratching it off. A more gentle approach could be to massage, talk to and care for the area that one wants to harm, or to stroke, talk to and care for another being such as a family pet.

Whether young people self-harm or are at risk of self-harm, Gov.UK (2013) champions empowering pupils to share their concerns in a safe environment, with schools providing this so mental health and wellbeing can be promoted positively to support underlying causes. Hawton and Rodham (2006) advise that the support that young people who self-harm primarily want is someone to talk to about the underlying issues that lead to self-harm, and primary prevention should be to improve coping skills for those underlying causes.

Both Gov.UK (2013) and the Camelot Foundation (2006) agree that good mental health should be promoted in schools through a whole-school approach with a range of known positive health strategies including counselling, creative arts and exercise. Further, they recommend that schools should not be afraid to try new and innovative strategies that should then be evaluated and good practice shared, as self-harm is a relatively new issue in schools and strategies to prevent or manage self-harm are still developing and need to be developed and evaluated further. Research into self-harm is 'patchy' (Camelot Foundation 2006) and not fully evaluated. The wide range of services available need research in order to evaluate them and further research is needed into the types of interventions and their effectiveness in different settings. Research is also recommended based on age, gender, ethnicity, sexuality and the resulting implications for race, religion and culture to ensure inclusion for all young people.

Disclosure of self-harm brings its own challenges and issues. Young people who self-harm often see it as a means of controlling their own lives and disclosure creates a risk of losing that self-control, with support being put in place without discussion or consent. The Camelot Foundation (2006) heard young people's voices about being laughed at when they disclosed self-harm and one young person was excluded from school permanently upon disclosure. The other side of the disclosure discussion is also concerned with having the knowledge and skills to listen and respond to disclosure, as teachers, parents and young people were concerned that they would say the wrong thing to a young person disclosing self-harm (Young Minds and Cello 2012).

Self-harm is a real concern for young people today as most people who self-harm are of school age and certainly the vast majority of young people who start to self-harm do so in the early years of secondary school. It does seem that schools are the best place to raise awareness of self-harm and put strategies in place to support young people. However, Young Minds and Cello (2012) do warn that there is a huge challenge for schools dealing with a relatively new and unknown issue. As one teacher informed Young Minds and Cello (2012, p. 19), 'You are so worried about handling it badly that you avoid handling it at all', while another recognised that to support young people you have to build and maintain a good relationship with them and this is not always possible with the number of young people in each class and the time available for pastoral support.

Conclusion

It seems to be clear that self-harming is growing on an international scale and that schools are the best place to start providing support for young people and their families. However, the challenge to young people who self-harm, their families, schools and the health service is funding. It is encouraging that the government announced in 2014 that it would put £30 million into mental healthcare in Accident and Emergency departments (BBC 2014). This will lead to a multi-agency approach that can offer a range of support and treatments to respond to the individual needs of children and young people who self-harm.

Case study 9.1: Natalia

My name is Natalia and I moved to the UK a few years ago when I was 12 because of my Dad's work. It was hard leaving my friends and family behind but I was looking forward to making new friends. Back home, I loved school and was a high flyer getting top grades in all of my lessons. Once I came to the UK I struggled in my classes as English was not my first language. I also struggled to make friends – all the girls in my classes already had friends and no one seemed to want a new one. I felt isolated and lost my status in school – I was no longer the clever high flyer with a great friendship group, I was the one who was always behind and had to keep asking the teacher for help, sat on my own at the front of the class. Sometimes when I asked for help, I could hear some of the others sniggering behind me.

So here I was, in a new country with no friends and just my Mum and Dad for company – no 12-year-old wants their only friends to be their parents. I turned to the internet for company – Facebook, Twitter, Instagram – I 'met' lots of people who were kind to me but then after a while some of them turned nasty, criticising how I looked and things I said. One person told me to 'get a makeover or kill myself'. That really hurt. I knew that this person didn't really know me and I would never meet them but their comment stuck in my head. Other people online were kind and listened to me when I was upset about it. One boy told me how he dealt with feeling sad and angry – he cut himself and said it made him feel better. He even sent me photos of his cuts and scars. At first I couldn't understand how anyone could do that to themselves. I'd heard of people harming themselves but never thought I'd meet someone who actually did it.

A few days later, the nasty comments escalated online – people started ganging up on me and I remember sitting in my bedroom sobbing. My parents were downstairs but I knew they wouldn't understand. They might even blame me for meeting people online. I couldn't imagine ever feeling happy again and so I decided to take that boy's advice. I had nothing to lose. I found a pencil sharpener and with a pair of craft scissors removed the blade. I felt apprehensive, worried it would hurt and so the first time I tried, I didn't break the skin so I did it again. On my thigh so no one would see – I didn't want to get into trouble. This time it bled. And he was right. All off a sudden I had a rush of relief and all of my focus was on the blood and the pain. It made me feel better.

It's now a year later and my thighs are covered in scars. I have to make excuses to my parents about keeping covered up in the summer – no more wearing shorts for me. I wish I hadn't started cutting myself but it seemed the only way out of my misery. I wish there had been another option. I still cut myself and want to stop but I don't know how. I tried stopping but I didn't have the willpower. I know I need help but I don't know where to go. I have a good teacher at school but if I ask them for help then other people might find out and they might think I'm trying to kill myself. I'm really not – I just want the emotional pain to stop.

Key questions:
- If you were Natalia's teacher, what signs were there when she first joined your class that she might need support?
- If you were Natalia's friend, how would you respond if Natalia told you that she was self-harming?
- What could schools do to support young people like Natalia?

Suggested reading

Camelot Foundation and the Mental Health Foundation (2006) *Truth Hurts: Report of the National Inquiry into Self-harm among Young People*. Available at: https://www.mentalhealth.org.uk/sites/default/files/truth_hurts.pdf

This is essential reading for all involved in self-harm as it gives an understanding of how people who self-harm can be supported and how further damage can be caused through ignorance of the issues involved. It is accessible reading for young people, practitioners and families.

References

Association for Young People's Health (2013) *Adolescent self-harm*. Available at: www.ayph.org.uk/publications/316_RU13%20Self-harm%20summary.pdf

BBC (2014) Self-harm hospital admissions among children 'at five year high'. Available at: www.bbc.co.uk/news/health-30414589

Bell, L. (2003) *Managing Intense Emotions and Overcoming Self-Destructive Habits*. Hove and New York: Routledge.

Camelot Foundation (2006) *Truth Hurts – Report of the National Inquiry into Self-harm among Young People*. Available at: www.mentalhealth.org.uk

Child and Adolescent Self Harm in Europe (2004) *Evidence to the National Inquiry into Self Harm Among Young People*. London: National Children's Bureau.

Cooper, J., Murphy, E., Webb, R., Hawton, K., Bergen, H., Waters, K. and Kapur, N. (2010) Ethnic differences in self-harm, rates, characteristics and service provision: Three-city cohort study. *The British Journal of Psychiatry*, 197 (3), 212–218.

Duperouzel, H. (2004). *People with Learning Disabilities Who Self-Injure: A Phenomenological Study of Their Personal Perspectives and Perceived Support Needs Whilst Living in an NHS Forensic Service.* Calderstones: NHS Trust.

Fox, C. and Hawton, K. (2004) *Deliberate Self Harm in Adolescents.* London: Jessica Kingsley.

Gov.UK (2013) Edward Timpson speaks about mental health services for young people. Available at: https://www.gov.uk/government/speeches/edward-timpson-speaks-about-mental-health-services-for-young-people

Gov.UK (2015) Mental health behaviour guidance to be issued to schools. Available at: https://www.gov.uk/government/news/mental-health-behaviour-guidance-to-be-issued-to-schools

Hawton, K. and Rodham, K. (2006) *By Their Own Young Hand: Deliberate Self-harm and Suicidal Ideas in Adolescents.* London: Jessica Kingsley.

Mental Health Foundation (2006) *The Truth About Self-Harm.* Available at: https://www.mentalhealth.org.uk/publications/truth-about-self-harm

Millard, C. (2015) *A History of Self-Harm in Britain.* Hampshire: Palgrave Macmillan.

Moran, P., Caffey, C., Romaniuk, H., Olsson, C., Borschmann, R., Carlin, J. and Patton, G. (2012) The natural history of self-harm from adolescence to young adulthood: A population-based cohort study. *The Lancet*, 379, 236–243.

Royal College of Psychiatrists (2010) *Self-harm, Suicide and Risk: Helping People Who Self Harm.* London: Royal College of Psychiatrists.

Smith, G., Cox, D. and Saradjian, J. (1998). *Women and Self-harm.* London: Women's Press.

Soni-Raleigh, V. (1996) Suicide patterns and trends in people of Indian subcontinent and Caribbean origin. *England and Wales in Ethnicity and Health*, 1, 55–63.

The Priory (2005) *Adolescent Angst.* London: The Priory Group.

Turrell, S. C. and Armsworth, M. W. (2000) Differentiating incest survivors who self-mutilate. *Child Abuse & Neglect*, 24 (2), 237–249.

Walsh, B. (2006) *Treating Self Injury: A Practical Guide.* New York: Guildford Press.

Whitlock, J. (2010) Self-injurious behaviour in adolescents. *PLoS Medicine*, 7 (5).

World Health Organisation (2014) WHO calls for stronger focus on adolescent health. Available at: www.who.int/mediacentre/news/releases/2014/focus-adolescent-health/en/

Young Minds and Cello (2012) *Talking Self-harm.* London: Young Minds.

10 The mental health needs of refugee pupils

Shirley Hewitt

This chapter explores:

- the impact of changes to SEND provision in England in relation to mental health;
- the teacher's role in supporting the mental health of pupils;
- the specific mental health issues relating to refugee pupils;
- the nature of effective provision for refugee pupils and all pupils with social, emotional and mental health needs.

Introduction

In 2014, the Children and Families Act (CFA, 2014) came into force in England. For the first time emotional, social and mental health difficulties (SEMH) were recognised as a dimension of Special Educational Need (SEN). Although linked to other aspects of SEN, the introduction of mental health as an identified need has led to education providers considering elements of their provision within the new framework.

Previously, 'social, emotional and behavioural disorders' (SEBD) were identified as attributes of SEN but debate arose as some felt that 'behaviour' was an ambiguous term often used by professionals to excuse a lack in effective provision (DCSF, 2009; Steer, 2009). However, the new term of SEMH also raises issues with regard to the accurate identification of need. Each pupil will have different characteristics of need that can be classified under this 'label'. These, in turn, will be influenced by many factors, thus requiring a personalised approach for each individual. Therefore, an inflexible approach to provision which refers only to global principles and generalised pedagogy will not meet the needs of these pupils (Norwich and Eaton, 2015).

The term SEMH creates tensions between the medical and social models of inclusion. The classification of children and young people into categories of need creates a struggle between prescriptive and responsive approaches to provision (Norwich and Eaton, 2015). For example, are practitioners' reactions merely formulaic: attributing certain behaviours and therefore certain 'remedies' to children based on the 'label' that has been allocated, or are the responses meeting the individual needs of a particular child in a specific situation, having considered the holistic development of the child? This becomes more evident when specific groups come into focus, for example refugees. Consideration needs to be given to the expectations placed on teachers in responding to diverse experiences and responses and this will inevitably lead to a

142 Shirley Hewitt

debate as to whether teachers have the knowledge and capabilities to meet these wide-ranging needs.

Debate 1: The teacher's role in promoting mental health well-being

The mental health of children and adolescents has become an increasing concern and this is reflected in media coverage and political soundbites. Lindo et al. (2014) report an increase in the need for mental health services in the USA. Similar trends are evident in the UK (Young Minds, 2016). Cefai and Camilleri (2015) identify that approximately 20 per cent of school children experience social, emotional and behavioural difficulties such as anxiety, depression and Attention Deficit and Hyperactivity Disorder (Hyperkinetic Disorder). This may rise to 50 per cent for pupils from socially disadvantaged areas. Issues such as these may require access to mental health services for a variety of reasons, either as a direct result of the identified need or as a supplementary support mechanism. Often these pupils create challenging situations for teachers and support staff who can sometimes respond negatively to the individuals concerned. Factors which influence staff responses can stem from a variety of causes, for example from a lack of training or from personal reactions caused by pre-conceived attitudes or stress-related factors. Delays in initiating appropriate interventions can lead to these pupils withdrawing from education and social interactions, which can ultimately lead to other mental health symptoms. This, in turn, has an impact on long-term outcomes for these children and young people (Lindo et al., 2014; Soppitt, 2016).

The chances of such issues arising are heightened by certain circumstances and pupils who have more than five of these predictors (see Figure 10.1) have a 75 per cent chance of developing mental health problems (Cefai and Camilleri, 2015).

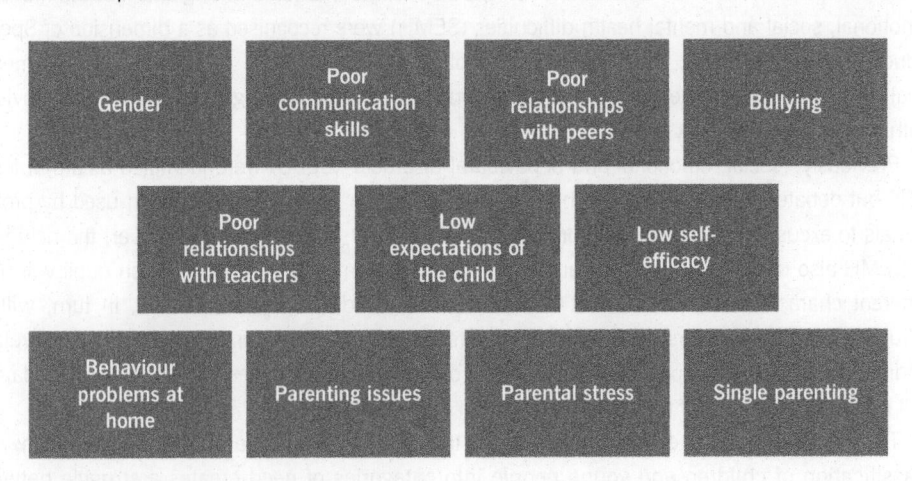

Gender	Poor communication skills	Poor relationships with peers	Bullying
	Poor relationships with teachers	Low expectations of the child	Low self-efficacy
Behaviour problems at home	Parenting issues	Parental stress	Single parenting

Figure 10.1 Predictors of mental health issues

> ✎ **Activity: Predictors of mental health**
>
> Consider the predictors of mental health issues. Why do these factors have a particular impact on the mental health of children?

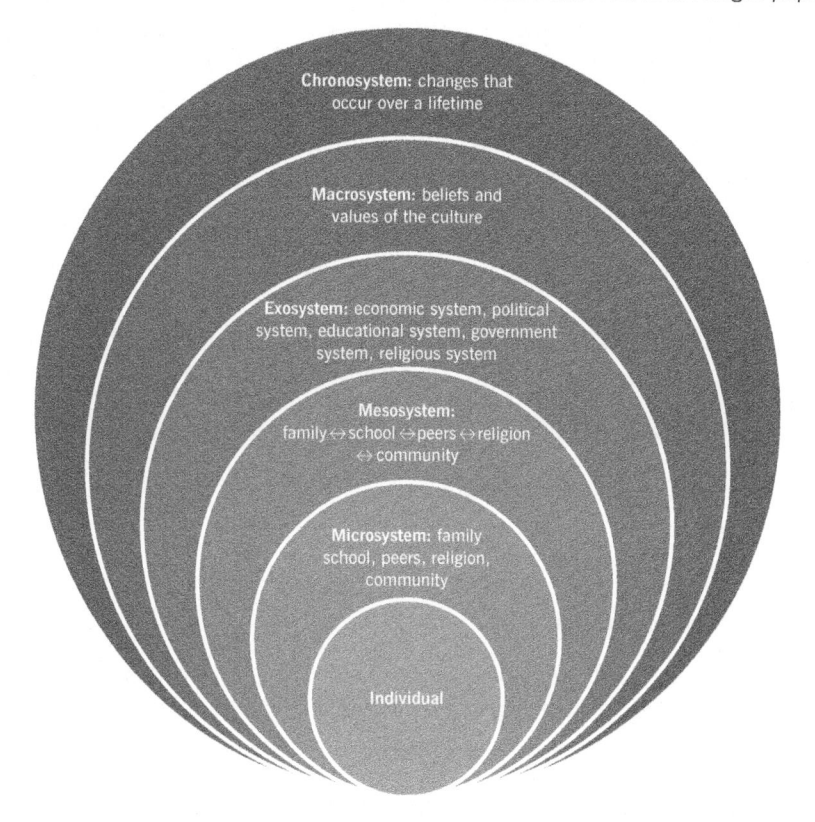

Figure 10.2 Bronfenbrenner's (1994) ecological framework

In 1989, Bronfenbrenner formalised an ecological framework for human development (Bronfenbrenner, 1994). There are various layers to the environments that influence a child's development: the microsystem, the mesosystem, the exosystem, the macrosystem and the chronosystem. In reflecting on this framework, it becomes evident that the microsystem has a fundamental influence on the development of these pupils. The microsystem requires consideration of the individual student, their home and community as well as class setting and wider school influences.

> **Activity: Bronfenbrenner's ecological framework**
>
> Consider Bronfenbrenner's ecological framework and identify which aspects of the microsystem impact on pupil development and why this is the case – for example, how can friends, or the lack of them, influence a child's mental health?

Early involvement in shaping the microsystem is essential in order to lower the chances of the trigger behaviours becoming fixed. Lawson *et al.* (2006), DfE (2014), Lindo *et al.* (2014) and Cefai and Camilleri (2015) identify a range of appropriate interventions and responses which would include those shown in Figure 10.3.

144 *Shirley Hewitt*

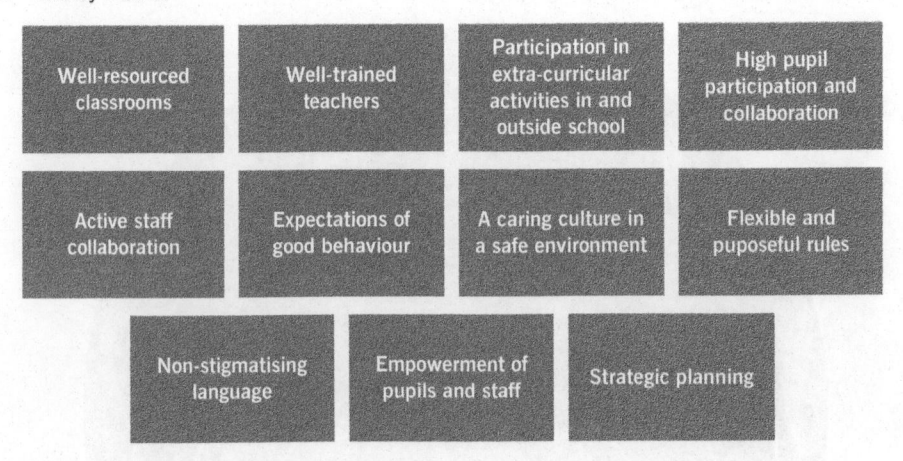

- Well-resourced classrooms
- Well-trained teachers
- Participation in extra-curricular activities in and outside school
- High pupil participation and collaboration
- Active staff collaboration
- Expectations of good behaviour
- A caring culture in a safe environment
- Flexible and puposeful rules
- Non-stigmatising language
- Empowerment of pupils and staff
- Strategic planning

Figure 10.3 Interventions which shape the microsystem

> **Activity: School initiatives**
>
> Consider which specific initiatives schools could introduce to meet the needs of these pupils. What are the challenges in promoting these initiatives?

Wolpert *et al.* (2013) identify that there is evidence to suggest that interventions led by school staff can be as successful as those led by external professionals. Healthy teacher–pupil relationships will increase the chances of effective learning, both academically and emotionally (Hattie, 2009; Lindo *et al.*, 2014). The argument that teachers find these relationships particularly difficult to establish with more challenging pupils comes to the fore at this point. Even teachers who would be amenable to spending time in developing these bonds might find this yet another hurdle to overcome, especially when high academic targets are set by school leaders. Therapeutic interventions such as art therapy, drama therapy and play therapy have been shown to have a positive influence on mental health but often need to assume a different format within the school environment so that academic expectations can also be met (Lindo *et al.*, 2014).

Engaging parents in supportive and effective home–school partnerships can also be problematic, although evidence shows that it has a profound effect on pupil development (Desforges and Abouchaar, 2003; Harris and Goodall, 2007). However, schools, colleges and other educational providers, as well as individual teachers, have an essential role in sign-posting parents to other supporting services and professional advice (Lawson *et al.*, 2006). Listening and responding to parents is an intrinsic part of many educational systems, including those in the UK and USA as can be seen by the introduction of various strategies such as Achievement for All in England (Achievement for All, 2016). However, there continue to be struggles between the views of professionals and those of parents, children and young people, for example in relation to appropriate interventions, desired outcomes and behaviour management (Reid *et al.*, 2016; Home Room, 2016).

Meeting the needs of these particular pupils requires consideration of a range of approaches such as the development of resilience (to be discussed in Chapter 11), self-efficacy and positive psychology.

Building on the child's assets as well as developing caring environments, both at school and at home, all benefit emotional well-being. Knowledge of the risks and positive aspects of the microsystem surrounding the pupil is vital in ensuring effective provision (Cefai and Camilleri, 2015). This may, however, be affected by the personal circumstances of the teaching professional whose judgements may be influenced by their own mental health and well-being (BBC, 2016). Questions arise, therefore, as to whether it is the teacher's role to provide an inclusive, supportive environment adopting a social disability model or whether the role extends to more direct interventions, attaching to a medical model of need (as discussed in Chapter 8). If these direct approaches are required, it is necessary to consider whether teachers have the knowledge to work at this level and whether the support mechanisms are in place to ensure that teachers are able to meet the challenges of this; for example, should professional counsellors be required to attend supervision meetings in order to support their own mental health (DfE, 2015; BACP, 2016)?

Wolpert *et al.* (2013) discuss the Targeted Mental Health Support (TaMHS), a national initiative which attempted to improve the psychological and mental health of children and young people throughout England. Similar initiatives have emerged in Australia (the KidsMatter programme) and the USA (for example, the School-Wide Positive Behavioral Interventions and Supports framework). The focus of TaMHS was on pupils aged 5–13 years of age who were at risk of developing mental health problems. It built on existing programmes of intervention and developed school-based and local provision. Various conclusions were drawn after reviewing this project which identified certain benefits and aspects for improvement. Firstly, locating the provision in schools was found to develop collaboration between different agencies and increased access to the services. However, the lack of a common language across the agencies created barriers to effective provision. Timing was seen to be an important issue and primary educators were more open to the initiative than secondary. It was felt that if secondary schools could identify a link between intervention and academic attainment, they may be more inclined to participate. There were also questions in relation to the nature of the provision and whether it should be universal or aimed at targeted groups. Finally, there were conflicts in relation to the ownership of the programme and the need for evidence-based practice (Wolpert *et al.* 2013; Norwich and Eaton, 2015).

Norwich and Eaton (2015) also draw attention to the International Classification of Functioning (ICF) of the World Health Organisation. This is an attempt to synthesise the medical and social models of difference which have been tested in various European states (WHO, 2001). It presupposes that a 'disability' occurs from the interaction of the individual with personal and environmental influences and therefore all relevant factors need to be considered. This bio-psycho-social model has had little impact in the UK in relation to educational provision which, in turn, suggests that there is likely to be a lack of appropriate identification systems.

✎ Activity: The ICF

Browse the ICF at www.who.int/classifications/icf/en/ and consider the social, medical and bio-psycho-social models of difference. Which model or models should teachers adhere to in their professional role? What are the advantages or disadvantages of taking certain approaches?

Debate 2: Who is responsible for meeting the mental health needs of refugees and what are the challenges?

Following on from the challenges that schools face in meeting the needs of pupils with social, emotional or mental health needs, it is important to consider the needs of specific groups. Recently, there has been increasing press coverage of the number of refugee families seeking asylum in Western states and the impact of this (*Guardian*, 2015, 2016; *New York Times*, 2016). This, in turn, has encouraged some consideration of the ways in which host nations can meet the needs of the escalating numbers of refugee families. A refugee is defined as:

> A person who is outside his/her country of nationality or habitual residence; has a well-founded fear of persecution because of his/her race, religion, nationality, membership in a particular social group or political opinion; and is unable or unwilling to avail himself/herself of the protection of that country, or to return to there for fear of persecution.
>
> (UNHCR, 2011)

The United Nations High Commissioner for Refugees (UNHCR) registered more than 4 million refugees living in Turkey, Lebanon, Jordan, Iraq and Egypt; more than half are under 18 and 40 per cent are under 12 years of age (Sirin and Rogers-Sirin, 2015). In 2012, there were 23,000 applications for asylum in the UK with over 1,100 being unaccompanied minors, defined as individuals who are under 18 years of age and who have no primary caregiver with them (Fazel, 2015). Fazel (2015) identifies that these children and young people experience a range of challenging circumstances in their country of origin (pre-migration), journey (peri-migration) and in the new host country (post-migration) (see Figure 10.4). Refugee children might have experienced many issues during the three

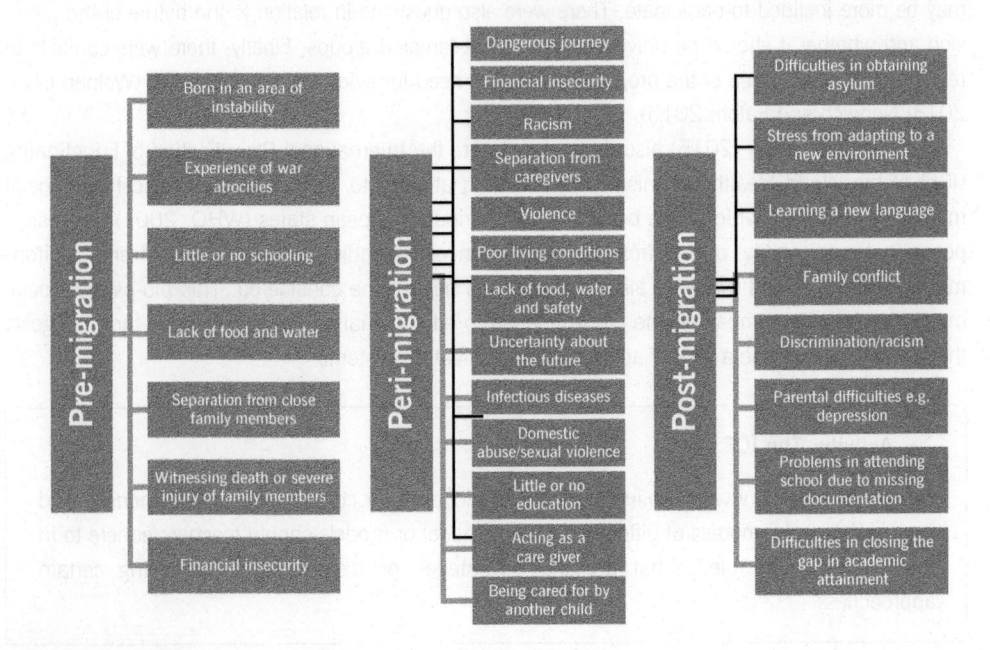

Pre-migration:
- Born in an area of instability
- Experience of war atrocities
- Little or no schooling
- Lack of food and water
- Separation from close family members
- Witnessing death or severe injury of family members
- Financial insecurity

Peri-migration:
- Dangerous journey
- Financial insecurity
- Racism
- Separation from caregivers
- Violence
- Poor living conditions
- Lack of food, water and safety
- Uncertainty about the future
- Infectious diseases
- Domestic abuse/sexual violence
- Little or no education
- Acting as a care giver
- Being cared for by another child

Post-migration:
- Difficulties in obtaining asylum
- Stress from adapting to a new environment
- Learning a new language
- Family conflict
- Discrimination/racism
- Parental difficulties e.g. depression
- Problems in attending school due to missing documentation
- Difficulties in closing the gap in academic attainment

Figure 10.4 Factors faced during the migration process

different stages. Reflecting on the experience of different refugee populations allows identification of negative factors which can impact on a child's life experiences during migration (Anderson et al., 2004; Ragonesi and Martinelli, 2013; Measham et al., 2014; Fazel, 2015; Sirin and Rogers-Sirin, 2015).

In considering the adverse events that can occur prior to and post resettlement, it becomes evident that the likelihood of undesirable events does not decrease after leaving the country of origin but potentially escalates. Fazel (2015) comments that in Denmark, it was identified that stresses during exile and after migration were more predictive of psychological problems than experiences in the country of origin (pre-migration). In 2015, Sirin and Rogers-Sirin report that 45 per cent of Syrian refugee children displayed symptoms of Post-Traumatic Stress Disorder (PTSD) and 44 per cent had symptoms of depression. The main stresses which appeared to be causing these responses were linked to economic hardship, language barriers, social isolation and discrimination. Many of these relate to the fundamental aspects of need which were identified by Maslow (1954) such as basic psychological needs, safety and social needs.

> **Activity: Maslow's (1954) hierarchy of needs**
>
> Refer to Maslow's hierarchy of needs and the factors faced during the migration process: see McLeod (2016), available at www.simplypsychology.org/maslow.html. Why do you think that these children and young people were demonstrating these particular symptoms associated with mental health disorders?

Many of these children will resettle in Europe and the USA. It is therefore imperative that these issues are addressed by the host countries. Trauma can have different levels of impact depending on cultural background although, encouragingly, children can have more resilience to ordeals than adults (Anderson, 2004). However, with the intense nature of the events and the chances of multiple triggers, it is likely that these children and adolescents will develop responses, such as mental health issues, that require informed interventions. Without satisfactory interventions, these problems can multiply and escalate into adulthood (Kelly and Bokhari, 2012). Many of these children can suffer from PTSD, anxiety, depression, survivor's guilt and personality disturbances (see Figure 10.5). Often children will try to create meaning around the events that have happened by revisiting the incidents during their interactions with others and on their own, for example through play, drawing, verbal interactions or in their private thoughts (Kelly and Bokhari, 2012).

Few children under the age of eight would be able to cope with prolonged separation from their parents without some impact on their mental health (Frater-Mathieson, 2004; Kelly and Bokhari, 2012) and those who have started the migration process under the age of eight are more likely to develop oppositional or conduct traits at school. These may be displayed as aggressive, defiant and angry behaviours with individuals often being resentful and blaming others. Those who have had some stability in the country of origin before the age of eight are less likely to develop these traits (Frater-Mathieson, 2004). It has also been observed that pupils between the ages of 6 and 12 tend to develop problems in concentration with additional responses such as re-enactment of the loss, feelings of guilt, episodes of aggression, demanding behaviours, social isolation, passivity and other physical symptoms including anxiety in relation to death. Adolescents, however, often tend to adopt the role of an adult and therefore have issues in forming a clear identity.

148 *Shirley Hewitt*

> **Anxiety disorder:** a variety of fears or concerns which are present for the majority of the time. Can be accompanied by panic attacks and/or phobias. An individual may restrict activities to avoid triggers.

> **Post-Traumatic Stress Disorder:** a range of intrusive memories, flashbacks or nightmares. Can be accompanied by irritablilty, anger, lack of concentration, poor recall of traumatic events, sleep problems, self-blame, physical symptoms which have no known cause and a sense of detachment.

> **Depression:** low mood or irritability in children, tiredness, loss of interest in activities. Additional symptoms may include poor appetitie, sleep disruption, lack of confidence, poor concentration, tension, acts of self-harm, suicidal thoughts, feelings of guilt, hopelessness for the future, lack of purpose, worry about health, physical symptoms without any obvious cause.

Figure 10.5 Characteristics of prevalent mental health disorders

They also can demonstrate self-destructive behaviours, feelings of doubt, isolation, pessimistic frames of mind and can participate in anti-social acts.

Trauma can also impede the short-term memory of individuals which can, in turn, impact on learning (Frater-Mathieson, 2004). Bronfenbrenner (1994) discusses the impact of the macrosystem on an individual's development and, in particular, considers the cultural impact. Trauma can affect individuals in different ways depending on cultural background and therefore it is not possible to draw universal conclusions based on previous experiences with different cultural groups. Although it would be applicable to acknowledge the effects of migration on refugees, each experience will be different and the responses to these events will be unique.

In order for the chances of successful outcomes to increase for these pupils, it is important to develop a sense of security, a supportive social network and opportunities for the children to develop and succeed (Frater-Mathieson, 2004). Schools can begin to achieve this by considering the experiences of refugees and highlighting positive ways of handling difficult events. Other aspects to consider in addressing the needs of these pupils are: language difficulties, educational experiences, cultural difficulties, lack of resources and establishing a correct diagnosis of need based on informed cultural understanding (Measham et al., 2014). Possible interventions should therefore match social and cultural norms and allow children to develop a sense of belonging within a safe environment. These might include the use of art, music, dance, poetry and story-telling (Frater-Mathieson, 2004).

Activity: School and community responses

Consider the aspects which are identified by Anderson (2004) and Hamilton (2004) in relation to school and community responses. What specific interventions could be created by schools and the local community?

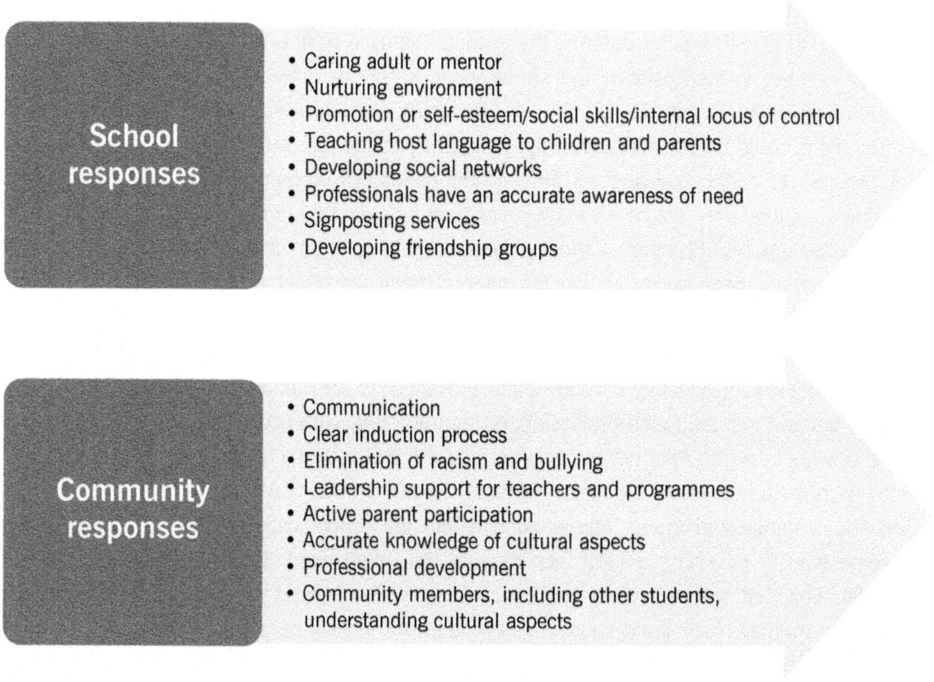

School responses
- Caring adult or mentor
- Nurturing environment
- Promotion or self-esteem/social skills/internal locus of control
- Teaching host language to children and parents
- Developing social networks
- Professionals have an accurate awareness of need
- Signposting services
- Developing friendship groups

Community responses
- Communication
- Clear induction process
- Elimination of racism and bullying
- Leadership support for teachers and programmes
- Active parent participation
- Accurate knowledge of cultural aspects
- Professional development
- Community members, including other students, understanding cultural aspects

Figure 10.6 School and community responses

Betancourt et al. (2015) advance the proposition that financial and language barriers impede academic progression and social support. Ragonesi and Martinelli (2013) support this by identifying that parents' illiteracy creates serious impediments to children's progress in school. Parents with limited communication tend to presume that children are progressing well, even when this is not the case. Language is therefore seen as the cornerstone in developing effective teaching and learning strategies within the host country. Ragonesi and Martinelli (2013) continue to suggest ways in which effective communication can be used to facilitate the stability and security of the refugee child. Identification of a specific professional to work with these families is deemed to be most effective. If the professional cannot speak the language of the country of origin, then he/she should be accompanied by an interpreter. This professional should be the link between the child, family and school. This specialist should provide information on the local education system, addressing misconceptions, reporting on educational progress, encouraging a personalised approach to learning and teaching, providing support for homework tasks and encouraging teachers to develop professionally through practical experiences with the families. However, this relies on a sufficient number of interpreters who are respected within the community and can speak a range of languages and dialects, as well as sufficient funding to support the programme.

Fazel (2015) recognises further barriers which include the fact that children will not arrive at the normal transition points in the year and, therefore, may be excluded from induction procedures. Some will be in foster care, or with adults other than their own parents, and so may face several moves to different locations, as well as problems in accessing school through a lack of a parent advocate or missing paperwork. If the child is demonstrating mental health issues which, as can be seen by the figures discussed earlier, is likely, the support services may seem very remote. Even if the child is with his/her parents, the parents themselves may be unaware of mental health support procedures in the host country. These services may be different, or may not even exist, in the country of origin. It may be felt that by accessing such provision, asylum applications and parenting rights could be affected adversely. Temporary residence conditions may also mean that it is not possible to access support for longer-term needs. Unaccompanied minors face an even bigger hurdle as they may not be aware of procedures or even be attuned to the fact that they need mental health support. Children without parents escorting them show a greater risk of mental health issues than those accompanied by parents (Kelly and Bokhari, 2012; Sirin and Rogers-Sirin, 2015).

Effective responses which may address the needs of these children have their roots in the methods advocated for effective mental health provision for all pupils. The cooperation of educational settings and mental health professionals is paramount, with access to mental health support within the school environment, where most pupils will feel a sense of security. Collaboration with services such as the Child and Adolescent Mental Health Service (CAMHS) in the UK and working on individual, family and group interventions within the school with the support of interpreters, goes some way in providing a rapid response to individual need. In a study by Fazel (2015), pupils identified that teachers were one of the most well-informed groups to initiate referrals to such services as they had a good knowledge of the pupils in their care.

Community-based approaches are more likely to lead to positive outcomes with project teams aiming to meet psychological needs through social support and 'fun-based' activities within a well-known environment (Sirin and Rogers-Sirin, 2015). The type of interventions which Kelly and Bokhari (2012) and Sirin and Rogers-Sirin (2015) identify as having particular impact include:

- helping pupils to learn the host language while supporting their first language;
- bridging the gap in knowledge and skills;
- enabling them to settle in the host country without losing ties to the country of origin;
- working with families to address issues using culturally appropriate skills;
- training educators to recognise trauma and manage it;
- educating those working with refugees and ensuring that they are familiar with research on refugee populations, including cultural backgrounds;
- adequate access to translation services.

> **Activity: Community-based approaches**
>
> Consider the areas of intervention which have been identified as particularly effective for this group of learners. Which of these fall within the usual remit of the teacher and which would be considered as additional to their normal role?

Solutions

Mental health issues are identified as an area of assessment in the new Ofsted Framework (Ofsted, 2015) which asks school inspectors to make judgements as to how well pupils are able to make choices about their emotional and mental well-being. Therefore, schools need to ensure that there is effective provision to enable pupils of all ages to overcome mental health disorders as well as meeting a universal need for healthy lifestyle choices. Positive mental health outcomes will be affected by the availability of support from the family and community and will be influenced by cultural, political and historical factors. Positive input from educational settings which is linked to establishing comprehensive, effective and culturally acceptable services is also required, particularly when this enables families to develop strong and supportive links with the local community. Specific programmes can be introduced to deal with identified need but also an inclusive approach should be taken to ensure universal coverage. Consideration should also be given to developing a personalised approach to interventions with a view to creating a more developed model of disability which fully meets the need of the individual. This should also address the needs of the facilitators in ensuring that they too have strategies to consider their own mental well-being in an increasingly demanding role.

Educators are now coming to terms with an increasing focus on the mental well-being of pupils and how to effectively address this within individual settings. This requires practitioners to be proactive in developing skills and accessing training to meet the needs of pupils within their care. They need to be aware that pupils will have individual needs which will change throughout their education and 'one-size-fits-all' remedies are not suitable. Added to this are the needs of refugee pupils who have experienced particularly traumatic events such as war and bereavement. These pupils will often have acute mental health problems which will need to be addressed but also have cultural, environmental and language barriers which influence intervention approaches. The issue which transcends both debates is whether educational professionals are the appropriate people to carry out such work and if this is the case, whether they are being given access to sufficient support and resources to carry out these duties.

Case study 10.1: Interventions in a UNICEF Transition Camp

In Mafraq, Jordan during November 2012, Syrian refugee children show Jane MacPhail, a UNICEF child protection worker, pictures they have drawn which depict events that they have witnessed. They show acts of revenge and violence towards others. On seeing these pictures, she asks them to consider what they would draw if they lived in a world which did not contain aggression, hostility and war. The children then begin to draw pictures which include flowers, trees and animals and she asks them which world they would prefer to live in and why.

Jane MacPhail believes that this will encourage children to consider the more positive qualities of their lives and help them to remember what it is like to be a child without the fears and worries faced by adults. She believes that it will help them to relinquish the responsibilities that they may have acquired during the events preceding their resettlement in Jordan.

This is part of a wider intervention that is being adopted within the camp to meet the needs of children who have experienced trauma and stressful events as part of their migration from Syria. The wider programme aims to educate teachers and child protection workers in the psycho-social needs of these children. It provides the workers with a better understanding of the needs of the children and how to address the issues that may have been created through their life experiences so far. There is a six-day training course which trains adults to 'reconnect the feelings part of the brain'. Songs and dance are used to create enjoyable activities which develop links to self, family and community.

Many of the children have witnessed violent events and now re-enact that violence themselves, often talking about revenge attacks. Children feel that they no longer have to conform to the accepted social norms and they have become disconnected from their community. They see their new environment as far removed from their previous life and have started to adopt practices which would have been unacceptable in their former lives. They need to be reminded of how they would have behaved in their country of origin and that this is the behaviour that is expected in their new environment. The children have an emotional burden which means that they have become detached from the world around them, unable to establish normal social bonds with others. Equally, they have also lost the ability to relate effectively with themselves, becoming disconnected from their previous behaviour patterns. These responses have many causes, but even the lack of food can impact emotional well-being leading to lapses in short-term memory and the inability to plan for the future. Jane MacPhail adds that children lose the ability to imagine and this has a detrimental impact on child development.

One of the techniques used is the 'heart contract' where children create a contract of rules which they feel are important. Examples of these rules include 'don't fight', 'love our families' and 'respect our teachers'. If children fail to observe these agreements, they can be shown the contract and reminded of the rules that they have created. This helps to remind them of the expected behaviours and enables staff to work effectively with them.

Working with the children and allowing them to connect again with their emotions, as well as other people, allows the whole community to develop and recuperate. The ability of the children to reconnect with their parents and community allows the adults to begin to rebuild their lives.

Jane MacPhail says the importance of this work with children cannot be underestimated, as, once children begin to reconnect to their feelings it has a ripple effect and begins to impact on the community itself. It is the children's renewed connection with their parents and communities that helps the adults, themselves, to recover.

Source: Adapted from Bruere (2016) for UNICEF

Key questions
- What type of interventions are seen as effective for these pupils? How do you feel that these could be transferred to mainstream education in Western cultures?
- How does the microsystem influence the children's behaviours? How do the workers begin to make links between the children and their new environment?
- Overall, do you think that these approaches are feasible within mainstream education? Justify your response.

Conclusion

Meeting the mental health needs of the young is now becoming a priority in many educational settings. Children and young people are reacting to changes in their environment, academic expectations, cultural and social structures and practitioners are increasingly being asked to manage and address issues arising from related mental health needs. This often impacts on the mental health of the practitioners themselves, particularly when their needs are not met within the support mechanisms of the educational setting. The situation is further complicated when supporting the needs of particular groups such as refugee children who face traumas before, during and after migration which can increase the risk of mental health problems. An essential factor in meeting these needs is a theoretical knowledge of effective responses and the ability to put them into practice. The development of suitable training and support for professionals working to nurture the mental health of the young in educational settings, is therefore a priority and an essential element in sustaining the community and inclusive education.

Suggested reading

Fazel, M. (2015) A Moment of Change: Facilitating Refugee Children's Mental Health in UK Schools. *International Journal of Educational Development*, 41, 225–261.

This journal article discusses the issues faced in UK schools when staff have to meet the needs of refugee children, with particular reference to psychological and mental health needs. Short case studies are also considered and give an insight into the challenges that can be faced by practitioners.

Sirin, S. R. & Rogers-Sirin (2015) *The Educational and Mental Health Needs of Syrian Refugee Children*. Washington, DC: Migration Policy Institute.

This is a report which was prepared for a research conference at the Migration Policy Institute, which concentrates on young children aged from birth to ten years of age. It considers the well-being of children migrating from Syria and addresses aspects such as child development, psychology, sociology, health, education and public policy. It is useful in providing an overview of the current issues that are faced in meeting the needs of these children.

References

Achievement for All (2016) *Let's Pull Together and Get Education Working for Everyone*. Available at: www.afaeducation.org (accessed 04.08.2016).

Anderson, A. (2004) Resilience. In Hamilton, R. & Moore, D. (eds.) *Educational Interventions for Refugee Children: Theoretical Perspectives and Implementing Best Practice*. London: RoutledgeFalmer, pp. 53–63.

Anderson, A. Hamilton, R. Moore, D. Loewen, S. & Frater- Mathieson, K. (2004) Education of refugee children: Theoretical perspectives and best practice. In Hamilton, R. & Moore, D. (eds.) *Educational Interventions for Refugee Children: Theoretical Perspectives and Implementing Best Practice*. London: RoutledgeFalmer, pp. 1–11.

BBC (2016) Four in 10 Teachers 'Attacked by Pupils'. Available at: www.bbc.co.uk/news/education-35431782 (accessed 30.01.2016).

Betancourt, T.S. Frounfelker, R., Mishra, T., Hussein, A. & Falzarano, R. (2015) Addressing Health Disparities in the Mental Health of Refugee Children and Adolescents through Community-Based Participatory Research: A Study in Two Communities. *American Journal of Public Health*, 105:S3, 475–482.

British Association for Counselling and Psychotherapy (2016) About Us. Available at: https://www.bacp.co.uk/about_bacp/ (accessed 30.01.2016).

Bronfenbrenner, U. (1994) Ecological Models of Human Development. In *International Encyclopaedia of Education* 3, (2nd Edn). Oxford: Elsevier. Reprinted in Gauvain, M. & Cole, M. (eds.) (1993) *Readings* on the Development of Children, (2nd Edn, pp. 37–43). New York: Freeman. Available at: www.psy.cmu.edu/~siegler/35bronfebrenner94.pdf

Bruere, W. (2016) In Jordan, Syrian refugee Children Learn How to Recover from a Violent Past. Available at: www.unicef.org/infobycountry/jordan_66351.html

Cefai, C. & Camilleri, L. (2015) A Healthy Start: Promoting Mental Health and Well-being in the Early Primary School Years. *Emotional and Behavioural Difficulties*, 20:2, 133–152.

Children and Families Act (2014). Available at: www.legislation.gov.uk/ukpga/2014/6/contents/enacted

DCSF (2009) *Lamb Inquiry: SEN and Parental Confidence*. Nottingham: DCSF Publications.

Desforges, C. & Abouchaar, A. (2003) *The Impact of Parental Involvement, Parental Support and Family Education on Pupil Achievement and Adjustment: A Literature Review*. London: DfES.

DfE (2014) Mental Health Behaviour Guidance to be Issued to Schools. Available at: www.gov.uk/government/news/mental-health-behaviour-guidance-to-be-issued-to-schools

DfE (2015) *NFER Teacher Voice Omnibus: June 2015 Responses*. Available at: www.gov.uk/government/publications/teacher-voice-omnibus-june-2015-responses

Fazel, M. (2015) A Moment of Change: Facilitating Refugee Children's Mental Health in UK Schools. *International Journal of Educational Development*, 41, 225–261.

Frater-Mathieson, K. (2004) Refugee Trauma, Loss and Grief: Implications for Intervention. In Hamilton, R. & Moore, D. (eds.) (2004) *Educational Interventions for Refugee Children: Theoretical Perspectives and Implementing Best Practice*. London: RoutledgeFalmer.

Guardian (2015) 'We Can't Go Back': Families seeking Asylum Fear Destitution. Available at: www.theguardian.com/society/2015/aug/19/families-seeking-asylum-face-destitution-under-new-rules (accessed 04.08.2016).

Guardian (2016) Children Seeking Asylum in the UK Denied Access to Education. Available at: www.theguardian.com/society/2016/feb/02/children-seeking-asylum-in-uk-denied-access-to-education (accessed 04.08.2016).

Hamilton, R. (2004) Schools, Teachers and the Education of Refugee Children. In Hamilton, R. & Moore, D. (Eds.) (2004) *Educational Interventions for Refugee Children: Theoretical Perspectives and Implementing Best Practice*. London: RoutledgeFalmer.

Harris, A. & Goodall, J. (2007) *Engaging Parents in Raising Achievement: Do Parents Know They Matter? A Research Project Commissioned by the Specialist Schools and Academies Trust*. London: DCSF.

Hattie, J. (2009) *Visible Learning: A Synthesis of Over 800 Meta-Analyses Relating to Achievement*. Abingdon: Routledge.

Home Room (2016) *The Critical Voice of Parents in Education*. Available at: blog.ed.gov/2015/06/the-critical-voice-of-parents-in-education-2

Kelly, E. & Bokhari, F. (2012) *Safeguarding Children from Abroad: Refugee, Asylum Seeking and Trafficked Children in the UK*. London: Jessica Kingsley.

Lawson, H.A., Quinn, K.P., Hardiman, E. & Miller Jr., R.L. (2006) Mental Health Needs and Problems as Opportunities for Expanding the Boundaries of School Improvement. In Waller, R.J. (ed.) (2006) *Fostering Child and Adolescent Mental Health in the Classroom*. London: Sage.

Lindo, N.A. Taylor, D.D. Meany-Walen, K.K., Purswell, K., Jayne, K., Gonzales, T. & Jones, L. (2014) Teachers as Therapeutic Agents: Perceptions of a School-based Mental Health Initiative. *British Journal of Guidance and Counselling*, 42:3, 284–296.

Maslow, A. (1954) *Motivation and Personality*. New York: Harper.

McLeod, S.A. (2016) *Maslow's Hierarchy of Needs*. Available at: www.simplypsychology.org/maslow.html

Measham, T., Guzder, J., Rousseau, C., Pacione, L., Blais-McPherson, M. & Nadeau, L. (2014) Refugee Children and their Families: Supporting Psychological Well-Being and Positive Adaption Following Migration. *Current Problems in Paediatric and Adolescent Health Care: Primary Care for Refugee Children*, 44:7, 208–215.

New York Times (2016) Sweden Toughens Rules for Refugees Seeking Asylum. Available at: www.nytimes.com/2016/06/22/world/europe/sweden-immigrant-restrictions.html?_r=0 (accessed 04.08.2016).

Norwich, B. & Eaton, A. (2015) The New Special Educational Needs (SEN) Legislation in England and Implications for Services for Children and Young People with Social, Emotional and Behavioural Difficulties. *Emotional and Behavioural Difficulties*, 20:2, 117–132.

Ofsted (2015) *School Inspection Handbook: Handbook for Inspecting Schools in England under Section 5 of the Education Act 2005*. Available at: www.gov.uk/government/uploads/system/uploads/attachment_data/file/458866/School_inspection_handbook_section_5_from_September_2015.pdf

Ragonesi, I.C. & Martinelli, V. (2013) Somali Children in the Maltese Educational System. *Malta Review of Educational Research (MRER)*, 7:2. Available at: www.mreronline.org/wp-content/uploads/2013/12/MRER712P1.pdf

Reid, G., Peer, L., Strachan, S. & Page, J. (2016) Special Educational Needs: Parents' Perspectives. In Peer, L. & Reid, G. (eds.) (2016) *Special Educational Needs: A Guide for Inclusive Practice* (2nd Edn). London: Sage.

Sirin, S.R. & Rogers-Sirin, L. (2015) *The Educational and Mental Health Needs of Syrian Refugee Children*. Washington, DC: Migration Policy Institute.

Soppitt, R. (2016) Attention Deficit Hyperactivity Disorder (or Hyperkinetic Disorder). In Peer, L. & Reid, G. (eds.) (2016) *Special Educational Needs: A Guide for Inclusive Practice* (2nd Edn). London: Sage.

Steer, A. (2009) *Learning Behaviour: Lessons Learned: A Review of Behaviour Standards and Practices in our Schools*. Nottingham: DCSF Publications. Available at: www.educationengland.org.uk/documents/pdfs/2009-steer-report-lessons-learned.pdf (accessed 16.02.2016).

UNHCR (2011) *Handbook and Guidelines on Procedures and Criteria for Determining Refugee Status under the 1951 Convention and the 1967 Protocol Relating to the Status of Refugees*. Geneva: UNHCR.

WHO (2001) *The World Health Report Mental Health: New Understanding, New Hope*. Available at: www.who.int/whr/2001/en/ (accessed 04.08.2016).

Wolpert, M., Humphrey, N., Belsky, J. & Deighton, J. (2013) Embedding Mental Health Support in Schools: Learning from the Targeted Mental Health in Schools (TaMHS) National Evaluation. *Emotional and Behavioural Difficulties*, 18:3, 270–283.

Young Minds (2016) What's the problem? Available at www.youngminds.org.uk/about/whats_the_problem

11 The role of education in resilience

Andy Marshall

This chapter explores:

- the meaning of resilience;
- the context of resilience in education;
- the practical application of resilience in education.

What is resilience?

In an ever unstable and unpredictable world, we hear about resilience in multiple settings – in the home, in sport, at work and perhaps most frequently in our response to disasters, from natural hazards to terrorism, and infectious diseases to financial shocks. Resilience has breadth but it also has depth, it is a through-life concept that can be equally relevant to young and old alike. This chapter therefore initially examines the concept of resilience in more detail in order to develop a better understanding of its broad context. It then seeks to encourage debate around whether education could or should have a role to play in developing it.

> **Activity: What is resilience?**
>
> Think about the term 'resilience'. How would you define it? Are there different ways that resilience can be interpreted and defined? How do your ideas compare to the ones below?

A review of key literature suggests that resilience can be codified into at least five main areas, each with its own variation on both definition and interpretation.

1. Science and medicine

Clarke and Nicholson (2010) trace the origin of resilience to the physical properties of a material to revert to its original state after being subjected to bending or stretching. They also underline the common reference to patients in medicine whose resilience may be a measure of how capable they are to withstand not only the stress of trauma or injury but also their ability to respond to intervention and treatment.

2. Individual vulnerability

Resilience is commonly linked with the study of vulnerable children and young adults who have been exposed to, or are at risk from, adverse behaviour such as sexual abuse and domestic violence and may have experienced formal social care intervention. Vulnerable children have typically been seen as passive, helpless actors whose safety and life chances have historically depended upon external intervention by education, prevention and therapy (Thompson, 2006). Thompson promotes a preventative culture where resilience is an enabler to empower children and young people to take responsibility for their own emotional development, to make them stronger in the face of adversity. She therefore agrees with core definitions of resilience as the 'capacity to bounce back: to withstand hardship and repair oneself' (Wolin & Wolin, 1993 in Thompson, 2006, p. 8) and 'the strengths humans require to master cycles of disruption and reintegration throughout the lifecycle' (Flach, 1998 in Thompson, 2006, p. 8). In so doing, she accepts the allied importance of developing resilient personalities (see Figure 11.1) who possess characteristics such as compromise, discipline, self-awareness, open-mindedness, a sense of humour, the ability to dream about the future, endurance of distress and a focus and commitment to life (Thompson, 2006, p. 8). The environment in which resilience is promoted and developed is a multi-agency construct,

Figure 11.1 Resilient personality characteristics (adapted from Thompson, 2006, p. 8)

centred on the community and underpinned by trust in all people and organisations (Thompson, 2006, p. 8).

Similarly, Gilligan (2009, p. 6) defines resilience as:

> [D]oing well in the face of adversity. Resilience comprises a set of qualities that may help a person to withstand many of the negative effects of adversity. A child displaying resilience has more positive outcomes than might be expected given the level of adversity impinging on their development.

As with Thompson (2006), Gilligan (2009) agrees that children are not bystanders in their personal growth so they can influence it with the aid of a supportive and positive environment, where formal professional interventions do not restrict the development of their own resilience. The approach is very much 'optimistic and pragmatic' (Gilligan, 2009, p. 9) and centred on empowering the child to develop skills and behaviours that will have enduring relevance throughout his or her life.

Cyrulnik (2009) echoes many of the concepts put forward by Thompson (2006) and Gilligan (2009). For example, the role of the individual is central to developing resilience and is seen as an emotional, character-based quality that can be developed throughout life by a person's interactions with his or her environment: 'resilience is a sweater knitted from developmental, emotional and social strands of wool' (Cyrulnik, 2009, p. 51) and 'resilience is an internal mechanism that allows us to cope with life's adversities' (Cyrulnik, 2009, p. 47).

While Cyrulnik accepts that there is a high price to be paid for experiencing adversity, people do have the capacity to bounce back to a position that is equal to or better than before. For example, he rejects the assertion that trauma inevitably leads to depression later in life and maintains that many 'at-risk' children actually go on to become 'well-rounded adults'. The key to achieving this for Cyrulnik is the close interplay, as outlined by Thompson and Gilligan, of the self and the environment: 'Resilience is not just something we find inside ourselves or in our environment. It is something we find midway between the two, because our individual development is always linked to our social development' (Cyrulnik, 2009, p. 284).

Thompson (2006), Gilligan (2009) and Cyrulnik (2009) all echo earlier views put forward by Newman (2004). Newman defines resilience simply as 'a quality that helps individuals or communities to resist and recover from adversities' (Newman, 2004, p. 35). However, he too argues that resilience, particularly for vulnerable children, lies in the individual linking to effective 'assets and resources', such as competent parenting, high-quality schools and teachers, community resources, connections to supportive adults and support networks and an internal sense of self-worth, self-efficacy and self-determination (Newman, 2004, p. 7). Like Cyrulnik (2009), the interplay between the individual and the environment is a key determinant of resilience as opposed to a singular focus on risks and associated risk-based interventions (such as placing a child in care) (Newman, 2004, p. 5). That is not to say that interventions are not important in promoting and developing resilience, particularly where multiple risk factors such as poverty, racism and low social capital are present. However, children commonly cite the main contributory factor for having succeeded 'against the odds' as the support provided by extended family, peers, neighbours and informal mentors and not the 'transient involvement of professionals' (Newman, 2004, p. 26).

Newman (2004) accepts that if resilience relies on strong community fabric, much the same as Cyrulnik's (2009) 'knitted sweater', the necessary environmental support mechanisms are more likely to be present in safe communities, strong in social capital (Newman, 2004, p. 20). This is not to say that children from socially challenged environments who are exposed to significant risk cannot be resilient as 'resilience has nothing to with vulnerability or invulnerability' (Cyrulnik, 2009, p. 284). In other words, resilience is a response to a unique individual and environmental situation in any place at any given time and overcoming adversity is more about the ability to adapt and evolve to these new and changing circumstances.

Limiting exposure to (or even removing) all risk because there is abundant social capital to do so, may also be counter-productive in terms of promoting resilience. As Cyrulnik outlines, resilience is an oxymoron: it can have positive outcomes but ultimately it is a natural defence against trauma: 'Resilience has a form and there is a price to be paid' (Cyrulnik, 2009, p. 287). Newman is therefore well placed to stress that developing coping mechanisms in children is ultimately also dependent on a necessary '[m]anaged exposure to risk' (Newman, 2004, p. 27).

> **Activity: Managing risk**
>
> Should children be exposed to 'managed' risks? If so, what should these be? Do schools allow managed exposure to risk and, if so, how do they manage it?

The Wakefield Resilience Framework (Wakefield Council, 2015) provides an example of a protective policy to help reduce the risk of adverse outcomes in vulnerable children and young adults aged 0–19. Based in West Yorkshire (UK), the Framework is a multi-agency approach offering advice, guidance and resources for teachers, youth support workers and early years teachers to promote interventions that reduce risk and 'motivate and help develop the practical skills and core competences children and young people need to be resilient'.

> **Activity: Activities to promote resilience**
>
> Think about how you would design a programme of activities to develop resilience across the 0–19 age range. What factors would you focus on developing? What methods would you use to deliver these? How would your approach change to suit different ages? When you have listed your ideas, visit the Wakefield Resilience Framework to see what key factors its programme focused on to develop resilience.

This echoes Gilligan's (2009, p. 8) view that formal interventions, where necessary, should:

> enhance resilience in young people in care or in need by positively influencing social experiences available to them, their carers and their family of origin without prolonging problems unnecessarily by failing to see the resilience potential in a young person or their social context.

3. Cognitive/behavioural

The literature suggests that a further area broadens the scope of resilience theory and practice beyond vulnerability in at-risk groups. Neenan (2009, p. 17), for example, defines resilience as 'a set of flexible, cognitive, behavioural and emotional responses to acute or chronic adversities, which can be usual or commonplace'.

From this Neenan outlines that resilience is rooted in the self, an emotional concept that interacts with the 'context in which you live' (Neenan, 2009, p. 17), very much as Thompson, Gilligan and Newman argued. However, the key departure from a simple focus on vulnerable or at-risk groups is that resilience is neither rare, nor is it the preserve of the few (Neenan, 2009, p. 17). We can all experience adversity and we can all, therefore, be resilient; resilience is ordinary and not extraordinary. Resilience is more about progression through life towards defined personal goals and how any individual negotiates adversity to attain these. Neenan (2009, p. 17) therefore questions the common interpretation of resilience as 'bouncing back', preferring to see it as 'coming back', a slower journey that promotes change through learning in order to meet established goals. This perhaps distinguishes Neenan (2009) from Thompson (2006), Gilligan (2009), Newman (2004) and Cyrulnik (2009); if resilience is based on behaviours, then resilience can be developed, in Neenan's case through Cognitive Behavioural Therapy (CBT) (Neenan, 2009) to build resilience to life's inevitable adversities in the context of the individual, the workplace, relationships and when dealing with difficult people.

Clarke and Nicholson (2010) argue that resilience is 'the ability to bounce back from tough times or even triumph in the face of adversity; to display tenacity, but not at the expense of reason'. Notwithstanding the distinction between 'bouncing back' and 'coming back' that is outlined above, this definition has much in common with Neenan (2009), primarily through the suggestion that resilience is a character trait (tenacity) and that it is applied with some degree of judgement (reason). Clarke and Nicholson (2010) argue that resilience is therefore a function of emotional intelligence and that the key to a better understanding of this is self-awareness. Resilience is therefore not a static concept and it can be taught: 'Crucially, we believe that these skills, attitudes and behaviours [i.e. resilience] can be refined, developed or, in some cases, learnt from scratch ... we really can learn to become more resilient' (Clarke & Nicholson, 2010).

This moves beyond Neenan (2009) in asserting that resilience can be measured and monitored over time. This is illustrated in the Nicholson McBride Resilience Questionnaire (NMRQ), consisting of 64 questions that explore key indicators of resilience. There are two key observations to make from this. First and foremost is the assertion that people have a unique Resilience Quotient (RQ) (Clarke & Nicholson, 2010). Second is the conclusion from the findings of the NMRQ that there are five common elements that are 'central' to resilience:

- optimism;
- freedom from stress and anxiety;
- individual accountability;
- openness and flexibility;
- problem orientation.

Not only does this re-emphasise the emotional drivers of resilience, but Clarke and Nicholson (2010) specifically point to the importance of childhood in the development of individual resilience. Drawing from interviews with 26 people who had experienced and triumphed over personal or professional adversity (the so-called R-Team), all participants remarked how events and experiences from their early childhood explain why they feel they had become so resilient (Clarke & Nicholson, 2010). This feedback is categorised into five themes, suggesting that childhood brings back vivid memories of one or more of the following:

- being in 'Troubled Times' leading to a sense of determination to succeed;
- being a 'Fish out of Water', feeling in some way different to other children (e.g. racial minority, academic ability);
- having an 'Unhappy Family', leading to a need to take on responsibility early in life;
- having 'Strong Role Models', from at least one adult to inspire ambition;
- having a 'Competitive Edge' at school through sport.

This is not to suggest that resilience can be developed solely in childhood, as respondents suggested that key moments in 'young adulthood' and the 'middle years' presented 'critical challenges' to their resilience (Clarke & Nicholson, 2010, p. 17). In the context of this chapter, it is simply important to consider the potential significance of childhood on the promotion and development of resilience. This is perhaps supported by the tendency for survivors of childhood trauma to display a sense of 'sublimation' (artistic, intellectual, ethical activities) and emotional self-control (time management, reduced anger and despair) (Cyrulnik, 2009); in other words children form their emotional response to adversity in the short term, but also shape their minds for how they will react to life events in the future in a more resilient way. Beyond this, the period of 'youth' is seen to have equal importance in the development of resilience and 'the most neurotic choices we make in our lives – choosing a career and choosing a partner – are basically made when we are young, and youth is a sensitive period' (Cyrulnik, 2009, p. 139).

Grotberg (2003, p. 1) defines resilience as 'the human capacity to deal with, overcome, learn from, or even be transformed by the inevitable adversities of life'. This underpins a strong sense that resilience is not just found in a lucky or celebrated few, but that it can be found in everyone, it can be developed, it can be promoted at any age and there does not need to be an instance of adversity for resilience to emerge (Grotberg, 2003). However, Grotberg (2003) echoes the study of resilience in the context of vulnerability by arguing that resilience in children is highly dependent on forming a trusted relationship with an adult role model, such as a family member, carer, teacher, youth worker or member of the Emergency Services. This idea is based on the 'International Resilience Research Project', conducted in 2000, where 1,225 parents and their children from 27 sites across 22 countries were interviewed. Based on this, Grotberg (2003) concluded that:

- every resilient person was helped to become resilient at some point;
- individual temperament was key to the successful development of resilience;
- the socio-economic environment of an individual does not necessarily determine their resilience;
- resilience is developed by a combination of allied factors and not a single source;
- cultural variations determine how resilience is promoted and developed;
- the age and gender of the child is related to their resilience.

Grotberg's (2003, p. 3) model consists of three 'factors' (I have; I am; I can), which can be linked to eight 'building blocks' (trust, autonomy, initiative, industry, identity, intimacy, generativity and integrity) to explain a situation in the context of resilience and promote strategies for improving it. Again, resilience is seen as a concept that exists in all, it can be developed and at its heart lies emotional intelligence interacting within each unique social context. More recently, Grotberg's (2003) model has been applied as a behavioural/cognitive approach to resilience to promote positive mental health in Australian schools (Worsley, 2014).

> **Activity: Resilience and character**
>
> 'Educational policy should promote good character as an essential life skill.' List as many arguments for and against this statement as you can.

A final application of the cognitive/behavioural resilience approach is when resilience is seen as a policy tool to promote social mobility by influencing factors such as character and behaviour. An example of this is the UK All-Parliamentary Group on Social Mobility's 'Character and Resilience Manifesto' (Lexmond et al., 2014). This draws on many of the themes that this chapter has highlighted by claiming that, for example, resilience is not reliant on birth: it can be taught and learnt throughout life; it is influenced by emotional intelligence; its promotion should start early; it should be tailored to meet changing age ranges and that positive parenting is crucial to embedding resilience from an early age. 'Children's attainment, well-being, happiness and resilience are profoundly affected by the quality of the guidance, love and care they receive during the first few years of their lives' (Lexmond et al., 2014, p. 21). Resilience is a universally applicable concept that should be seen not only as core business of education policy, but that a sense of character, coupled to a resilient outlook, are key determinants of positive life outcomes.

4. Disaster management

The main drivers of resilience theory in the field of disaster management lie within specific national, regional and local policies. In the UK, for example, resilience policy emanates from the Civil Contingencies Act 2004, produced by the UK government's Cabinet Office (2004). While the Act itself does not define the term 'resilience', it does outline what circumstances constitute an 'emergency' or 'major incident' before then placing specific legal duties on prescribed responder organisations to prepare to respond to, and recover from, events such as floods and pandemics. An organisation meeting its requirements under the Act could therefore be described as 'resilient', although there is no structure in place (other than perhaps the International Standard for Business Continuity (ISO 22301) and British Standard for Organisational Resilience (BS 65000)) to formally benchmark, assess, measure and report on compliance; it is therefore difficult for a UK responder or community to truly and objectively know how resilient they actually are.

Further non-statutory guidance is laid out in two supporting documents, Emergency Preparedness (Cabinet Office, 2006) and Emergency Response and Recovery (Cabinet Office, 2013). Within these, resilience is defined as the 'ability of the community, services, area or infrastructure to detect, prevent, and, if necessary to withstand, handle and recover from disruptive challenges'

(Cabinet Office, 2013, p. 229). Sector-specific policies and plans may also be developed which are linked to, but do not replace, national planning frameworks. An example would be the UK NHS's Emergency Preparedness, Resilience and Response (EPRR) Framework (NHS England, 2013), which lays out specific emergency planning guidance for NHS organisations and staff.

Resilience is also driven trans-nationally. For example, the UN Sendai Framework for Disaster Risk Reduction 2015–2030 clearly defines resilience (UNISDR, 2015, p. 9) but outlines the importance of nations incorporating this into policies, plans, programmes and budgets in order not only to focus on building resilience to actual disasters but also to reduce disaster risk itself and help promote sustainable development and poverty eradication (UNISDR, 2015). A multi-agency, multi-sectoral, people-centred 'enabling environment' is called for which is overtly broad in context, encompassing investment in the economic, social, health, cultural, educational, community, country, environment, technology and research systems across the globe (UNISDR, 2015, p. 11), in order to 'strengthen resilience' (UNISDR, 2015, p. 12). Within this, there are seven targets, thirteen guiding principles and four priorities for action. Included in the priorities for action are specific references to education:

- Priority 1: 24(m): To promote national strategies to strengthen public education in disaster risk reduction (UNISDR, 2015, p. 15).
- Priority 1: 25(f): To develop effective global and regional campaigns as instruments for public awareness and education … to promote a culture of disaster prevention, resilience and responsible citizenship (UNISDR, 2015, p. 16).

> **Activity: Resilience and global policy drivers**
>
> Consider how education policy and practice, both in the UK and internationally, might help to achieve the resilience-based outcomes of the UN Sendai Framework 2015–2030.

A clear link can also be made between UN and EU policy on resilience. The Roadmap for Europe 2030, for example, outlines how the EU plans to better inform investment and capability development in the higher education sector in order to meet the Sendai Framework's outcomes on disaster risk reduction. In so doing, it recognises the increasing importance of resilience in enabling communities to 'bounce back' after disasters (Amaratunga et al., 2015, p. 6).

5. Community resilience

Community resilience is a highly contextualised relative of disaster management theory and is more about promoting effective prevention, preparation, response and recovery by joining local networks in response to specific, recognised local hazards or risks (Ronan & Johnston, 2005). Key to this is a coalition of groups, specifically schools, youth and families, who share a high degree of motivation, typically born out of a shared risk or hazard, to be prepared to 'bounce back' after a disaster (Ronan & Johnston, 2005, p. 10). Community resilience is a force for positive change, an 'impetus for transformation within a community' (Ronan & Johnston, 2005, p. 10).

Others argue that risk is one of a number of drivers of community resilience. Cultural history and epidemiology may also lead to a heightened sense of togetherness in adversity in certain

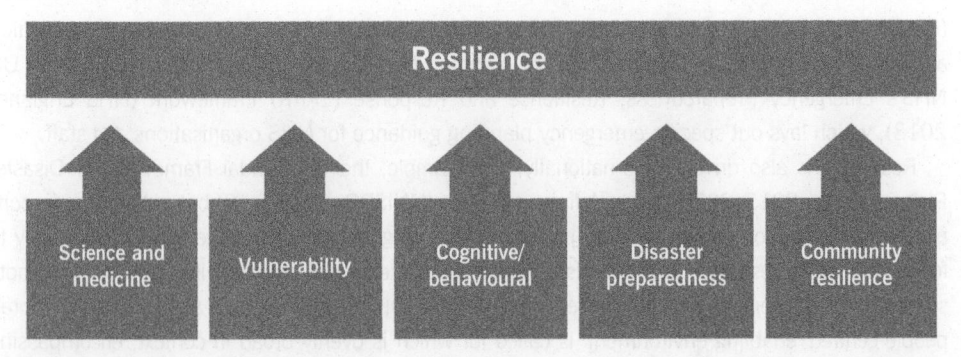

Figure 11.2 The five main areas of resilience

communities (for example, the Inca/Mayan tradition is claimed to have fostered an enduring sense of social solidarity in Latin American communities), along with social humour, good governance, spirituality and collective self-esteem (Suarez-Ojeda in Grotberg, 2003).

An example of a formal community resilience strategy, driven by learning from the Fukushima earthquake in 2011, is the Japanese Disaster Resilience Handbook. This establishes legal obligations on organisations and communities to prepare for disasters, while also providing resource material for communities to build individual and collective resilience. This is done through an 'educational climate' that promotes local knowledge of risk, a spirit of collective solidarity and the practical ability to be able to evacuate an area in an emergency (Japanese Government Cabinet Office, 2015).

Education and resilience

The literature has indicated that education already has a key role to play in resilience. However, it does this compartmentally, acting within each discrete area outlined above. It is difficult, therefore, to evidence an attempt, successful or otherwise, of a genuinely holistic approach to resilience that joins the concept specifically across the vulnerability, cognitive/behavioural, disaster management and community resilience spectrum. Newman (2004) suggests that there is traction in the latter approach, given that resilience is most effective when promoted as part of a wider strategy; yet he too finds it difficult to cite clear examples where strategies of comprehensive resilience strategy have been validated and replicated.

Perhaps the closest examples of holistic approaches to resilience can be found in curriculum development. Curriculum mapping in Australia shows how the teaching of resilience can be segmented across Science, Geography, History and Health and Physical Education (Dufty, 2014; dk2 Pty Ltd Australia, 2014) and split into discrete units of work (Australian Government Attorney General's Department, 2012). The US Department for Homeland Security also provides a Youth Emergency Preparedness 'Be a Hero' curriculum that contains extensive cross-curricular teaching materials across Humanities, Science and Mathematics for application from first to twelfth grade (US DHS, 2015). Finally, the Regional Consultative Committee (RCC) on Disaster Management (2007) outlines the key drivers for integrating disaster risk reduction into mainstream education and a range of suggested steps for designing and influencing such a programme.

However, the literature highlights a range of consistent themes which suggest that a more holistic approach to 'resilience education' (Brown et al., 2004 in Newman, 2004, p .58) could be feasible:

- Resilience is widely understood to affect us all as individuals in some way and at some point in our lives, irrespective of age, gender, nationality, cultural identity and social background. As Neenan (2009, p. 7) outlines, resilience is 'routine'.
- It can be taught and developed at any stage in life, but the earlier it is taught, the more effective it is. Delivery must also be flexible and adaptable to suit a particular age range (Barusch & Strutman, 2003 in Grotberg, 2003, p. 49).
- It is founded on a network of social factors, including family, community organisations and adult role models. School lies at the heart of this network and can therefore be central for targeting the most at-risk members of a community but also in building resilience that lasts into the immediate and long term. 'Schools are a centrally located part in any community that links the adults of tomorrow with the majority of the adults and households of today' (Ronan & Johnston, 2005, p. 2).
- It can help people become more aware of, and therefore help reduce exposure to, risks.
- Children are often seen as 'agents of change' (UNISDR, 2015, p. 23) in promoting risk knowledge transfer to family members and adults.
- It may have an economic benefit. For example, if it is accepted that resilience is about promoting a culture of prevention (Ronan & Johnston, 2005; Thompson, 2006), there is potential synergy between individual public service providers through reducing the frequency and cost of formal interventions (particularly when it is claimed that the monetary benefit to society of implementing initiatives to promote resilience is '2.8 times that of the cost of delivery'; Lexmond et al., 2014). The 'Life Skills Project' in the UK is an example of a range of joint outcomes being shared across a broad range of organisations (public health, fire and rescue service, local authority, civil contingencies unit, third sector etc.) and attained through the promotion of 'personal health, safety, mental and physical wellbeing' across all ages (Garner, 2015).
- It is about managing change (Neenan, 2009) and it may also impact positively on social mobility. Newman (2004, p. 59), for example, argues that schools may well influence social mobility through resilience development by tackling the 'subversion of achievement' and 'learned helplessness'. A further example is given by Thompson (2006) who describes the intervention of a mentor to enable rather than direct the 'change process' to support a student in the US who aspired to attend college. In an informal report, the educational system 'had no time to work with this student … parents don't have a clue anyway. The mother is an immigrant and the father is an absentee career soldier. They surely wouldn't be invested in their child's education' (Thompson, 2006, p. 6). Following support from her mentor, the student went on to obtain a doctorate in Counselling and Educational Administration from the College of William & Mary and hold adjunct professorships at three universities.
- It is driven by international collaborative frameworks which encourage the development of policy to incorporate resilience through risk awareness and preparedness in education.
- It may well promote resilience through emotional intelligence. Paphazy (2003, in Grotberg, 2003, p. 105) argues that resilience should in fact become the 'Fourth R' in schools, and that

the role of teachers should be 'to help children develop a variety of problem-solving and social/inter-personal skills. Teachers do this by modelling and promoting resilience'.
- Education, and specifically the role of teachers, is therefore about building resilience to deal with the routine challenges of life (Paphazy, 2003 in Grotberg, 2003). This is further supported by Thompson (2006), who argues that the role of education is to provide significant influence or 'sigfluence' on the emotional development of children, citing the earlier development of an 'emotional development curriculum' as an example of this. Wellington College, a private fee-paying school in the UK, has taught resilience as a core curriculum subject since 2006, with positive effects on students' emotional intelligence (BBC News, 2014). However, a recent study claims that 'character and resilience' contributed to only 0.5 per cent of achievement at GCSE exams, despite a £5 million investment by the UK government in 2014 to promote resilience in students (Griffiths, 2016).

The literature also suggests that there are a range of factors which indicate that developing resilience as a combined educational offering is open to challenge. Consensus on what resilience is, and therefore how to define it, is difficult to achieve: 'Resilience is an intriguing yet elusive concept ... elusive in that the concept resists a definitive definition' (Neenan, 2009, p. 3). A consistent, shared definition of resilience would require significant impetus around joint policy development, potentially requiring consensus across multiple disciplines and, in the context of funding, typically across multiple government departments.

Benefits realisation is typically difficult to articulate as the measurement of resilience outcomes relies on a complex range of factors. How, for example, would a resilient person, community or organisation be defined and how would this be measured? Moreover, benefits realisation may take considerable time, potentially across generations, and be problematic to apportion to a single intervention. This was highlighted in a study of 'public value' generated by the construction of a fire station as a 'community hub' in the UK (Barber, 2012). When assessing the community engagement and intervention that accompanied this strategy (e.g. by co-locating with a local college and supporting a joint educational programme), it was difficult to define how many incidents (e.g. fires) had been prevented by the Fire and Rescue Service *alone* as 'there are a multitude of cross-cutting interventions delivered by a range of partners all aimed at reducing the occurrence of incidents within a locality' (Barber, 2012, p. 42).

Key considerations

- In the context of formal schooling, how and where would resilience sit within already crowded curricula and are teachers best-placed and adequately trained to deliver it?
- While it is claimed that children are enablers of knowledge transfer, it is also claimed that this is often based on assumption (Dufty, 2014). In other words, can children effectively transfer knowledge about being resilient and if so where is the evidence?
- It cannot be assumed that people will act appropriately in response to a risk or hazard (such as flooding) simply because they know about it (Boura, 1998 and Paton et al., 2003 in Dufty, 2008).
- When resilience is seen as a promoter of social mobility or life skills, it may be problematic to define what desirable character and behaviour are, without them being perceived as a potentially

partisan concept, 'some new modern code word for moral fibre or moral character' (Gilligan, 2009, p. 8).
- Learning takes place in non-formal and informal contexts (Dufty, 2014), particularly with the proliferation of social media (see Chapter 12). This presents a further challenge to measuring how resilient we are as individuals and communities as social media is not part of the formal curriculum.
- If resilience is really something that affects us all, then it must equally be seen as a through-life concept. Much focus has been placed in this chapter on the role of education and resilience in the context of the formal education of children. However, genuine resilience, in its widest sense, must be equally applicable to the very young (pre-school) and adults who are no longer in formal education.

Conclusion

Resilience is a complex concept that has multiple meanings in multiple contexts. It has increasing resonance due to the proliferation of global risks and the global policy consensus contained within the UN Sendai Framework 2015–2030 that sees building resilience as a means to not only improve disaster response, but as a lever for social change; education is overtly seen to have a key role in achieving these outcomes. This chapter has highlighted the broad definitions of resilience to illustrate its application in the contexts of science, vulnerability, cognitive behaviour, disaster management and community resilience. This has shown that despite such divergent interpretations, a number of key themes emerge such as the importance of emotional intelligence to individuals and communities, suggesting the potential for combining resilience outcomes to achieve multiple goals. Education could be the catalyst for such a combined effect.

The review of resilience highlights a number of potential areas for further research. These include:

- the definition of resilience;
- the measurement of resilience;
- resilience curriculum mapping;
- cost-benefit analysis of resilience programmes in education;
- the use of children as agents of knowledge transfer;
- the implementation of the Sendai Framework priorities for action for education;
- the relationship between social mobility and resilience.

Case study 11.1: The Pillowcase Project – a combined approach to promoting resilience in schools

The Pillowcase Project is a Red Cross initiative that was established in the United States in 2013 with sponsorship from the Walt Disney Company to promote resilience through awareness of emergency preparedness. The Pillowcase Project stems from the aftermath of Hurricane Katrina in August 2005 when evacuees arrived at Red Cross emergency shelters carrying their belongings in pillowcases. The Project has now been rolled out across the US and an international pilot has been run by the Global Disaster Preparedness Center (GDPC) in six further countries: the UK, Australia, Hong Kong, Mexico, Peru and Vietnam. The next phase of the Project is to extend the scheme to up to 75,000 children aged 8–11 in 15 further countries.

Delivery of the Pillowcase Project is based on a core curriculum, aimed chiefly at children aged 7–11, although the content of the lessons can be adapted to reflect the most pressing local risks and hazards. The generic lessons cover awareness of safety in the home, including the need to make and test a fire safety evacuation plan, how to evacuate in the event of fire, the reason for having smoke alarms and the importance of testing them. They then focus on building awareness of specific local risks and what to do in the event of them happening, before then looking at coping strategies in times of stress and building a 'communications plan'. The final activity encourages students to draw on their pillowcase that they are issued with at the start of the lessons, in order to illustrate the key messages that they have learned and show what emergency equipment they will put in their pillowcase when they take it home at the end of the lesson.

The Pillowcase Project may at first appear like simply risk-specific emergency training. However, there are a number of elements within it that illustrate the broader potential appeal of resilience in education. Firstly, delivery can be multi-agency. For example, in Peru the Pillowcase Project is delivered by local Red Cross volunteers and members of the local Civil Defence organisation. There is an expectation that children will take the learning back into their families and communities to transfer knowledge to adults. Chelsi Monroe, a teacher from Louisville, Kentucky in the US, stated that, 'By teaching kids, they absorb everything like a sponge. The hope is that when you teach one kid, they go home and teach a household' (American Red Cross, 2016). A similar sentiment was echoed from the experience of Pisco and Chincha in Peru, an area which was hit by an earthquake in August 2007, killing 600 people: 'A key selling point to teachers and Civil Defence workers was attitude change in regards to the role of the child ... now this child will share information and definitely be a multiplier, an agent for change for their peers, their parents, their families' (GDPC, 2015).

The Project is aligned with relevant national curricula. For example, in the US the Project is aligned with the Common Core State Standards for Grades 3–5, while in the UK it is provided with suggested links to the National Curriculum in Personal, Social and Health Education (PSHE), Geography, Science and Spiritual, Moral, Social and Cultural (SMSC) learning (British Red Cross, 2015). The learning outcomes include the development of emotional intelligence, such as self-efficacy, adaptive capacity, problem solving, coping skills and management of stress, awareness of local networks and communication skills. Learning is universally applied, irrespective of wider vulnerability, cognitive ability, gender, cultural or racial background. It can be applied internationally. With necessary cultural variation (understanding in Peru, for example, that children who live in jungle areas do not have pillows as they sleep in hammocks), the key underlying messages are consistent and transportable.

Key questions
- Watch the Peru video case study online at http://bit.ly/1SKdH2b.
- List examples in the film that evidence the following:
  - risk awareness and adaptation of material based on risk;
  - leadership;
  - knowledge transfer by children;
  - community engagement.

Suggested reading

Cyrulnik, B. (2009) *Resilience: How Your Inner Strength Can Set You Free from the Past*. London: Penguin Books.

An excellent overview of resilience through the experience of children who have experienced and overcome adversity.

Ronan, K. R. & Johnston, D. M. (2005) *Promoting Community Resilience in Disasters: The Role for Schools, Youth and Families*. New York: Springer.

A detailed introduction to community resilience research and practice and the key role that schools and public education might have in this.

References

Amaratunga, D., Faber, M., Haigh, R., Indirli, M., Kaklauskas, A., Lill, I., Perdikou, S., Rochas, C., Sparf, J., Perera, S., Thayaparan, M. and Velazquez, J. (2015) *ANDROID Report: Disaster Resilience Education and Research Roadmap for Europe 2030*. Disaster Resilience Network. Available at: www.disaster-resilience.net

American Red Cross (2016) *Pillowcase Project*. Available at http://rdcrss.org/1R2LlwH

Australian Government Attorney General's Department (Australian Emergency Management Institute) (2012) *Mt Macedon Disaster Resilience Education Units of Work: Lower Primary, Middle Primary, Upper Primary & Lower Secondary*. Available at: http://bit.ly/1KfvX1M

Barber, R. (2012) *Staffordshire Fire & Rescue Service – Strategic Change and Its Influence on Public Value*. Stoke-on-Trent: Staffordshire University.

BBC News (2014) Character can and should be taught in schools, says Hunt. Available at: http://bbc.in/1g57pGE

British Red Cross (2015) *The Pillowcase Project: Links to the National Curriculum in England*. Available at: http://bit.ly/1WhCv0v

Cabinet Office (2004) *The Civil Contingencies Act 2004*. Available at: http://bit.ly/242aDDs

Cabinet Office (2006) *Emergency Preparedness: Guidance on Part 1 of the Civil Contingencies Act 2004, Its Associated Regulations and Non-Statutory Arrangements*. Available at: http://bit.ly/1TeAX8d

Cabinet Office (2013) *Emergency Response and Recovery: Guidance for Staff of Responder Agencies, Particularly Senior Officers or Managers Involved in Emergency Response and Recovery Preparations*. Available at: http://bit.ly/1oz1odC

Clarke, J. & Nicholson, J. (2010) *Resilience: Bounce Back from Whatever Life Throws at You*. Richmond, UK: Crimson.

Cyrulnik, B. (2009) *Resilience: How Your Inner Strength Can Set You Free from the Past*. London: Penguin Books

dk2 Pty Ltd Australia (2014) *National Emergency Management Project – Educating the Educators – Mapping of Disaster Resilience Education Resources Against the Australian Curriculum – For Schools and Agencies*. Available at: https://schools.aemi.edu.au/content/national-curriculum

Dufty, N. (2008) A new approach to community flood education. *The Australian Journal of Emergency Management*, 23:2, 4–8.

Dufty, N. (2014) Opportunities for disaster resilience learning in the Australian curriculum. *The Australian Journal of Emergency Management*, 29:1, 12–16.

Garner, J. (2015) *Stoke-on-Trent and Staffordshire Lifeskills Resource Needs Analysis and Outcome Framework*. Stafford: Entrust.

Gilligan, R. (2009) *Promoting Resilience: Supporting Children and Young People Who Are in Care, Adopted or in Need*. London: British Association for Adoption & Fostering (BAAF).

Global Disaster Preparedness Center (GDPC) (2015) *Pillowcase Project International Pilot Peru: Video Case Study*. Available at: http://bit.ly/1SKdH2b

Griffiths, S. (2016) A hard truth about lessons in grit. *The Sunday Times News Review*, 21 February 2016, p. 8.

Grotberg, E. H. (ed.) (2003) *Resilience for Today: Gaining Strength from Adversity*. Westport, CT: Praeger.

Japanese Government Cabinet Office (Disaster Management Office) (2015) *Implementation Handbook for Disaster Resilience Education at the Regional Level*. Available at: www.bousai.go.jp/index.html

Lexmond, J., Paterson, C. and Tyler, C., (2014) *The Character and Resilience Manifesto*. London: The All-Party Parliamentary Group on Social Mobility. Available at: http://bit.ly/2ORvfPJ

Neenan, M. (2009) *Developing Resilience: A Cognitive Behavioural Approach*. Hove: Routledge.

Newman, T. (2004) *What Works in Building Resilience?* Nottingham: Barnardo's.

NHS England (2013) *NHS England Emergency Preparedness, Resilience and Response Framework*. Available at: http://bit.ly/242bmEG

Regional Consultative Committee (RCC) on Disaster Management (2007) *Integrating Disaster Risk Reduction into School Curriculum – Mainstreaming Disaster Risk Reduction into Education*. Available at: http://bit.ly/1QbqbKJ

Ronan, K. R. & Johnston, D. M. (2005) *Promoting Community Resilience in Disasters: The Role for Schools, Youth and Families*. New York: Springer.

Thompson, R. A. (2006) *Nurturing Future Generations: Promoting Resilience in Children and Adolescents through Social, Emotional and Cognitive Skills* (2nd edn). New York: Routledge.

UNISDR (2015) *Sendai Framework for Disaster Risk Reduction 2015–2030*. Available at: www.unisdr.org/we/coordinate/sendai-framework

US Department of Homeland Security (DHS) (2015) *Be a Hero!* Available at: http://1.usa.gov/OB2DGT

Wakefield Council (2015) *The Wakefield Resilience Framework*. Available at: www.riskandresilience.org.uk

Worsley, L. (2014) *Building Resilience in Three Australian High Schools, Using the Resilience Doughnut Framework*. In Prince-Embury, S. and Saklofske, D. H. (eds.) (2014) *Resilience Interventions for Youth in Diverse Populations*. New York: Springer-Verlag. Available at: http://bit.ly/1SMMope

12 Education and the digital revolution

Tom Staunton

This chapter explores:

- various theoretical perspectives on the nature of technology;
- the effects that the digital revolution is having on education;
- how education should respond.

Introduction

> We stand on the brink of a technological revolution that will fundamentally alter the way we live, work, and relate to one another ... The First Industrial Revolution used water and steam power to mechanize production. The Second used electric power to create mass production. The Third used electronics and information technology to automate production. Now a Fourth Industrial Revolution is building on the Third, the digital revolution that has been occurring since the middle of the last century. It is characterized by a fusion of technologies that is blurring the lines between the physical, digital, and biological spheres.
>
> (Schwab, 2016)

Klaus Schwab, founder of the World Economic Forum, sets out the basic theme of this chapter, the fundamental change to the world that has been brought about by the digital revolution. The advent of the internet, social media, mobile devices and other technological breakthroughs is creating a decisive change to our world equivalent to the advent of the industrial revolution. Schwab (2016) sees this change as one which is 'blurring the lines between the physical, digital, and biological spheres'. This blurring can be seen in the way practices such as recruitment and dating increasingly have digital elements; or how products such as Google Glass and smartwatches change how we interact with the world around us; or in the debates around who owns online data and who has the right to delete it.

This chapter will explore how education could rise to the challenge of the digital revolution. This will be done by exploring the intersection between different understandings of the digital world and education. The debate of this chapter will be around the question: What should education do in response to the digital revolution?

Digital literacies

> ✎ **Activity: Digital literacies 1**
>
> Before reading this section, consider how you would define the term 'digital literacy'. Can you make a list of various aspects that describe someone who is digitally literate?

Digital literacies aim to describe the underpinning abilities that are needed to interact with digital technology. Just as traditional literacies aim to describe an individual's ability to work with words and numbers, digital literacy aims to describe how an individual works with digital technology and digital environments. Jisc (2015) describes digital literacies as the 'capabilities which fit someone for living, learning and working in a digital society'. This describes how in a 'digital society' something fundamental has changed that has led to these skills being needed. This supports Schwab (2016) and Wheeler and Gerver's (2015) analysis that the world has been fundamentally changed by the digital revolution; therefore education must now put digital literacies alongside other literacies in the curriculum.

There is a wide range of different frameworks that describe digital literacies. Belshaw (2011) identifies eight essential elements of digital literacy as shown in the table below:

Table 12.1 Elements of digital literacy (adapted from Belshaw, 2011)

Cultural	Uses technology appropriately in different contexts
Cognitive	Effectively uses different tools, softwares and platforms
Constructive	Creates and shares new resources as well as remixing and reusing existing ones
Communicative	Able to effectively communicate across different devices, platforms and networks
Confidence	Is a self-learner, developing personal learning systems and practices
Creative	Takes risks to create new artefacts of value to themselves and others
Critical	Is aware of the power structures behind the digital world and is aware of how they will be received by others
Civic	Uses digital resources to enhance and engage in a wide range of networks as a global citizen

This chapter is less concerned with the exact details of what constitutes digital literacies and instead focuses on what the concept of digital literacies in general implies about the nature of education. The implication made by Belshaw (2011) and others who attempt to describe digital literacy is that an individual who develops the capacities described above will be equipped to live a fulfilling life in the digital world in which we live. Following on from this, education's role is to develop learners with this set of skills. Similarly to Schwab (2016), we see the claim that because the world is encountering a digital revolution we need to therefore revolutionise teaching in order to impart different skills for different ages. This view of education sees the curriculum as having to match and keep pace with the changing digital world and its demands.

There are two responses to this that we should consider. Firstly, we need to consider to what extent digital literacies can actually be taught. Prensky (2001) is famous for popularising the idea of digital natives and digital immigrants. A digital native is someone who has grown up inside a technological environment and is what Prensky (2001) would see as digitally fluent. This is in contrast to digital immigrants, people who come from non-digital generations and cultures and need to learn to adapt to the new languages and cultures of the digital world. Prensky's work cultivates the idea that education has little to say to natives who have developed their digital literacy informally through constant exposure to a digital environment. Going slightly further, Law (2012) raises the question of whether education's attempts to step into the digital space which young people are already native to is a form of imperialism whereby digital space is colonised.

There are some significant problems with Prensky's (2001) analysis. Longridge and Hooley's (2012) research, for example, has provided evidence that just because someone grows up around technology does not mean that they can use it effectively, especially when it comes to high-level skills such as critiquing online information or curating an online identity. Similarly, Livingstone (2008) has shown that just because someone may access more information online does not mean that they have the critical capacities to understand what they find. This suggests a need to teach digital literacies across the spectrum to digital natives and digital immigrants.

But Prensky (2001) still raises an interesting point. The idea of a digital native stems from the notion that individuals are exposed to and learn how to use technology outside of formal education. Wheeler and Gerver (2015) describe how individuals combine personal web tools and online personal learning networks to create a personal learning environment or PLE. The focus here is on personal; social media and online tools allow individuals to build their own networks, resources and learning tools away from institutions. No longer do individuals need to go to an institution, such as a school, university or library, to learn. We only need the smartphone in our pocket and its access to Google, Twitter and YouTube to engage in a wide range of learning. The danger with some discussions around digital literacy is they do not always recognise how technology has challenged the institution as the place where learning occurs.

Our second response to digital literacy comes from Lankshear and Knobel (2015) who claim that digital literacy is often conceived of in abstract terms. In their words digital literacy 'consists in so many lists of abstracted skills that a proficient person can "do". Once they "have" these "skills" they can use them purposefully at work, at home, at school etc., and function "competently"'. They point to the work of sociocultural theorists such as Street (1984) who complain about the idea that any literacy can exist in abstract. Literacies instead 'take on very different forms when embedded in different social practices involving different purposes and where different kinds of meaning are at stake' (Lankshear and Knobel, 2015, p. 17). This view of literacy challenges the view that we can prepare people with literacies in general before launching them into the real world. Learning about how to exist in the digital world takes on different social practices, it is born out of the social situations of the individual learner. Lankshear and Knobel (2015) challenge us that learning is contextual and personal; these claims chime with social constructivist views of education put forward by thinkers such as Dewey (1916) and Piaget (1995). Here education grows out of an individual's own experiences of the world and the meaning they attach to them, in this case their own involvement in the digital world and what that means to them.

In conclusion, we may learn some important things from digital literacy as a concept, but note that it is potentially weak by being abstract and inadequately describing the context that learning occurs in. Digital literacy rightly points out that different skills and abilities are needed in a digital world, but it could be argued that it does not go far enough to adequately engage with the importance of social context.

> **Activity: Digital literacies 2**
>
> What do you think of the concept of digital literacies? Do you think becoming digitally literate is something that you can actually teach someone? Is focusing on digital literacies a helpful approach for institutions to take? Be prepared to justify your answer.

Digital disruption

We noted above that the digital world disrupts the primacy of educational institutions for where learning occurs. The digital revolution creates the potential for learning to take place in informal online communities. Knowledge and learning is no longer monopolised by institutions such as schools, universities and libraries.

This has led to theorists such as Siemens (2005), Downes (2010) and Cormier (2008) to argue that there is a need for new theories of learning to respond to this change. Connectivism, as espoused by the above theorists, attempts to give this account. Siemens (2005) sees Connectivism underpinned by the realisation that in the digital age "know-where' has replaced 'know-what' as the most important aspect of learning. Siemens (2005) claims that traditionally knowledge is viewed as long lasting and held inside institutional bodies such as public libraries and universities; however, the digital age has radically increased the scale of knowledge alongside humanity's capacity to access it and increasingly knowledge is found in online communities and networks away from institutional dominance. Connectivism is therefore the belief that the task of education is to equip learners to access informal online communities and engage in their own learning as an ongoing life-wide activity. Siemens (2005) has produced a series of principles that underpin connectivism as an educational theory:

- Learning and knowledge rests in diversity of opinions.
- Learning is a process of connecting specialised nodes or information sources.
- Learning may reside in non-human appliances, e.g. computers.
- Capacity to increase knowledge is more critical than what is currently known.
- Nurturing and maintaining connections is needed to facilitate continual learning.
- Ability to see connections between fields, ideas and concepts is a core skill.
- Currency (accurate, up-to-date knowledge) is the intent of all connectivist learning activities.
- Decision-making is in itself a learning process.

Cormier (2008) similarly argues that the digital revolution has profoundly altered the nature of knowledge and how it is created and accessed. Especially, according to Cormier, the idea of institutional expertise is no longer valid in the digital age. Cormier (2008) describes how a rhizomatic model of learning may create an alternative model for learning:

In the rhizomatic model of learning, curriculum is not driven by predefined inputs from experts; it is constructed and negotiated in real time by the contributions of those engaged in the learning process. This community acts as the curriculum, spontaneously shaping, constructing, and reconstructing itself and the subject of its learning in the same way that the rhizome responds to changing environmental conditions.

Rhizomatic learning is therefore best seen as a mode of informal learning that particularly challenges authoritarian views of knowledge and education. It focuses on the potential for online communities to create learning which is personal, dispersed and driven by a learner's own motivations and subjective understandings of the world. Cormier's (2008) approach can be summed up by his expression that the 'community is the curriculum'; knowledge is not vetted and defined by experts but exists in a variety of expressions in a variety of communities. Though rhizomatic learning is not necessarily uniquely enabled by the digital age, it is a response to how the digital revolution has challenged traditional ideas of knowledge and is enabled by the ability of digital technologies to create the context for communities that support rhizomatic learning.

While it is perfectly possible to take digital literacies and add them to the pre-existing list of learning outcomes a school offers to its students, this approach is not possible with connectivist approaches to learning and teaching. Connectivism fundamentally argues for a different relationship between student and teacher to underpin education, as well as education being moved to a fundamentally different place away from the monopoly of an institution. While digital literacies are an additional set of aims for education which can sit alongside others, connectivism argues for the transformation of education.

It is important to focus on what makes connectivism unique when we attempt to see how it responds to the 'Fourth Industrial Revolution'. The re-articulation of the relationship between student and teacher found in connectivism very much echoes Freire's (2007) banking model of education, with the focus on an individual's interest and learning in the real world as opposed to the classroom linking in with the social constructivism of Dewey (1916) and Vygotsky (1978). What is unique about connectivism is how it takes themes from radical, social constructivist and informal understandings of education and re-purposes them for the digital world.

As part of this debate there are two critiques of connectivism we want to consider. Firstly, it is worth noticing connectivism's description of knowledge, and especially new knowledge, as the outcome of education. Connectivism links in heavily with the idea that knowledge is expanding too fast for traditional models of education to cope. There may be a general feeling in society that the speed of knowledge creation is moving at an increasingly exponential rate; it is worth asking if this applies equally to all forms of knowledge. Is the rate of expansion in fields such as engineering, computing and some parts of the natural sciences the same as in mathematics, social sciences or humanities-based disciplines? This raises the question whether connectivism applies equally to all types of knowledge or whether there is an unconscious focus on some areas more than others. Similarly, it could be argued that this description and focus on knowledge fits better with subjects (such as technology and science-based subjects) where knowledge and facts are more central to how the curriculum is structured. Other subject areas that focus more on building skills, attitudes and tacit knowledge do not fit so easily into the categories which connectivism uses. This is not to say that connectivism is only useful to some subject areas but that its central premise on the nature of knowledge does not fit equally with all subject areas across the educational spectrum.

The second critique of connectivism is around how it views technology and the internet. Why is the internet necessary for connectivism as a theory? As we have noted before, connectivism holds much in common with social constructivism and informal learning; connectivism argues for learning to be individualised, lifelong and lifewide and that this happens through accessing and making use of online communities. Connectivism argues that these aspects are enabled by the internet but it is unclear whether this can only be done online, especially when we consider our previous critique about how connectivism understands knowledge. Connectivism appears to have an assumed positivism around the internet; that it must be good and will make our lives better. Connectivism sets out to describe how the internet has and could reform learning in the digital age, but the answers it comes up with are universally positive about the potential for the internet to transform learning. As we will see in the last section, this overlooks important critiques of learning in the digital age which we would be wise to consider.

In conclusion, an understanding of the implications of digital disruption for education contains an important perspective for debate. The ideas that have been discussed from connectivism provide a fresh outlook on what education could look like in the fourth industrial age. Connectivism responds to the changing nature of knowledge in the digital world and provides a perspective on education that is decentralised, personal and social. That said, there are some concerns about how knowledge is understood by connectivists and if technology is entirely necessary for this pedagogical approach.

Connectivism

Connectivism argues for the need to rethink the relationship between teachers and pupils in the digital age. What might the advantages and disadvantages be of rethinking this relationship? What place does this give to traditional institutions in the digital age?

Digital scepticism

The two perspectives we have considered so far in this debate have both assumed that technology is positive and that education can benefit individuals by helping them make better use of it. In our critique of connectivism in particular, we questioned whether some of their pedagogical ideals necessitated the use of technology. The final perspective we will consider in this debate, digital scepticism, challenges the assumption that education should be uncritically wedding itself to technology.

Though there are a variety of criticisms that could be made of the assumption that education should make use of technology, we are going to focus on critiques linked to technological determinism. Technological determinism is the idea that the technologies that society makes use of are deterministic of the shape of these societies. This is an idea originally associated with Marshall McLuhan and his book *Understanding Media* (1994). McLuhan famously coined the phrase, 'the medium is the message'. In other words, it is the media itself rather than how it is used which determines the effect it has on society. He goes on to say that 'the "message" of any medium or technology is the change of scale or pace or pattern that is introduced into human affairs ... it is the medium that shapes and controls the scale and form of human association' (1964, p. 2). This is to say that media have a profound effect on society beyond the specific content it contains or how people choose to use it. How education responds to the digital age should be grounded not just in how digital technologies could be used, but also in the effects digital technology has on society. McLuhan (1994) was not necessarily a sceptic about technology and he did not live to see the advent of the digital revolution, but his ideas create a starting point for understanding explicitly sceptical positions. In order to explore this further, the next section will consider three main effects that technology has on society and what this means for education: speed, individualisation and privacy.

Speed

As Mejias (2013) discusses, digital networks remove distance as a property from human relationships – we can connect with information and people on the other side of the world. There is a temptation to see this speed as inherently positive – quicker is better. Virilio (2012) describes this differently, noting how societies have developed a 'cult of speed'. As Virilio (2012) argues, society has become dominated by the instant, but we have little space for reflection and critique if we are constantly assaulted by the new. This is similar to Rushkoff's (2013) concept of 'present shock' where society's ability to discuss the future is diminished by a variety of forces, including digital technology, which create a world which is 'always on' and so trapped in the present. What Virilio (2012) and Rushkoff (2013) argue is that our ability to think about and understand the world around us is decisively changed by how technology brings speed into our lives. This should be of great concern for education. How we think and how we consider the future appear self-apparent aims for education.

Individualism

Technology could be seen to heighten a sense of individualism with individuals on personal devices making their own personal decisions. But this individualism obscures educational problems. Duckworth and Cochrane (2012, p. 589) note that this casts the learner as an entrepreneur in an environment in which 'learners are expected to succeed against the odds and if they do not, the fault is their own and not [due to] structural inequalities many encounter'. Selwyn (2016) proclaims that there is a tendency to call for individuals to be resourceful and nomadic in their pursuit of learning online, but those who call for this often fail to account for the fact that this flexibility is often linked to being economically and socially positioned to do so. Technology, here, creates the conditions for inequality to exist and prosper. Mejias (2013) makes a similar point by arguing that social media inevitably creates inequality because they require individuals to compete for attention and connections online, something which some are better able and better positioned to do. Andrew Keen (2012) picks up the same point, noting that networks are dominated by a few super-nodes who disproportionately benefit from the network. Because technology has individualised learning it both puts unfair pressure on individuals to be responsible for what is out of their control and obscures how digital networks create the conditions for some individuals to thrive more than others. Finally this individualisation has implications for the nature of education; as Selwyn states, 'If we are all immersed in our own personalized learning journeys, what implications might this have for education as a social, supportive and shared endeavour?' (2016, p. 78).

Privacy

Van Dijck (2013) argues that the organisations behind social media sites are creating a different friction between individuals' desires for privacy and control over their data and commercial organisations' desire to access this data. Van Dijck (2013) sees social media sites on the one hand reassuring users that they are in control of their privacy while on the other encouraging commercial organisations to exploit this information through advertising, among other activities. As Mejias (2013) notes, this creates a situation where users are increasingly encouraged to put their lives online where the information is consumed by corporations whose use of this data is largely hidden and not accounted for. This creates a challenge for educators about whether or not they should encourage students to engage in this sort of environment. Though it may be tempting to say that educators can still enthusiastically promote digital technology while encouraging individuals to protect their digital identities online, Mejias (2013) notes how corporate organisations and government agencies sidestep these privacy controls. This can be of particular concern for people with marginal political views or who have misdemeanours in their past. Though education may have values of allowing people to develop in safe environments where they can move on from their mistakes, it is not clear if this is equally true online. This creates a situation where individuals have to increasingly control their identities online and present a socially acceptable vision of themselves. Foucault's (1977) concept of the panopticon describes how the fear that someone may be watching forces individuals to conform to socially acceptable behaviour so that they are in effect 'trapped' by this fear. Keen (2012, p. 77) discusses how the internet heightens the control mechanism Foucault describes, stating 'if visibility is a trap, then hypervisibility is a hypertrap'. It is important to note that Foucault (1977) and Keen (2012) are discussing the fear of being observed – it is this fear that controls behaviour beyond whether anyone is even watching. In the context of this debate we need to ask if this fits in with liberal educational values of enabling people to become individuals confident in themselves.

In light of these three phenomena it seems important to ask how education equips people to respond to the digital age and if education needs to ask if it is actually initiating people into this digital world, with its apparent difficulties, without thinking through the consequences. These sceptical voices create a position that asks education to be more critical of the digital age and to equip learners to do the same.

In the context of this debate there are two main responses to these views. Firstly, technological determinism ignores the power of individuals to make decisions and respond to the problems they face. Particularly in the context of education it could be argued that though these concerns are worth noting, it does not follow that education should step back from technology entirely. Secondly, there are concerns about how practical these positions actually are. We live in a technological age, the digital revolution has occurred and we cannot ignore it. A critical response to this digital scepticism is it just encourages Ludditism that is not practical in the real world. Should education not be about preparing people for the real world rather than postulating about what we want society to be like?

> ✎ **Activity: Digital scepticism**
>
> Mejias (2013) argues that individuals should step 'off the network' as a response to the inherent difficulties with networked life such as encouraging individualism, widening inequality and compromising privacy. What reasons might students of education have for encouraging this? Is this realistic in the digital age in which we live?

Debate conclusion

When we step back and look at the three positions that have made up this debate we see that we have a debate centred on the nature of technology and the nature of education.

Firstly, let us consider technology. From the position of digital literacy, technology is seen as something that is under the control of the individual and which does not represent a substantial change to the world. This leads to a position where structures such as education can stay as they are and can respond by adding in the extra set of requirements that technology requires. Technology is additional rather than transformational. Connectivism takes the position that technology is transformational rather than additional; we have undergone a paradigm shift with the advent of the digital age which has disrupted domains such as politics, the media, social life and education. But in connectivism, as in digital literacy, people are ultimately agents able to respond to make use of technology in this new environment. This is in contrast to the view of digital scepticism which focuses on the effect that technology has on individuals outside of their control. Like connectivism, it focuses on the paradigm shift that technology brings but while connectivism sees this as an opportunity for the individual to make use of, digital scepticism argues there are substantial negative changes beyond the individual's control, including how individualism and privacy operate in a digital world. To summarise, we see two fundamental questions around technology emerging from this debate: To what extent has technology changed society? And to what extent is technology an instrument for individuals?

Secondly, among the views we have discussed, there are differences in the approach to education. When we consider approaches from digital literacy and from connectivism the primary difference is about where the centre of power resides. Much discussion around digital literacy maintains the position of institutional authority and adds digital literacy to the list of outputs it determines. Connectivism, by contrast, explicitly takes aim at this institutional dominance and aims at producing learners able to manage their own learning in a digital environment, learners who are nomadic and able to make their own decisions about what to learn. It should be noted that digital literacy is often discussed as a skill by connectivists, the two terms to blur with each other. We are more contrasting the general approach to digital literacy that many institutions take, which preserves their own power structures, with connectivism's focus on disrupting them. This then creates a question about whether education in the digital age should preserve or challenge institutional authority. Digital scepticism creates an interesting departure for us here because though it has a lot to say about education it has no explicit plan for delivery. Authors such as Selwyn (2016) and Keen (2012) highlight problems with education's relation to technology. These sceptical views encourage us to think philosophically and sociologically about the world around us before engaging in it. This, in itself, can create a valid approach to education. It helps us move past the distinction that Collini (2012) sees education as often having between 'useful' and 'useless' knowledge.

180 Tom Staunton

Education should as much be about understanding the essence and the effects of technology as it is about preparing people to use it. We are left then with two key questions: What place should institutional authority play in education? And should education be about helping people live differently or understanding the world differently?

Case study 12.1: LinkedIn and education

Consider this fictional situation. Jane recently returned to education in her 30s and has started a law degree. At a recent talk one of her lecturers encouraged students to join the social media network LinkedIn to network with lawyers to help them gain work experience and work towards landing a lucrative training contract. Jane had not heard of LinkedIn before and thought the site looked really interesting. She is very keen to pursue a career in law after her studies, but is nervous by how the legal sector is based around networking. It appears that neither Jane nor anyone she knows has any personal contacts in the legal profession. LinkedIn, with its focus on building professional networks, therefore looks like it might be of real benefit to Jane. Despite this, she has a number of concerns.

Firstly, Jane is finding it difficult at university to get used to using technology in general. She has always avoided using social media. She doesn't like what her friends say about it and how easy it seems to be to make mistakes. She is also worried as it seems the media is full of stories of people being compromised on social media, either through bad news about them personally or through falling victim to a scam. All of this makes Jane very nervous about using social media in any form.

Secondly, Jane is worried because of something that happened in her past. Three years ago Jane's brother was involved in a difficult child protection case that made it into the local press. He is now spending time in jail having being found guilty. At the time Jane wanted to stand up for her brother and went on record in the press protesting his innocence. She feels like she did the right thing, but knows that it would be easy for people to find the story and what she said online as they share a surname. She knows she has committed no crime but feels the story does not paint her in a good light as a prospective lawyer. She is worried that by joining LinkedIn more people will start looking her up online and may come across the news story.

Thirdly, Jane is already struggling with her degree and time management. She is a single mum with three children to look after as well as holding down a part-time job while she studies. She already feels stretched with time and LinkedIn just feels like another thing for her to worry about. She's worried she's not keeping up with all of the reading she needs to study law as it is. Is LinkedIn really worth the bother? She doesn't want to start it and find out she doesn't have the time to see it through.

Key questions

- How might the various theoretical positions mentioned in this chapter help us understand Jane's situation?
- What might someone be able to teach Jane to help her resolve her situation?
- What is your response to Jane's situation? What does this say about how you might naturally relate to technology? How do you feel about this?

Suggested reading

Wheeler, S. & Gerver, R. (2015) *Learning with 'E's: Educational Theory and Practice in the Digital Age*. Camarthen: Crown House Publishing.

This provides a helpful and accessible introduction to learning and teaching in the digital age. It is particularly helpful for separating practice that uses technology from understandings of education that conceptualise technology.

Selwyn, N. (2016) *Is Technology Good for Education?* Cambridge: Polity Press.

Neil Selwyn's short book provides a much-needed counterpoint to some of the extremes of positivity around education and technology and is a helpful companion to Wheeler and Gerver. Selwyn raises pertinent questions to how education is currently making use of technology and critiques some of the common claims of technological enthusiasts.

References

Belshaw, D. (2011) *What is Digital Literacy? A Pragmatic Investigation*. Available at: http://dmlcentral.net/wp-content/uploads/files/doug-belshaw-edd-thesis-final.pdf

Collini, S. (2012) *What Are Universities For?* London: Penguin.

Cormier, D. (2008) Rhizomatic Education: Community as Curriculum. *Innovate: Journal of Online Education*, 4(5). Available at: http://nsuworks.nova.edu/cgi/viewcontent.cgi?article=1045&context=innovate

Dewey, J. (1916) *Democracy and Education: An Introduction to the Philosophy of Education*. New York: Macmillan.

Downes, S. (2010) New Technology Supporting Informal Learning. *Journal of Emerging Technologies in Web Intelligence*, 2(1), 27–33.

Duckworth, V. & Cochrane, M. (2012) Spoilt for Choice, Split for Choice. *Education Training*, 54(7), 579–591.

Foucault, M. (1977) *Discipline and Punishment* (trans. Sheridan, A.). New York: Pantheon.

Freire, P. (2007) *Pedagogy of the Oppressed*. New York: Continuum.

Jisc (2015) *Developing Students' Digital Literacy*. Available at: https://www.jisc.ac.uk/guides/developing-students-digital-literacy

Keen, A. (2012) *Digital Vertigo: How Today's Online Social Revolution Is Dividing, Diminishing, and Disorienting Us*. London: Macmillan.

Lankshear, C. & Knobel, M. (2015) Digital Literacy and Digital Literacies: Policy, Pedagogy and Research Considerations for Education. *Nordic Journal of Digital Literacy*, 9, 8–20.

Law, B. (2012) *Digital Literacy*. Available at: www.hihohiho.com/newthinking/EVColonist.pdf

Livingstone, S. (2008) Taking Risky Opportunities in Youthful Content Creation. Teenagers' Use of Social Networking Sites for Intimacy, Privacy and Self-Expression. *New Media & Society*, 10(3), 393–411.

Longridge, D. & Hooley, T. (2012) An Experiment in Blended Career Development: The University of Derby's Social Media Internship Programme. *Journal of the National Institute for Career Education and Counselling*, 29(1), 39–46.

McLuhan, M. (1994) *Understanding Media*. London: Routledge.

Mejias, U. A. (2013) *Off the Network: Disrupting the Digital World*. Minneapolis: University of Minnesota Press.

Piaget, J. (1995) *Sociological Studies*. London: Routledge.

Prensky, M. (2001) Digital Natives, Digital Immigrants Part 1. *On the Horizon*, 9(5), 1–6.

Rushkoff, D. (2013) *Present Shock: When Everything Happens Now*. London: Penguin.

Schwab, K. (2016) *The Fourth Industrial Revolution: What It Means, How to Respond*. Available at: www.weforum.org/agenda/2016/01/the-fourth-industrial-revolution-what-it-means-and-how-to-respond

Selwyn, N. (2016) *Is Technology Good for Education?* Cambridge: Polity Press.

Siemens, G. (2005) *Connectivism: Learning as Network Creation*. Available at: www.elearnspace.org/Articles/networks.htm

Street, B. (1984) *Literacy in Theory and Practice*. Cambridge: Cambridge University Press.

Van Dijck, J. (2013) 'You Have One Identity': Performing the Self on Facebook and LinkedIn. *Media, Culture & Society*, 35(2), 199–215.

Virilio, P. (2012) *The Administration of Fear* (trans. Polizzotti, M.). Los Angeles: Semiotext(e).

Vygotsky, L. S. (1978) *Mind in Society*. Cambridge, MA: Harvard University Press.

Wheeler, S. & Gerver, R. (2015) *Learning with 'E's: Educational Theory and Practice in the Digital Age*. Camarthen: Crown House Publishing.

13 The future of education

Vanessa Cottle and Anne O'Grady

This chapter explores:

- how policy can give hints about the future of education;
- a future curriculum;
- the economy and social mobility.

Introduction

There are two main challenges for this chapter and both relate to definitions: what is meant by the concepts of firstly 'the future' and secondly 'education'. Throughout the chapter clues about the future of education have been taken from government policy and this has given rise to one particular conceptualisation of education about which, through various activities, you are invited to join the debate. The chapter will explore the future of education in the compulsory, further and higher education sectors. It is worth noting that some current policy documents have deadlines of 2020 – which may well be the year you are reading this and the future has suddenly become the present, or even the past!

Is it possible to predict the future?

Of course, it is an impossible task to accurately predict the future – there were two national events in the UK in 2016 which exemplify this. Football fans may remember that Leicester City won the Premier League championship in May 2016 and at the beginning of the season the odds for this happening were 5000:1 according to one betting organisation. Approximately one month later, on 23 June 2016, the United Kingdom voted, by referendum, to leave the European Union – an outcome which has become known across the world as Brexit. This outcome came as a complete surprise, even shock, to all involved including politicians and voters on both sides of the strongly fought campaign. It is clear then, that any predictions about the future of education, which is often quoted as being an area of life where the one most predictable aspect is change, simply may or may not be correct.

Dictionaries explain the term 'future' variously, for example, it is a point in time after the present, or an indefinite time yet to come. The problem is that by the time we arrive in the future there are changes in the imperatives that caused the original plans to be made. These changes might be caused by 'big-picture' external factors such as a change in government or by more local, context-specific factors such as recommendations arising from evaluations of changes – we never arrive at an absolute conclusion.

The term 'education' is no more straightforward than 'future' and means different things depending on a person's world view or perspective, which will, in turn, be informed by their context. The government's Department for Education (DfE) is responsible for compulsory schooling but refers to schooling by using the term 'education'. Nick Gibb, Minister of State for Education (2015), describes education as the engine of our economy, the foundation of our culture and essential preparation for adult life. The tendency to translate the term education into schooling is also shared by school teachers for whom the process of teaching and learning is a prime concern; by parents who think of education in terms of what happens to their children at school and by employers who want educated people to meet the needs of business, industry and commerce. The outcome of a good education could be seen as someone who has financial benefits from being employed in a well-paid profession either directly as a result of school or progression into further or higher levels of learning. The opportunity to access these financial benefits is often predicated upon achievements measured by national tests and qualifications which, in turn, are used to reflect the quality of the practitioners who deliver the learning and the locations in which learning takes place. It can be concluded from these perspectives, therefore, that education is a process of learning which takes place in schools, further education and higher education. The success, or products, of this process is measured in terms of qualifications, employability and financial security for individuals and a strong economy for the country.

> **Activity: What is education?**
>
> 1. Are you aware of your responsibility for the country's future economy?
> 2. Do you believe that the above is an accurate definition of education?
> 3. Look at this website for some alternative definitions of education: www.brainyquote.com/quotes/topics/topic_education.html. To what extent do these resonate with your own ideas?

Future purpose of school

As government is the key funding agent for education that takes place in schools, colleges and universities, it is not surprising that it has great influence on plans for the future. An example comes from Gove (2014) who, when making his inaugural speech as the then Minister for Education for the Coalition Government, claimed that there was a widening gap in achievement between rich and poor children and that to close this gap was an 'economic imperative' (Gove 2014). The speech goes on to explain that:

> Our jobs, our lives, our economies and our societies are going through dramatic and irreversible change. For the next generation to flourish, education systems must equip every child with the knowledge and skills, the qualifications and confidence they need to succeed.

Another example comes from the Conservative Party (Conservative Party 2016), currently in government, who claim that school standards and discipline need to be restored to ensure 'our children can compete with the world's best and enjoy a better future' and they also claim to be 'giving young people the chance to learn vital skills for work'. It is interesting to note that the implications here are that education/schooling is currently less than it should be and, therefore, in the future it must be improved.

These two examples reflect both the process and product of education. Strategies required to ensure children experience a disciplined and standards-driven curriculum are clues about future processes in schooling which, it is inferred, will facilitate three purposes: (1) a skilled workforce resulting in (2) a well-fuelled economy and (3) social mobility. What is not clear here is specifically what strategies should be employed, just what might happen in the everyday school experience of children and the practice of teachers, i.e. the curriculum, to realise these ambitions.

A future curriculum

The Conservative Party manifesto (2015, p. 33) claims that the government knows 'what works in education: great teachers; brilliant leadership; rigour in the curriculum; discipline in the classroom; proper exams' and that it believes 'that there is no substitute for a rigorous academic curriculum to secure the best from every pupil'. Although softened, these ideals are echoed within the DfE's (2016a) White Paper which sets out the government's vision for schools in England. There are hints here about the kind of strategies that might be evident in the classroom of the future as a result of Tory government policy. Readers may believe that implementing strategies to achieve 'great teachers; brilliant leadership; rigour; discipline; proper exams and rigorous academic curriculum' would not change what is already strived for and the suggestion that education needs to be improved is political rhetoric, painting an inaccurate deficit picture. The Conservative manifesto (2015, p. 34) goes on to lay down expectations of a future curriculum:

> every 11-year-old to know their times tables off by heart and be able to perform long division and complex multiplication. They should be able to read a book and write a short story with accurate punctuation, spelling and grammar.

and

> We will require secondary school pupils to take GCSEs in English, maths, science, a language and history or geography.

So, there are some specifics upon which future pupil success and teacher performativity will be measured and there are strong suggestions that the current system is failing.

Activity: Failing schools

1. Do you believe the current system in schools is failing? Read this 40-year-old pivotal report on the nature and purpose of education: www.educationengland.org.uk/documents/speeches/1976ruskin.html
2. What similarities and differences do you see when comparing today's future proposals for education with those of 1976?
3. Where you see similar proposals for the future, why do you think there seem to have been no improvements?
4. Do you think the past can inform the future of education?

Digital curriculum

Gradually – and it really is gradually – technology in the form of the digital revolution as discussed in Chapter 12 is informing pedagogy and is believed to affect how we all learn. The rate of improvements to the internet and mobile devices in terms of speed, innovative range of applications and memory size is challenging schools to keep up with opportunities for creative teaching and learning. Even the youngest student now has personal access to technology with smartphones overtaking laptops 'as the most popular device for getting online in the UK' (Martellozzo et al. 2016).

New understandings of what is meant by and taught about digital literacy is an area of growing concern and debate among school leaders and practitioners (digital technology is, of course, also especially important to employers now and in the future). The internet and social media sources are accessible to a lesser or greater extent, but alongside the perceived advantages of having not only an unfathomable quantity of information immediately at the fingertips, but also of keeping in touch with increasingly large circles of people, both known and unknown, there are dangers. Children and adults have become increasingly exposed to and have to deal with previously unlikely threats. Cyber bullying, grooming for sexual exploitation and radicalisation are prominent in the media and have the potential to become increasingly widespread as time progresses. For example, research (Martellozzo et al. 2016) commissioned by the Children's Commissioner and the National Society for the Prevention of Cruelty to Children (NSPCC) found that over half of children aged 11–16 have been exposed to online pornography. Clearly this is an area where all educational settings have a responsibility to help both young and adult learners alike. Curriculum design of the future should help learners understand the potential dangers arising from digital online worlds and how to navigate them safely and with positive purpose.

Other areas of technological concern for current and future educational settings include understanding how digital technology will affect children in terms of behavioural issues, cognition and even school readiness (Howard-Jones 2011). Gaining insights into how learners interact with and are affected by technology will provide schools with a basis to facilitate effective learning and appropriate safeguarding strategies. These strategies used alongside appropriate teaching and learning of digital technologies should insure that learners are able to cope with those 21st-century (and it won't be long before we begin to think about 22nd-century) employment skills and qualities required to support the economy.

Undoubtedly, there are positive outcomes from the use of digital technologies in education. Improvements in attainment, motivation and learning are consistently evidenced through research. However, research demonstrates that digital interventions are slightly less effective than other interventions when it comes to improving learning and attainment. According to Higgins et al. (2012), the effectiveness of technology on learning depends on the quality of school in which it is used – better schools being more effective. Higgins et al. (2012) also find that, as with any new intervention, gains made in learning are often due to its motivational novelty value. Therefore, supplementing, rather than replacing, normal teaching with technology is likely to be more effective. Also, as with non-digital interventions, they are likely to have more effect on the lower attaining students, those with special educational needs and those from disadvantaged backgrounds.

However, the outcomes of the Higgins et al. (2012) research were clear about the use of digital technology being 'more productive' when it is used to promote student collaboration, discussion, interaction and feedback. In the future, as enhanced connectivity pervades our everyday lives, these ideas will increasingly become the norm. For example, cloud functions will enable peer-to-peer work within school, between schools locally and even worldwide. These ideas should allay fears that future classrooms are likely to be isolating spaces which reduce communication and interaction.

Easy access to information suggests a compelling argument for future digital learning without the need for traditional teaching and learning of subjects. There are two arguments against this. Firstly, the volume of information available is such that 'letting learners loose on the internet is a little like sending teenagers into the British Library and expecting them to make successful forays to support their learning' (Higgins *et al.* 2012, p. 9). The second argument against completely replacing traditional pedagogies with a digital search engine is that information alone is not helpful. Information needs to be applied and synthesised by learners in order that it is understood and, therefore, useful.

Digital technology has similar implications for HE and FE as it does for schools. Pedagogically, as with schools, there is increasing evidence that teaching and learning are changing and will continue to do so. The arguments for and against digital technologies explain why there is not a simple trajectory into the future. Adaptations in the sense of cultural and political shifts, placement of resourcing and teacher education combined with theoretical understandings have to be achieved to successfully accommodate the new.

Activity: The Open University

The Open University accepted its first students in 1971. In the light of current digital technology, discuss why learners continue to learn in traditional institutions.

Outdoor curriculum

The aim for any innovation or intervention in education is to improve the educational process, i.e. experience for learners, and, therefore, its outcome, i.e. employability and a healthy economy; above we see that digital technology is a device that could contribute significantly to such an outcome.

However, digital technology is not the only aspect of teaching and learning that is becoming increasingly recognised for its ability to engage learners and facilitate effective learning. At the other end of the technology scale, outdoor learning (Potter and Dyment 2016) is becoming well established and proving to be beneficial for young learners of all abilities. For example, Lavington Park School Federation adopted outdoor learning in 2007 and this was reported by Ofsted (2012, p. 2) as a significant contributor to the 'marked improvement in the overall quality of teaching and in pupils' progress'. The schools in the Lavington Park Federation (2016) continue to underpin their curriculum through their forest schools, as do many other primary schools across the UK. Perhaps a future recipe which combines learning outdoors with digital technology will provide the perfect marriage of learning strategies.

> **✎ Activity: Digitial technology, teaching and learning**
>
> Explore these websites:
> www.ed.gov/oii-news/use-technology-teaching-and-learning
> www.forbes.com/sites/jordanshapiro/2015/04/30/4-fundamental-problems-with-everything-you-hear-about-the-future-of-education/3/#5a4e27742267
>
> 1. What do you think are the benefits and limitations of online contexts for learning?
> 2. What digital technology opportunities have you experienced in your previous and current learning contexts?
> 3. Have you taken advantage of these?
> 4. Could your learning experiences be enhanced?
> 5. What more could be done with digital technology to enhance your current and future learning experiences?
> 6. Do you believe that learning should be fun?

The future of education for further education and higher education

This section of the chapter demonstrates that the priorities established to influence the future of further and higher education, as with the compulsory sector, fundamentally emphasise learning for economic benefits – for individuals and society. While this is, arguably, quite rightly an important purpose of our education provision, this economic trajectory presents some challenges and limitations for us as a society and misses the point – on a number of levels – in relation to social justice, social mobility and social cohesion.

> **✎ Activity: Further and higher education**
>
> As an undergraduate student, you will have experienced some form(s) of further education and higher education. Think about the following:
>
> - Why did you engage with FE – was it just to get into HE?
> - Why are you studying in HE – is it just to get a job?
> - Do you think these are sound principles on which to study?
> - Think about how people engage with each of these sectors. Do you think there is any difference based on: social class, career ambitions or qualifications?

Further education

When people in England refer to FE it is generally within the context of 'going to college', often to undertake vocational-type courses with qualification outcomes that lead directly to employment opportunities. However, FE has traditionally encompassed a wide variety of learning opportunities, from traditional academic subjects to vocational courses, from retaking 'failed' school examinations to learning for pleasure and, more recently, over the last decade or so, to undertaking 'access to higher education' courses, or to study higher education courses within a FE environment. Thus, FE has to meet the needs of the whole community for which the provision is made.

The Post-16 Skills Plan is currently the key policy document for FE with reform at its heart. Its aim is to ensure the sector is providing high-quality technical education which meets the needs of business and industry, and to ensure an available workforce is appropriately equipped to meet and drive up productivity, enabling economic growth. The Plan offers a vision for the future of the post-16 system going forward, shaped through dialogue with employers, colleges and others, for implementation through a road map of reform to be realised by 2020.

Activity: Post-16 skills

Access the Post-16 Skills Plan here: www.gov.uk/government/uploads/system/uploads/attachment_data/file/536068/56259_Cm_9280_print.pdf Read the Executive Summary, and then have a look at Figure 2: Post-16 skills reform timeline (July 2016–2020) on page 44 for an outline of the review plan and key milestones.

1. How ambitious do you think this plan is in reforming the current FE sector?
2. What do you think might be lost from the system as a result of the refocusing of the sector on skills?

It is very early days since the implementation of this agenda for change of the post-16 sector, and there are some unsurprising events. As a result of a refocusing and reallocation of resources, some providers have considered merging with other providers, while some have decided to review and adapt their curriculum offer.

What is apparent in this review is what will no longer form part of the FE sector. Firstly, the renaming of the sector to a post-16 skills sector tells us there is little room for learning for pleasure or for learning which does not lead directly to employment opportunity. As the Skills Plan is implemented, financial resource will drive learning providers to collaborate, but there also needs to be a discussion about how potential learners are enabled, financially, to engage in such provision.

Located within the FE sector the government has set a target of three million apprentices by 2020 – compare this to 500,000 in 2014–15 (Delabarre 2016). When launching the Apprenticeships Inquiry (Sub-Committee on Education, Skills and the Economy 2016), Neil Carmichael, Chair of the Education Select Committee, reinforced the message that technical and professional education was important to the economy and that greater numbers of quality apprenticeships would boost the country's ability to compete internationally. However, there is a need to ask questions of this narrow model of FE based on a skills agenda which generates a system without provision for learning beyond an economic purpose.

Higher education

As noted elsewhere (O'Grady 2013, p. 43), higher education (HE) is 'a well-established strand of education', based on the pursuit of 'higher learning' and the transmission of such knowledge through the generations. Today, current HE policies and key performance indicators, and the surrounding discourses, reveal a clear imperative for those engaged in HE in the form of knowledge acquisition closely associated with 'skills development' and economic success. This does not appear to be too different from the discourse we have considered in relation to FE education and even compulsory education, but let's take a closer look at some policies which will frame the future of HE.

Reflecting the notion that change often re-dresses old ideas, the Higher Education Green Paper (DBIS 2015) echoes the much earlier Robbins Report (Committee on Higher Education 1963) as both propose to increase participation by students from disadvantaged and under-represented groups in higher education. In addition, the Higher Education Green Paper seeks to:

- introduce a Teaching Excellence Framework (TEF);
- introduce a single gateway for providers to enter the sector;
- reshape the funding and regulator architecture for the higher education system.

The Higher Education and Research Bill 2016–17 aims to operationalise these ambitions and build on the previous significant legislative reform affecting the FE and HE sectors from more than two decades ago (Great Britain 1992). At its core, the Bill aims to support the government's mission to raise life chances for the population, providing opportunities for social mobility and enhancing the country's economic competitiveness and productivity. It encourages competition between HE providers, choice for potential HE participants by building flexibility into courses, innovation and raising productivity. Two metrics which are identified as key to driving this agenda forward are the Research Excellence Framework (REF) and the Teaching Excellence Framework (TEF).

Research Excellence Framework and Teaching Excellence Framework

The REF has been established in HE for a number of years, whilst the TEF is currently being introduced to the HE sector. Both these frameworks aim to support the HE sector to be able to demonstrate their commitment to high-quality research as well as high-quality teaching, allowing employers to recruit students who have the knowledge and skills required for high-level employment positions. The Stern Review (2016) considered the future of the REF for the HE sector and concluded that research undertaken in HE was 'crucial to the future of the UK in a rapidly changing and sometimes turbulent world' (p. 32). Therefore, we can be pretty confident that research will continue to be a strong aspect of higher education. However, the review concluded that there was a need for HE to raise its research quality and to work in potentially new ways, for example, interdisciplinary and collaboratively.

For many HE providers, an external metric which focuses on their teaching quality is new, and is likely to require a degree of change in thinking – particularly of staff who have to date, arguably, prioritised their academic competence as a researcher rather than a teacher. The metric outcomes associated with TEF and REF will be used to provide HE providers with a rating on their performance (similar to Ofsted ratings). The carrot to encourage compliance is that providers who are rated highly will be eligible to charge higher fees for their courses.

What about individual needs?

For many years there has been political and cultural will to ensure that learners receive an appropriate education by addressing their individual needs. The terms 'personalisation', 'individualisation' and 'differentiation' have been core to every practitioner's thoughts as they construct creative and innovative teaching experiences to ensure that learning abilities, styles, needs and approaches are addressed. With this in mind, it is interesting to anticipate if the characteristics of individual learner needs will change in the future. Again, current government policy offers clues with specific categories of individual need being highlighted. These include looked after children, traveller families, SEND in mainstream care, individuals for whom English is not their first language and LGBT groups who face challenges of gender transition and associated concerns. The imperative to be concerned about learners in these categories is driven by the need to assure employability skills for all, global issues of immigration, cultural acceptance of difference and better understanding of how to manage what might have previously been seen as learning deficits. With ongoing improved cultural understandings and medical advances which mean that recovery from injuries or congenital birth differences is far better than in the past, it is fair to predict that the demand for future developments to cater for individual needs will not diminish.

Freedom to learn

The freedom for students to learn what they want in a way that they want, is likely to become increasingly limited. FE providers are increasingly required to merge to meet reduced financial resource demands and to provide a curriculum that responds to employers' skills needs. The urban–rural challenges for students may result in a two-tier system where students in rural areas are unable to source a course because the transport infrastructure is more limited, technological connectively is weakest and the economic opportunities more limited, resulting in lack of apprenticeship opportunities. People will have to travel greater distances to access learning opportunities, which has costs in time, finance and personal energy. Resources to embed digital technology physically and culturally will have to be much improved to meet these challenges. As HE providers are tasked not only with evidencing excellent teaching and research, but also application of learning to employment, students are increasingly likely to be required to attend lectures, undertake assessments and meet learning outcomes, rather than explore a particular topic of interest based on curiosity. The tension between this and the rise in recognition of, and demand for, the student voice in the future crafting of the FE and HE sectors should not be underestimated. HE will be judged by a range of indicators including, but not exclusively or exhaustively, the National Student Survey, the Destinations of Leavers from Higher Education, the TEF and the REF within a marketisation agenda. The extent to which widening participation is squeezed or minimised – and the nature and role of that agenda – is one that should be fought for.

The lines between FE and HE are becoming increasingly blurred with many colleges providing higher education courses and some now having been granted the status to award their own degrees. Similarly, the distinctions between pre-16 and post-16 FE are no longer clear, as schools increasingly look to offer a curriculum which incorporates more vocational and apprenticeship-type courses. Additionally, FE colleges across the country are increasingly feeling priced out of the market as funding for courses is withdrawn – particularly those which might have historically been seen as informal and/or for pleasure.

Education and social mobility

Part of the rationale for achieving an education system that has a focus on improved employability opportunity, and in turn a strong economy, is that by doing so there is the potential for that education system to indirectly facilitate an individual's social mobility. In September 2016, the UK's prime minister, Theresa May (May 2016), formally announced her government's decision to reintroduce support for a grammar school system. For many, the grammar school process of selecting the best children and labelling others as failures is an unpopular concept and the introduction of new grammar schools was banned in 1997 by the then Labour government. However, there are pockets of the grammar school system remaining in England and throughout Northern Ireland and Theresa May (2016) argues that even without grammar schools a covert sort of selection remains because 'selection exists if you're wealthy'; that is a child's chances in life can be determined by whether or not their parents can afford to live near an outstanding school or pay for private education.

The tension here is that while selection is potentially contentious and unpopular, it is being upheld as a strong mechanism within the social reform agenda to establish improved social mobility – an ambition shared by all political parties. Taken from this perspective, an education system designed to fuel the economy and thereby create an upwardly mobile society is beneficial.

> **Activity: Social mobility**
>
> Share with your peers a Google search for comment about 'school and social mobility'. In the light of reflection on your own experiences to date, consider the extent to which you believe education could have an effect on future social mobility.

For FE and HE policy, discourse around social mobility and embracing diversity is arguably located within an economic framework. The objectives to develop a fair and just society, based on social integration and cohesion at its heart seem weak, at best. As we increasingly observe challenges and divisions emerging in our society, for example, through the rise in 'hate crime', and increased violence in sporting stadia, surely FE and HE have a role to play in developing a society that is constructive and not socially fragile.

There seems to be a series of events of critical importance to the future of FE and HE. The structures are changing, and our agency towards the degree of choice we have in relation to the courses we study is similarly changing. The power of government through policies driven with an economic intent is clear in the determination to drive through an agenda for apprenticeships throughout the post-16 landscape, the increased academisation of post-16 provision, the raising of the school-leaving age and the expectation that higher education degrees have a clear line to graduate employability.

> **✏ Activity: Potential of FE and HE**
>
> To what extent does the future of further education and higher education have to serve all members of our society in terms of economic and social potential? Think about:
>
> - the responsibility of these sectors in facilitating and supporting social justice and civic responsibility in the future;
> - costs to students in terms of finance and time;
> - whether the apprenticeship model could be the answer.

Conclusion

There is evidence through numerous government policy initiatives that our schools, FE and HE education systems are prepared for, and react to, economic imperatives. There is significantly less evidence, however, that there are any plans or strategies that prioritise, or indeed focus on, the need to build a socially responsive and responsible society through our education system.

There will be winners and losers in society as a result of these changes. Teachers' professional identity will be eroded, learners' freedom to learn and engage in a wide-ranging curriculum will be diminished, and as the cost of engaging in FE and HE increases, some aspects of education will become inaccessible. Technological advances will fundamentally change learning spaces – people will be able to learn in a wide range of locations. Additionally, employers will become increasingly responsible for the development of courses and qualification outcomes through a model of apprenticeship. This may well result in driving up the skills expertise of the available workforce, but it may not! What is certain is that learning will continue to be lifelong – but not necessarily as we have known it, seen it or experienced hitherto. Let's wait and see.

The role, purpose and value of education was formed on the basis of knowledge acquisition, to encourage curiosity and ultimately to provide hope for us all to co-exist in a cohesive, democratic society. Our hope is that the education of the future does not limit itself to an economic imperative but retains a holistic focus on its commitment to serve all of its population as it is instrumental in shaping our society. We recognise the importance of a strong economy for everyone, however, it should not be forgotten that at the heart of the economy are the individuals that make up our society. Surely, therefore, the key to an education of the future is to hold learners at its heart.

> **Case study 13.1: *Educational Excellence Everywhere***
>
> The following three statements are taken from the 2016 White Paper *Educational Excellence Everywhere* and together represent the characteristics that each child, young person and adult should have experienced in an English education in the 21st century.
>
> > The best possible education for adult life in 21st century Britain is one that equips children and young people with the knowledge, skills, values, character traits and experiences that will help them to navigate a rapidly changing world with confidence.
> >
> > (p. 91)

> A 21st century education should prepare children for adult life by instilling the character traits and fundamental British values that will help them succeed: being resilient and knowing how to persevere, how to bounce back if faced with failure, and how to collaborate with others at work and in their private lives.
>
> (p. 97)
>
> A 21st century education also promotes integration so that young people can play their part in our society. Schools and other education providers have an important role to play in promoting the fundamental British values of democracy, the rule of law, individual liberty, and mutual tolerance and respect of those with different faiths and beliefs, while developing the knowledge, critical thinking and character traits that enable pupils to identify and challenge extremist views.
>
> (p. 100)
>
> **Key questions**
> 1. Deconstruct each statement into its component parts.
> 2. Where, in the education landscape, do you believe the responsibility for achieving these characteristics lies?
> 3. What kind of curriculum would you devise to achieve the outcomes?
> 4. What challenges might you face?

Suggested reading

www.educationengland.org.uk/

While this chapter aims to capture what will come in the future, ideas from the past can be very useful to help understand how we get to be where we are in the present; in turn this helps to plan for the future. Browse this website for a fabulous history of UK education.

Tarlau, R. (2016) If the past devours the future, why study? Piketty, social movements, and future directions for education. *British Journal of Sociology of Education*, 37:6, 861–872.

Rebecca Tarlau has real concerns about education in the future from a sociologist's perspective.

www.gov.uk/government/organisations/department-for-education

While government policies change continuously, they are perhaps the best predictor of the direction of education we have. Browse this website to review UK government policy.

http://unesdoc.unesco.org/images/0024/002437/243724E.pdf

For a global view of the future of education up to 2030 read the World Education Forum 2015 Final Report.

References

Committee on Higher Education (1963) *Higher Education: Report of the Committee Appointed by the Prime Minister under the Chairmanship of Lord Robbins 1961–63*, Cmnd. 2154. London: HMSO.
Conservative Party (2015) *The Conservative Party Manifesto 2015*. Available at: https://s3-eu-west-1.amazonaws.com/manifesto2015/ConservativeManifesto2015.pdf
Conservative Party (2016) *Our Long Term Economic Plan*. Available at: https://www.conservatives.com/plan/bestschoolsandskills

Delabarre, J. (2016) *Appenticeship Statistics: England (1996–2015) Briefing Paper No 06113, 13 July 2016.* London: House of Commons Library.

Department for Business, Innovation and Skills (DBIS) (2015) *Fulfilling our Potential: Teaching Excellence, Social Mobility and Student Choice: Higher Education Green Paper.* London: Stationery Office.

Department for Education (DfE) (2016a) *Education Excellence Everywhere.* London: Department for Education.

Gibb, N. (2015) The purpose of education (speech). Available at: www.gov.uk/government/speeches/the-purpose-of-education

Gove, M. (2014) Michael Gove speaks about the future of education reform (speech). Available at: https://www.gov.uk/government/speeches/michael-gove-speaks-about-the-future-of-education-reform

Great Britain (1992) *Further and Higher Education Act.* London: Stationery Office.

Higgins, S., Xiao, X. and Katsipataki, M. (2012) *The Impact of Digital Technology on Learning: A Summary for the Education Endowment Foundation.* Available at: https://v1.educationendowmentfoundation.org.uk/uploads/pdf/The_Impact_of_Digital_Technologies_on_Learning_FULL_REPORT_(2012).pdf

Howard-Jones, P. (2011) *The Impact of Digital Technologies on Human Wellbeing.* Available at: www.nominettrust.org.uk/sites/default/files/NT%20SoA%20-%20The%20impact%20of%20digital%20technologies%20on%20human%20wellbeing.pdf

Lavington Park Federation (2016) *Forest School.* Available at: http://graffhamandduncton.w-sussex.sch.uk/forest-schools (accessed November 2016).

Martellozzo, E., Monaghan, A., Adler, J. R., Davidson, J., Leyva, R. and M. A. H. Horvath (2016) *'... I Wasn't Sure It Was Normal To Watch It ...' A Quantitative and Qualitative Examination of the Impact of Online Pornography on the Values, Attitudes, Beliefs and Behaviours of Children and Young People.* London: Middlesex University.

May, T. (2016) Britain: The great meritocracy (speech). Available at: www.gov.uk/government/speeches/britain-the-great-meritocracy-prime-ministers-speech

Ofsted (2012) *Lavington Park Federation – Good Practice Example.* Available at www.gov.uk/government/publications/improving-teaching-and-learning-using-the-outdoor-environment-in-west-sussex

O'Grady, A. (2013) *Lifelong Learning in the UK.* London: Routledge.

Potter, T. G. and Dyment, J. E. (2016) Is outdoor education a discipline? Insights, gaps and future directions. *Journal of Adventure Education and Outdoor Learning,* 16:2, 146–159.

Sub-Committee on Education, Skills and the Economy (2016) *Apprenticeships Inquiry.* Public Accounts Committee. Available at: www.parliament.uk/business/committees/committees-a-z/commons-select/education-skills-and-economy/inquiries/parliament-2015/apprenticeships-15-16/

Stern, N. (2016) *Building on Success and Learning from Experience: An Independent Review of the Research Excellence Framework.* London: Department for Business, Energy and Industrial Strategy.

INDEX

Page numbers in **bold** refer to a table, *italics* to figures.

Abdullaeva, D. 47
Abrahms, M. 38
academies 25–6, 57–9
Academies Act (2010) 57
accountability 53, 57–8, 88
Achievement for All strategy 144
Adams, R. 59
adolescence: LGBT students 99–100, 104; mental health issues 7; refugees 147; self-harming 132–3
Amabile, T. M. 66, 70, **73**
anxiety 7, 132–4, 142, 147, *148*
Apprenticeships Inquiry (2016) 188
apprenticeships 91, 188, 191
Asprey, A. 124
attainment gap 26, 60, 85, 100; see also educational attainment
Attention Deficit and Hyperactivity Disorder 142
Australia, education initiatives 145, 162, 164
autistic spectrum 121, 122, 123–4
autonomy 57, 59

Bartlett, S. 13
behaviours 19, 65, 124; behavioural resilience 160–2; creative children 65–6, 76; extremists 33–4; refugee children 141, 145, 147–8; teacher 68, 73, 107–8
Bell, L. 130
Belshaw, D. 172
benefit system 18–19, 20–1; Child Benefit 89, 90
Benn, M. 61
Bhui, K. 35

Bin Laden, Osama 37
biopower 121–2
bisexual individuals 104–6; see also LGBT individuals
Blatchford, P. 121
Blower, C. 26
Bowl, M. 114
Bradshaw, J. 22
British: naturalisation 44; values 9–10, 33–4, 40, 44, 193
British Standard for Organisational Resilience (BS 65000) 162
Bronfenbrenner, U. 148; ecological framework *143*
Browne Review (2010) 10–11
bullying 7, 133–4, 136; cyberbullying 185; LGBT students 99–101, 104–6

Camelot Foundation 129–30, 132, 136–7, 139
Cameron, D. 44, 90
categorisation, Special Educational Needs and Disability 120–6
Cefai, C. 142
Centre for Social Justice 20
charter schools (USA) 25
Child and Adolescent Mental Health Service (CAMHS) 150
Child and Adolescent Self-Harm in Europe (CASE) 133
Child Benefit 89, 90
Child Exploitation and Online Protection (CEOP) Centre 44
child obesity 21, 22

child poverty 16–18, 121; consequences 21–2; factors affecting 19–21; impact on educational attainment 18, 22–3; interventions 24–8; UK trends 18–19, 20–1
Child Poverty Act (2010) 24
Child Poverty Strategy (2014) 24
Childline 136
children: agents of change 165; behaviour and personality 65–7; creative and gifted children 64–7, **65**, 74–6; looked after children 133, 149; physical health 21–2; resilience 157–62; unaccompanied refugees 150; vulnerable children 157, 159–60
Children and Families Act (2014) 119–20, 141
citizenship 9, 44
City Academies 25
City Technology Colleges 22
Civil Contingencies Act (2004) 162
Clarke, J. 160–1
classroom environment 66–73, 110
Clegg, N. 89
Coalition government policies 89–90, 92, 183
Cognitive Behavioural Therapy (CBT) 160
cognitive resilience 160–2
coming out see disclosure
commodification: of education 55–6; students 56, 57
communities: counter-extremism 41, 45; refugees *149*; resilience 159, 163–4, 166; role of schools 57, 165
community schools 27–8
competition in education system 53–7
connectivism 174–6, 179
Connexions 88, 89
Conservative government policies 18, 27, 82, 90–1, 183–4
Contest strategy 39–42
coping strategies 129, 133, 134, 137
Corbyn, J. 60, 89
Cormier, D. 174–5
counter-extremism 38–9, 42–3
counter-terrorism 39–42, 43–4
Counter-Terrorism and Security Act (2015) 40
Creative Problem Solving (CPS) 67–8
creativity 63–7, *64*, **65**; barriers to 72–3, **73**; creative thinking 70–1; educational goal 12; fostering 66–73, **67**, 74–6

Crime and Courts Act (2013) 43
Criminal Justice and Immigration Act (2008) 43
Criminal Justice and Public Order Act (1994) 42
Csikszentmihalyi, M. 66–7
curriculum 4, 13; future 184–7; impact of technology 172–3, 175; National Curriculum 12, 59, 81, 168; outdoor 186; promoting resilience 164, 166
cutting (self-harm) 130–1, 135, 137
cybercrime 36, 43–4
Cyrulnik, B. 158–9, 161, 169

Davis, G. A. **65**, 66, 71–2
De Souza Fleith, D. **67**, 70
democracy 9–10, 33–4
Denmark, refugees 147
Department for Education 183; educational attainment 22–3; family intervention programmes 24–5; future of education 184; Prevent strategy 40; promotion of British values 9–10
depression 7, 132–4, 142, 147, *148*
deprivation 6, 16, 120–1; see also poverty
Desailly, J. 78
Dewey, J. 9, 175
DfE see Department for Education
differentiation 71, 190; fostering creativity 74–6
digital literacies 172–4, **172**, 175, 179, 185
digital technology 190; digital disruption 174–6; digital natives 173; digital scepticism 176–9; use in teaching 185–7; see also internet
Dijk, L. van 114
dilemma of difference 122–4
disabilities 119–26
disaster management 162–3, 164
disclosure: self-harming 136, 137; sexuality 101–3, 108–9, 110–13, **112**
discrimination 10, 40, 42; LGBT students 100, 103–4
diversity 5–6, 108, 191
dramatics 66, 71–2
Durkheim, E. 5
Dyson, A. 121, 123

Early Years Plan 25
earn or learn policy 91
Easton, M. 10
ecological framework 143, *143*, 145, 148

economic factors: child poverty 20–1; terrorism 34, 37
economic growth, through education 3–5
economic sanctions 38
ECOSOC (United Nation's Administrative Committee on Coordination Economic and Social Council) 17
education 1–2, *2*, 6–7, 175, 183; fostering creativity 12; individual needs 190–1; for knowledge transmission 57; for mental health 7; promoting economic growth 3–5; promoting nationalism 7–9; purpose 2–9, 12, 184, 191–2; for resilience 164–9; for socialisation 5–6; *see also* teachers
Education Act (2000) 27–8
Education Act (2002) 6–7
Education and Adoption Act (2016) 58
Education, Health and Care Plan (EHCP) 120
Education for the Knowledge Economy (EKE) 4
Education (Provision of Meals) Act (1906) 27
Education Reform Act (1988) 9
Education Select Committee 188
Education and Skills Act (2008) 90
education system: digital revolution 171–80; future 182–93; marketization 53–6; Prevent Duty 40–1, 46
educational attainment 22–3, *23*, 25–6, 185; attainment gap 26, 60, 85, 100; impact of child poverty 22–3
Educational Maintenance Allowance (EMA) 88–9
Emergency Preparedness, Resilience and Response (EPRR) Framework 163
emergency response 42, 162–3
emotional intelligence 160, 162, 166, 168
employment: transition to 81, 88; youth unemployment 82–4; *see also* NEETs (Not in Education, Employment or Training)
English: as additional language 121; educational attainment 22–3, *23*
Entry to Employment programme (E2E) 88
Equality Act (2010) 42, 120
ethnic minorities 89, 111, 133
Eurofound 81
Europe: International Classification of Functioning (ICF) 145; NEETs (Not in Education, Employment or Training) 84; Roadmap for Europe (resilience policy) 163; self-harming 130, 133
European Commission against Racism and Intolerance (ECRI) 43

European Convention on Human Rights (ECHR) 42–3
European Union 18; Commission to Protect Future Generations from Radical Violence 45; Internet Referral Unit (EU IRU) 44
Evans, J. R. 72–3
extended services in schools 27–8
extremism 9, 32–4; counter-extremism 38–9, 42–3; *see also* terrorism

failing schools 25, 184
family intervention programmes 24–5, 28
Family and Parenting Institute 20
Fatah 37
Fazel, M. 146–7, 149, 153
FE sector *see* Further Education
Ferracuti, F. 37
Figlio, D. 57
Flowers, P. 103
Football Offences Acts (1991, 1999) 42
formal learning 174, 183, 190; *see also* institutional learning
Foucault, M. 121–2, 178
foundation schools 58
fourth industrial revolution 175, 176
France, A. 94
Frater-Mathieson, K. 147–8
free school meals (FSM): as socio-economic indicator 22–3, 85, 120; Universal Infant Free School Meals (UIFSM) 24, 26–7
free schools 57, 59
freedom of speech 42–3
Freire, P. 175
Friedman, M. I. 54
friskolor (Sweden) 25
Full Fact charity 41
Full Service Extended Schools 27–8
funding 53, 57–8, 183; Pupil Premium Grant (PPG) 26–7, 60
Furedi, F. 10, 41
Further Education: digital learning 186; future of 187–8, 190–2; marketization 53, 56; Prevent Strategy 40; *see also* institutional learning; vocational education

Gardner, H. 64, **65**
Gay, Lesbian, Straight Education Network (GLSEN) 99, 101

gay individuals *see* LGBT individuals
GCSEs 22–3, *23*, 26, 59
Get Safe Online 44
Gibb, N. 81
Gilligan, R. 158
Global Coalition against Daesh 44
Global Disaster Preparedness Center (GDPC) 168
Goodey, C. 124
Gove, M. 89, 183
government policies: child poverty 18, 24–8; counter-extremism 38–9, 42–3; counter-terrorism 39–42; education system 4, 6–7, 183–4, 191; employment 82; free school meals (FSM) 24, 26–7; NEETs (Not in Education, Employment or Training) 87–92; sexuality 107; Special Educational Needs and Disability (SEND) 119–21; *see also* interventions
grammar schools 60, 191
Gray, B. 122
Greenberg, E. **67**, 70
Greening, J. 58, 60
Grotberg, E. H. 161–2
group work 67–8, 70, 185
Guilford, J. P. 64–5, **65**
Gunaratna, R. 45
Gupta, D. K. 34

Hamas 37
Hancock, N. 84
Hansen, J. B. **67**, **73**
Hawton, K. 130–1
HE *see* Higher Education
Heacox, D. 74
Head Start programme (USA) 25
health (children's) 21–2; mental health 7, 22, 141–4; refugee's mental health 145–53
Health in Pregnancy Grant 20
Healthy Start scheme 24
Hezbollah 37
Higgins, S. 185–6
Higher Education 10–11, 56; access to 91; digital learning 186; future 189–92; LGBT students 99; marketization 52–3; Prevent Strategy 40; *see also* institutional learning
Higher Education Academy (HEA) 11
Higher Education Policy Institute (HEPI) 11
Higher Education and Research Bill (2016–17) 189

Hirsch, D. 21
Hobbes, T. 34–5
Home Office 33, 36; Workshop to Raise Awareness of Prevent (WRAP) 39
home-school partnership 41, 144
homophobia 100, 104, 105
House of Commons Communities and Local Government Committee 41
human capital 3–4
Human Development Index (HDI) 16
Hussain, R. 32
Hutchinson, J. 86–7
Hyperkinetic Disorder 142

Iceland, LGBT students 101, 107
ICT (Information and Communication Technologies) 35–6; *see also* digital technology; internet
identity: online 173, 178; private/professional 108–9
immigration 44; *see also* refugees
inclusion 124–5, 141
individuals 177; needs 8, 190–1; privacy 178–9; resilience 157–62; socialisation 5–6, 8
inequality 5–6, 42, 120, 121
informal learning 167, 173–6, 177
institutional learning 173, 174, 179–80; *see also* formal learning; Further Education; Higher Education; schools
insurgents *see* terrorism
Integrated Household Survey (2015) 98
intelligence services 39
intelligences 64–5, 70; emotional 160, 162, 166, 168
International Classification of Functioning (ICF) 145
international comparisons: NEETs (Not in Education, Employment or Training) 6, 84; Programme for International Student Assessment (PISA) 56; self-harm incidence 130
International Covenant on Civil and Political Rights (ICCPR) 42–3
International Resilience Research Project 161–2
International Standard for Business Continuity (ISO 22301) 162
internet 35, 171–2, 176, 185; online communities 174–5; online identity 173, 178; social media 36, 173, 177, 178, 180, 185; use in radicalisation 35–6, 43–4; *see also* digital technology
intersectionality 111

interventions: counter-terrorism 39–42; developing resilience 157, 158–9, 165–6; digital 185; family programmes 24–5, 28; microsystem *144*; NEETs (Not in Education, Employment or Training) 86–92; promoting mental health 142–3, 144–5; refugee pupils 147–8, 150–2; Special Educational Needs and Disability (SEND) 120–1, 123; *see also* government policies
Isaksen, S. G. 70
Islamic groups 37
Islamic State 36, 38
Italy, terrorists 35, 37

Japan, Disaster Resilience Handbook 164
Johnson, A. P. 71–2
Jordan 151
Joseph Rowntree Foundation 16, 18, 21

Kaplan, S. 75
Keddie, A. 57
Keen, A. 177, 178
Kelly, E. 147, 150
Kenya, educational goals 7–9
Khan, M. H. 47
KidsMatter programme 145
King, J. 109
Kjaran, J. I. 101
knowledge 174–5
knowledge driven economy 3–5, 55, 57
Kolczynski, R. G. 71
Kosciw, J. G. 99, 102

labelling, Special Educational Needs and Disability (SEND) 120–6
Labour government policies 18, 82, 87–9, 92, 191
language barriers 121, 149, 150
Lankshear, C. 173
Lauder, H. 54
Lavington Park School Federation 186
Leadbeater, C. 4
league tables 53, 55, 59
learning 74–5, 183, 188; barriers to 85; digital 172–4, 175, 179, 185–7; formal 174, 183, 190; informal 167, 173–6, 177; lifelong 174–5; outcomes 13, 56, 74; outdoors 186; personalisation 173, 177, 190; rhizomatic model 174–5

learning difficulties 124–5
learning environment 69–71, 73, 110
Learning and Skills Council (LSC) 88
lesbian individuals *see* LGBT individuals
Lewis, A. 126
Lewis, O. 19–20
Lexmond, J. 162
LGBT individuals: bisexual individuals 104–6; disclosure of sexuality 102–3, 110–12; LGB population 98; LGBTQ (Lesbian, Gay, Bisexual, Transgendered and Questioning) 97–8; self-harming 133; students 97–106; teachers 106–14
Life Skills Project 165
lifelong learning 174–5
LinkedIn 180
Littky, D. 12
Little, W. 5
local education authorities 58–9
Local Government Acts (1986, 2003) 107
Locke, J. 35
looked after children 133, 149

McCormack, M. 114
McKenna-Buchanan, T. 112
McLuhan, M. 176–7
MacPhail, J. 151–2
McVeigh, T. J. 37, 48
mainstream education 120, 122, 190
maintained schools 25–6
marketization of education 5, 52–5, 59; accountability 57–8; information requirements 56–7; profitability 55–6
Marmot Review (2010) 22
Maslow's hierarchy of needs 72
mathematics, educational attainment 22–3, *23*
May, T. 39, 60, 191
medical model of need 120, 145
Medicines and Healthcare Regulatory Agency (MHRA) 44
Mejias, U. A. 178
mental health: disorders *148*; educational goals 7, 141–4; LGBT students 100; predictors of issues 22, *142*; refugees 145–53; self-harm 129–39; terrorists 35
Mental Health Foundation 132–3, 139
Mexico, poverty 19
microsystem (ecological framework) 143, 145

migration process 146–7, *146*
military campaigns 38
military intelligence 39
Mirza-Davies, J. 84–5
mobile devices 171–2, 173, 185
moderate learning difficulties (MLD) 121
Molesworth, M. 61
Monroe, C. 168
Morgan, N. 26
Morris, M. 104
Moutaux, G. 37, 46
Multidimensional Poverty Index (MPI) 16
Muslim communities 41
Mwaka, M. 7–8

naming, Special Educational Needs and Disability (SEND) 120–6
National Crime Agency 44
National Curriculum 12, 59, 81, 168
National Cybercrime Unit 44
National Student Survey 190
National Union of Teachers (NUT) 41
nationalism as educational goal 7–9
naturalisation (British) 44
nature versus nurture 34–5
Neenan, M. 160, 165
NEETs (Not in Education, Employment or Training) 6, 81–6; Europe 84; interventions 86–92
neoliberalism 5, 82, 90
Neuberger, L. C. 35
Neumann, P. 34
New Zealand, LGBT students 100
Newman, T. 158–9
NHS emergency response 163
Nicholson McBride Resilience Questionnaire (NMRQ) 160
Nigeria, rehabilitation of terrorists 45
Norwich, B. 122–3, 126

obesity, child 21, 22
Office of Cyber Security and Information Assurance (OCSIA) 44
Ofsted 27, 53, 57; inspection framework 10, 150–1
online communities 174–5
online identity 173, 178
Organisation for Economic Cooperation and Development (OECD) 6

Organisational Resilience, British Standard (BS 65000) 162
Osborn, A. F. 67
Osborne, G. 82
outdoor curriculum 186

panopticon 107, 178
parental choice 53, 54, 56–9
parental engagement 144
parenting skills 28
Parentline 136
participation: Higher Education 189; Raising of the participation age (RPA) 90, 92
Peer, L. 120–1
performance indicators 53, 54, 55, 59
personalisation 177, 190; personal learning environment (PLE) 173
personality traits 65–7, 157–8, 160
Peru, Pillowcase Project 168–9
Piirto, J. 66, **67**
Pillowcase Project 167–9
Playfair, E. 55
playmaking 72
political factors: child poverty 20; radicalisation 37
Post-Traumatic Stress Disorder (PTSD) 147, *148*
Potter, T. G. 186
poverty 16–18; consequences 21–3; factors affecting 19–21; impact on educational attainment 18, 22–3; interventions 24–8; relative poverty 16, 18, 27; UK trends 18–19, 20–1
Prensky, M. 172–3
Prepare strand (Contest strategy) 42
Prevent Strategy 9, 39–41
primary education 6–7, 26, 145
privacy 178–9
private/professional identity 108–9
privatization 53–4
profiling (Prevent Strategy) 41
profitability of education 55–6
Programme for International Student Assessment (PISA) 56
Protect strand (Contest strategy) 42
Public Order Act (1986) 42–3
Puerto Rico, poverty 19
Pupil Premium Grant (PPG) 26–7, 60
Pursue strand (Contest strategy) 40